A
Z
A

Volume
One

Journal of Korean Literature
& Culture

L

E

A

Korea Institute Harvard University
2007

AZALEA

Journal of Korean Literature & Culture

Volume One ~ 2007

Publisher: Korea Institute, Harvard University

Editor: David R. McCann

Managing Editor: Young-Jun Lee

Editorial Board: Bruce Fulton, Brother Anthony, Hwang Jong-yŏn, Kwon
Youngmin, Heinz Insu Fenkl

Copy Editor: K.E. Duffin

Design: Wayne de Fremery

Proofreader: Phyllis Coyne et al.

AZALEA (ISBN 978-0-9795800-0-0) is published yearly by the Korea
Institute, Harvard University, with generous funding by the International
Communication Foundation, Seoul. Translations from the Korean original
were supported by the Korean Literature Translation Institute.

Subscriptions: $30 (one year); $55 (two years); $80 (three years). Oversea
subscriptions: $45 (one year, air mail only).

Inquiries to: *AZALEA*, Korea Institute, Harvard University, Center for
Government and International Studies, South Building Room S228, 1730
Cambridge Street, Cambridge, MA 02138
Phone: (617) 496-2141 Fax: (617) 496-1144 Email: korea@fas.harvard.edu
Submissions are welcome. Submitted manuscripts and books sent for
review become the property of *AZALEA*.

CONTENTS

FEATURE : ANOTHER PERSPECTIVE

POETRY

BOOK REVIEW

INTERVIEW

KOREA FROM THE OUTSIDE

Editor's Note

AZALEA is about Korean literature and literary culture, and therefore about writing, publishing, translating, and reading. The writing has already happened, the translation too, but now for the reading! We have looked at original works, wondering who might best translate a gem. Or we have discovered a strong translation and asked, "Can we publish it?" And how might artwork of various kinds, or perhaps photographs of Korea contemporaneous with the literary works, be added to the mix? The occasional hortatory note, such as my own in this issue about the 1953 short story "Cranes" by Hwang Sunwǒn, may add another edge, perhaps, to the reader's framing and reframing of the piece.

We hope that our readers will write to us with suggestions of works, translations, and translators, and especially with ideas about other ways to read Korean literature. Watch, in that connection, for our issue in the not-too-distant future with a CD inside for examples of yet another way to read Korean literature—out loud!

David R. McCann
August 2007

Writer in Focus: Kim Young-ha

This Tree of Yours

by Kim Young-ha
Translated by Dafna Zur

1

When you were little, you read a story about an oak tree. You read it somewhere, in a very forgettable children's book—you can no longer recall the book's title or the look of its cover. The illustrations in this book—enormous trees with ferocious eyes and scowling mouths drawn on their trunks—were enough to send shivers down your young spine. They really started scaring you. Tree—outstretched roots wild as a madwoman's hair, the eerie crackle of their leaves—those trees were there before you were born, and will most likely be there long after you're gone.

Back then, a tree grew outside your house. A foul-smelling acacia. It hung over the roof, its branches draping a shadow over your window. Ants filed up its trunk and a hornet's nest swung from its thick branches. Every night, a bird—I think it was some kind of owl—hooted at you. You imagined how one day the roots would burst their way into the kitchen, and the branches would poke down through the roof. The ants would chew your bed to bits, birds would nest in the living room, and hornets, their bellies full of autumn venom, would sting your brother to death.

You felt much better after moving to the city. The trees looming over the streets at night were gone. You were no longer faced with those roots clawing fiercely at the earth. Spindly willows and ginkgos were all there were, and even they were not spared an annual spring pruning. Finally you were able to sleep soundly in the comfort of clean pavement, streetlights, and crosswalks.

In time, you learned to play video games, smoke cigarettes, and drive. You could tell the good people from the bad, and acquired the skill of picking up women who caught your fancy. You got yourself a passport and a credit card, and thought no more about those who'd disappeared from your life. You bought a pager and three years later upgraded to a cell phone, and now you could speed dial every last one of your friends. Such was your existence.

And now? You're looking at a tree. You're in a steamy, muggy place, you've come to a stop, and before you stands a fig tree that would dwarf a five-story building. You're listening to time, listening in the presence of this majestic life form whose origin no one can know, except that it sprang from a single seed lodged in the feathers of a passing bird.

The clouds scud by. The monsoon winds carry the scent of rain. Dark butterflies are first to catch the scent, and they swarm into the woods. Barefoot boys glide past you like butterflies. What brought you here, you wonder. This fig tree? That swarm of butterflies, flying thousands of miles across the sea to get here?

2

You were sitting in the living room with a cup of coffee the day it occurred to you to visit Angkor Wat. The coffee was no longer fresh—it tasted flat. It was quiet; no one was around to distract you. It was as if traffic had come to a standstill and all the children were cooped up in school. This oppressive silence was broken by a single clatter, as if from a faint tremor—barely audible—from the dishes settling in the dish rack. The movement was too slight to detect with the eye, and not forceful enough to disturb the stack. You knew, better than anyone, that this little clatter took place every day, not only in your dish rack but in other homes, everywhere, all the time. But to you that day, it came as a surprise. You figured it was natural for wet dishes to shift; in fact, according to the laws of gravity, that's what they'd be expected to do. That tremor was the most natural of movements, really. And in this world, weren't there such moments? You felt you had just witnessed one of them, a moment at which an insignificant clatter sets off a chain reaction leading to a momentous event.

The butterfly effect, that's what it's called. A butterfly flaps its wings in Beijing, and California is hit by a typhoon. This was still on your mind as you finished your coffee. That clatter, you were thinking, might just blow apart my life. It was just a hunch, but you couldn't shake it.

3

Leaving Bangkok, you arrived at the border village of Aranya Prathet, where you crossed over to Cambodia after a short stop at customs. You felt as though time were flowing backwards. Back in Thailand you were in your twenties, but here in Cambodia you felt younger. You saw barefoot boys, soldiers with automatic weapons slung over their shoulders, and a dirt road stretching all the way to the horizon. On the other side of this line—the border—lay a completely different world. You didn't look back. You simply hauled yourself into a pickup truck with some of the local people. It was smaller than a one-ton pickup, but it managed to carry you and sixteen other passengers. The vehicle rocked wildly along the road, which had been pitted by the monsoon rains. There were three flat tires along the way, and the wooden bridges were damaged. The small truck pushed along for six hours, a constant swirl of dust clouded the windows, and the passengers held fast to the side handles to keep from falling out.

It was only when the driver had to change a flat tire that you got a brief moment of respite, and you took in the tropical paddies that extended to the horizon. Even the smoke from your damp cigarette was a relief from the humidity. Your shirt, heavy with dust and sweat, smelled faintly of papaya. A moment later, the car was surrounded by children. You bought some rice steamed in bamboo leaves from one of the little girls whose scalp was ravaged by psoriasis. You unwrapped the leaves and took a bite out of the dense ball of rice inside. Another pickup truck full of people flew by in a whirl of dust. The dense, starchy rice stuck in your throat. With a genial smile, the driver urged you back on the truck. He walked with a noticeable limp. As you hopped in, you wondered what had compelled you to come to this place.

4

The day of the clatter, you got the message from your girlfriend that she was leaving you. You knew it was coming. A dish clattered, its tremor upsetting dishes in other homes, making dogs bark, which in turn set babies crying, which upset their mothers, whose anxieties were whisked along the phone lines to the workplaces of their husbands, one of whom ended up upsetting your girlfriend who was working with him at that moment. As far as the butterfly effect goes, it could have been a lot worse.

She didn't give a reason—not that you expected one. *I don't know what's wrong with me. The thing is, I'm losing my mind. I just can't stand to be with you any longer. Whenever we're together, I feel all knotted up inside. Like a guitar string wound so tight it only produces high notes. Have you ever seen a guitar with a broken neck? Strings usually snap when they're wound too tight, but the strings you've drawn across me just won't give in to the pressure.*

I'm going to miss touching you, you told yourself. Do you know what stays with a man longest when he breaks up with a woman? It's the feel. Bottom. Breasts. Bouncing belly. The way our hips dig into each other. My teeth hitting yours. The dampness between your toes. How slick and wet you are when you're ovulating.

Your reaction that day was inappropriate, and you know it. You wouldn't have said what you did if you knew how to love someone. You should have played desperate—said don't leave me, I need you, I can't live without you. But you didn't. There you were, talking to her on the phone, and all you could hear was that clatter of dishes. There was a reason you gave in so easily. You knew, you were certain it was all because of the morning clatter. That clatter was driving you both toward disaster. Your tone of voice grew more strained, her strings tighter.

"When I first held you in my arms, I had a sense of you not so much as a person but as an animal. Your hair and nose gave off a female scent, your skin was sticky with resin. I don't remember a single word I said to you. All that's left of you is your feel. Alright then, go. Your messages on my cell phone have been erased, your voice is no longer on my answering machine. The words you left with me are gone."

You didn't mean for it to happen, but your words dug into her body like the teeth of a saw.

5

You were completely sapped of strength when you arrived in Siem Reap, the nearest city to Angkor. It had been twelve hours since you left Bangkok, and the last six were a nightmare. But then again, you were the one who hadn't listened when someone said it was crazy to travel to Angkor by land. The smart thing would have been to start from Phnom Penh and go up the Mekong, but you ignored that, too. And your reward was a body grimy from the heat and dust.

You threw your bags down in a dollar-fifty-a-night guesthouse. The wall against your bed crawled with spiders the size of your fist and lizards. You closed your eyes and sank into your bunk bed. When you woke up, it was morning. The spiders were gone. All through breakfast your eyes searched for them. They stayed out of sight. Those big black hairy spiders didn't seem to like being out and about during the day. You polished off your nice, warm bowl of chicken congee in silence.

That was the day you started your exploration of the sprawling ruins, beginning with the main temple, Angkor Wat. The sun scorched your skin, and the temple's red-hot sandstone radiated its store of fever, making you feel even hotter. The faces of the Buddha-like Hindu deities smiled at you mysteriously as if to say, what took you so long. You didn't have an answer. Avalokitesvara's four faces overseeing north, south, east, and west from the pillars and towers also questioned you: Where have you come from, and where are you going? As you climbed the steps of soaring Bayon Temple, its towers studded and bristling with hundreds of Avalokitesvara's faces, you knew. You knew that he was watching you from right and left, from above and below. That there was no hiding from him.

You prostrated yourself in his presence. A monk in a saffron robe accepted your one-dollar donation and recited a prayer, waving a stick of incense over your head. These heads of Avalokitesvara date from the twelfth century, and by now were worshipped as Boddhisattvas. The faces were holy in your eyes, as well. Their smile—you'd seen it many times before. It was the smile of Kwan'um, the Buddhist goddess of mercy, which had been looking down upon you from her pedestal in the temple.

And there you are, sitting in the heart of this forest of faces in Bayon Temple, having a smoke as you look down on the precise rectangular layout of the ancient city of Angkor Thom. Angkor. Something about it makes it feel like a city not of this world. And yet, you feel at home here. Birds flutter past, leaving fleeting shadows on Avalokitesvara's faces. One face had sprouted a tree between the nose and mouth. The sun is setting, and for you time is flowing steadily backward.

Her mother's suicide attempt happened a week or so after the clatter of the dish. When she called to ask for help, you weren't there. Her voice on your answering machine sounded hoarse. *Come to the hospital, please. She lost so much blood. I'm frightened. I'm sorry. I don't know why I'm calling you. Please don't be angry.* It was hard to understand her. She lived with her mother, just the two of them. Her mother was probably somebody's mistress. You got that feeling every time you visited them. Their house was completely devoid of any male presence. Even on holidays, there was nothing festive in the air.

When you finally got the message and went to the hospital, they were gone. A nurse explained that the mother had been transferred to another hospital for a bigger operation. Her arteries had to be reconnected. You hesitated, then hesitated again, then gave up and headed for home. Her mother might die. It would be a pathetic, lonely funeral. And your girlfriend would probably fall apart. A guitar, its neck snapped in two.

This is all because of the clatter, you kept thinking. A dish clattered, your girlfriend left you, and her mother slit her wrists. Your girlfriend's taut strings had loosened; she was probably lapsing into hysterical fits back home, trapped by the similarities between her mother's fate and her own fixed destiny.

The next day, she came to see you. *I'm sorry I called you. I wasn't thinking—my fingers were still bloody when I dialed your number. On my way over, I saw a motorcycle with a huge chrysanthemum garland, taller than me. Probably being recycled from a funeral. It wasn't wrapped in cellophane, so every time the guy accelerated, flowers went flying. Mother lost a lot of blood. The house stinks of it. I mopped it up and down with Clorox, but I just can't get rid of it. A taxi ran over the petals. Don't bother going to the hospital. My ex-husband is there. He's actually quite useful in these situations. More than you are, anyway.*

Angkor was built for all moments in time: morning and night, sunrise and sunset, dry seasons and monsoons. It changes shape with the shifting angle of the sun, but it is never more glorious than at sunrise. You spent an entire day close by Avalokitesvara with his four faces, moving from one vantage point to another. As the heated sandstone warmed your bones, cows roamed the ruins, munching away at the grass. They grazed the area clean, even the blades of grass poking out from among the dancing Apsaras on the pillars. Come nightfall, they forded the great moat surrounding Angkor Wat and returned to their pens. The single line of cows against the backdrop of the brown temple in the setting sun brought your time to a standstill.

And now, a week later, you're facing a tree. A kapok tree that has swallowed up the entire temple. It started with a single seed that rode the wind to the top of the temple, then slowly sank its roots toward the ground absorbing moisture and nutrients until finally it had wrapped itself all around the temple. The cameos of women bearing flowers that stand among the relentless roots have long since started to crumble. Each root of this tree is so strikingly massive you feel as teeny as an ant. And there, another tree, sprouting from Avalokitesvara's head. Its tentacles have snaked down between the eyes, grasping to claw at the ground. One of them has cracked the lips of the face, turning its gentle smile into more of a sneer. That scared you. Because you don't know what he's sneering at.

You tell yourself you could understand how someone like Paul Claudel, who came here in the early 1900s, cursed this place as the land of the devil. Anyone confronted by a towering, ten-story kapok tree coiled around the ruins would sense the evil hovering there. That one minuscule seed has the power to unmake man-made monuments is enough to humble us all into reflecting on our lives. Yourself included. You too thought back upon the tiny seeds that have blown into your life. About how one of them must have settled somewhere on your head, grown into a great tree and was crushing your brain, was now inseparable from you.

8

Her mother lost the use of her left hand. The girl started drinking heavily. You knew what it was all about: the butterfly's wings had fluttered, and the worst was yet to come.

How far will that clatter go, you wondered. Your patience was soon to be rewarded. There was a tremendous explosion in the city where you lived. A decrepit apartment building collapsed into a heap of concrete. It happened not four blocks from the girl's house. There had been a gas leak overnight and a cigarette set it off, and several apartments were blown up instantaneously, survivors fleeing the collapsing building. The police seemed to think someone had tampered with the safety valve on the gas line.

The girl's mother would have had an argument with one of the checkout girls at the supermarket. It was difficult to pay with only one good hand, and she would have hated for people to notice. The checkout girl would have rushed her, making her drop her wallet, and she would have flown into a rage prompted by her disability. They would have cursed at each other, and the people waiting in line would all have seen the scars from the operation on her wrists. Her failed suicide attempt made people uncomfortable.

Back home, the checkout girl and other customers would each have replayed that unpleasant fight in its entirety. The mother's hysterical soprano and scarred wrists and the checkout girl's fierce reaction would have stayed with everyone for a few days or more. Among those people, a few would have entertained a fleeting thought of suicide, would have exploded at their clueless husbands' drunkenness, and one of them would have severed the gas line with a Swiss Army knife.

If it hadn't happened at the supermarket, a bus stop or

department store would have worked just as well. This kind of chain reaction cannot be stopped. Nor can your thoughts. Again you wonder: what else will go wrong?

9

Late at night, the king spider showed up again. There it was, above the bathroom mirror. Startled by the sudden light, it froze, waiting for you to make a move. You approached slowly, lighter in hand. It may have been poisonous after all. The guesthouse clerk warned you. But you put fear aside and turned the flame up full blast. Just like that it dropped to the floor, then scurried off faster than you ever imagined possible, leaving behind a faint smell of scorched fur. You took aim at the fugitive with a hiking boot, but didn't throw it. The gesture was enough to make the spider and a lizard of similar size scamper up the wall and out of sight.

That spider is going to come back for you y'know, the clerk tells you, his countenance severe, after you briefed him on the skirmish. You then remember that spiders devour their mother at birth. A vision of a black swarm of the scorched spider's young surrounding your bed sends chills down your spine. You arm yourself with insecticide and mosquito repellant, and crawl under the netting over your bed. Turns out you're scared of a lot of things.

That night you fell ill. You tried to get up, but lay right back down, giving up on your plans for that day. Was this the spider's revenge? You lapsed into a constant stream of paranoid delusions. You were feverish, beaded in a cold sweat. A rain squall beat down sounding like galloping horses on the slate roof.

Maybe it was the fever, but for the first time on this journey you longed for her. The uptight one, taut like the stretched strings of a guitar. Did the neck really break in the end? Did her mother try to take her life again? Maybe she succeeded this time. How did you ever let those women intrude into your life, you think. Or maybe, you tell yourself, I summoned them. Maybe it wasn't the clatter that set everything in motion—maybe it was the other way around. What came first? You were confused. The one thing you know for sure is that they are far, far away, and for this one brief moment, you miss them.

And while all this is going on, the chain reaction from the clatter continues. The guesthouse manager hands you a newspaper in English with a front page article and photos about three bombings in Phnom Penh. The anti-Hun Sen party was presumed responsible. In a related incident, two monks were shot dead, after which water cannons, guns, and tanks were mobilized. A train had rolled off a cliff in India, killing hundreds, and a Swissair jet crashed in Canada, killing all aboard.

10

The woman is sitting back in the cushy chair, avoiding your eyes. You, the clinical psychologist, are giving her a Rorschach test. What do you see? you ask her as you show her cards with ambiguous ink blots and try to elicit her interpretation. A seated naked girl spreading her legs, she answers cheekily. Actually, it looks more like a vagina, she adds. It's not the first time a patient has answered this way—though a butterfly or a bat is the usual response. You carefully record her answers, noting whether she looks first at the details or the whole, whether she sees the blot as the foreground or the background, et cetera.

You show her the next card. Can you tell me what you see in this card? Looks like two cannibals devouring a woman. Where do you see that you ask, and she points with a long fingernail. Look, the woman is here in the middle, hanging upside down. And each of the men grab a leg. They're getting ready to eat her up, of course. And what kind of people eat other people? Cannibals, obviously.

You're not the therapist. All you do is take careful notes, judge her mental state, and send your evaluation to her therapist. You continue to record her answers in detail, one by one. When you hold up the final card, she says, and that's number ten, right? When are these silly tests going to stop, anyway? Rorschach, MMPI, TAT . . . I've answered so many questions, but I don't get any better. Did you know that there's a rock band called Rorschach Test? Have you ever heard their music? Did you know that Andy Warhol has a painting called *Rorschach Test* from 1984? It's a silly one. He splashed some paint on a canvas, folded it in half—and what did he get? Perfect symmetry with no clear meaning, of course. I see a bat, I see a vagina—I'm supposed to believe this is my subconscious at work? And if it is, what difference does it make? I know just as much as other people. So why don't you give up all your graphs and charts.

You've had four years of experience, and this throws you off. For one thing, you've got no idea who this Warhol person is, and if the patient has seen through the test then none of the tests you've given her are worth the paper they're printed on. But you can't just stop halfway. You don't have that kind of authority. Her doctor will want to see the results, and it's your job to provide them.

If that's the case, you ask her, why are you here? I guess I needed to talk. What do you think it's like for a divorcee and her abandoned mother to live in the same house? Do you think we spend all our time consoling each other with sweet words? Or that my married friends want to be the first in line to call me and hear how delightful it is to be single? At home there are so many knives . . . two kitchen knives, one fruit knife, even an electric knife sharpener to sharpen them. We live on the thirteenth floor. It's a long way down. But it's scariest on the fifth floor. Up on the thirteenth floor, you lose your sense of height. I'm looking down at least once a day. Even my dog hates me. And I never get invited to the Neighborhood Association meetings.

You heard her out. She knows that half the people in the psychiatry field are crazy, and she also knows what to say to get their attention. She managed to screw up the test results, and the charts and graphs came out all messed up. They led you to evaluate her as having severe symptoms of schizophrenia, delusion, and depression on the one hand, and borderline personality disorder on the other. And in the interviews, she led you down the wrong path, sounding logical one moment and flying off in all directions the next.

That was the day the seed planted itself on your head. And slowly it began to sprout.

11

You were advised time and again: never, ever get close to a patient. You broke the rule. Patients are like vipers. Lower your defenses, and they strike; move in too close, and they bite. That's why you're supposed to keep your distance at all times. But you ignored all that advice. The woman came to see you often. I like how you don't try to cure me, she said. You felt her teeth sinking deep into your neck, but you couldn't shake her off.

You're out drinking together in a bar in Kangnam. When I was young, you tell her, there was an acacia tree in front of our house. Come nightfall, its shadow would dance across the curtains, and I was haunted by an image of its branches snaking their way inside. There was a hornets' nest in the tree, and the air around us was thick with hornets that killed off my father's honeybees. The honeybees fought back violently, but then one hornet can easily kill hundreds of honeybees. When had that battle begun? Long before I was born. It was probably imprinted in their DNA.

The more you drank, the less clear it became who was counseling whom. And once that line had vanished, the two of you were in bed. It felt comfortable not to have to talk. She stroked you lovingly, maternally. She let you suckle at her breasts, she bathed you. You were still new to sex, but she guided you patiently. Don't be afraid, she said. It's like singing a song. It's all that time you spend listening to other people. All patients lie, you know—they want their doctors to think they're normal. That's why they get tripped up by the trick questions mixed in with the hundreds of other questions. So they automatically circle, "I read the editorials every day" and end up looking even more unreliable. Aren't you just sick of the psychiatry thing? Just stop listening to other people. Let's talk about you.

That's when it really hits you that you've spent your life listening to other people, and, in shame, you draw her close. Teeth clash, arms and knees intertwine. A clock chimes, she swallows your semen, you pull her by the hair. Your steamy love session comes to an end, and the two of you fall asleep wrapped around each other like two trees.

12

The woman improved dramatically. She was able to sleep without pills, the voices went away and the depression subsided. It wasn't clear whether it was the sex or having someone to talk to. Maybe it was a bit of both. She became infatuated with you, and you didn't leave her. Actually, the two trips you took together weren't bad. Sometimes she wouldn't come out of her room, but it never got serious. It seemed her only symptoms now were a slight trace of hysteria. Even that had its charm. Like most hysteria cases, the girl had a flair for drama, and once in a while she gave you a pleasant shock. You'd arrive to find wine and candles on the table, or she'd be waiting for you wearing a racy outfit.

But the better she got, the more uneasy you felt. She wants to have your baby, she told you. That shook you up even more. The seed was sinking its roots further and further. The spreading branches cast a shadow over your window. The branches lurched and swayed whenever the wind blew. You started to think that you liked her a lot better when she was your patient. Her obsession intensified, she suspected you had something going on with all your patients, the sex grew more violent and her phone calls and pages more frequent.

You talked about breaking up. She made one attempt on her own life, and two on yours. She didn't cry; she just picked up a knife. Every time you tried to leave her, it was the same. One time, the paring knife missed your neck and hit your shoulder instead, and the next time it was a jackknife grazing your thigh. You stayed put every time. And always the next day she greeted you with a bright smile, as if nothing had ever happened. She licked you up and down, cleaned the house top to bottom, and whipped up terrific meals.

Now you were the one who was slowly losing your mind. And perhaps you would have, if you'd kept it up much longer. You got yourself a counseling position at a college away from the city and didn't give her your new phone number. It took her two months to find you. I'm in treatment again, she said. The doctor is telling me I have to let you go. It's the only way I'll survive. I go and meditate every morning. I feel like I can breathe there. You should give it a try. I've decided I'm not going to bother you any more. And I've got a new boyfriend.

She knew you better than you knew yourself. You faltered. Two days later you were dialing her number.

13

As you stand looking at the tree, a barefoot monk in saffron robes passes by you, then stops. He addresses you in halting English. What are you looking at, he wants to know. The tree, you answer, as you bring your palms together in greeting. The monk gathers his robes about him. And what do you see in the tree, he asks. Time, you answer. The limited English you share makes your conversation Zen-like. Instead of replying, the monk sits himself down beside you on the stump. A breath of hot air caresses you both. The monk has pulled out something to eat from his satchel and is taking leisurely bites. He offers you some. You respectfully decline, but he does not retract his hand. The smell is overpowering. And yet you accept.

The tree frightens me, you say. The monk smiles. Why does it scare you, he counters, as he looks up at the tree whose roots have been eating away at the great stone Buddha for centuries. What scares me, you answer, is that these trees are crushing the statues and temples. The monk rises, placing the leftover food in its wax paper and back into his satchel. He brings his palms together, bows to the strangled stone statue, says, is the tree destroying the stone, or has the stone gotten in the tree's way?

But isn't that the way of the world? There is in each object a place where the seeds of its own destruction can grow. Until a few years ago all the temples of Angkor Wat were hidden by a thick jungle, but now Ta Prohm—the temple you see here—is the only surviving witness. A gust of wind ruffles the monk's robes and dries your sweat. The jungle did two things, the monk continues. First, the tree roots wore away at the statues and temples. At the same time, they forced the statues and temples to resist their own destruction and disintegration. Statues and trees have survived for 900 years in this embrace. Sandstone wears down easily here, he explained; if it were not for the trees, many of these temples would have been turned to dust long ago. But isn't that what life is all about?

The old Cambodian monk smiled brightly at you. He must be one of the few hundred monks that survived the Khmer Rouge slaughter. Judging by his age, he would have witnessed French colonialism, Lon Nol, the Khmer Rouge, the Vietnamese invasion of Cambodia, and, more recently, the civil war. He probably lives on alms from Buddhist followers and tourists. And here he stands, stroking a tree that is eating away at the Buddha; and then he ambles off. You look up again at the tree. It is silent in return.

14

You remain at the temple, observing the tree. A pair of black butterflies flutters overhead. Suddenly, it hits you: maybe for the woman you are this tree. Taking advantage of the aura of your appeal as a therapist, you tempted her into having sex with you at your convenience. In the end, it was you who were being treated. Her hysteria was just an excuse to get away. Which was more dangerous: your cutting remarks or the fruit knife she'd brandished? Who, after all, is the tree, and who the Buddha?

You climb back on your scooter, and ease your way back to the guesthouse. Alongside you, people are bicycling home from a day's work, pedaling laboriously. You glide past them and arrive to find the television in the lobby tuned to a short science clip on CNN— the final episode in the chain of events triggered by the clatter of the dish.

The clip reported a supernova sighted within the Magellan Galaxy, as bright as the supernova discovered by Kepler in 1604. A dish clatters, your girl left you, a woman attempts suicide, a gas explosion obliterates an apartment building, three bombs explode in Phnom Penh, an airliner crashes over Canada; that these events culminated in a supernova millions of light-years away comes to you as no surprise. That the explosion that made the supernova visible millions of light-years away has, in fact, taken place millions of years ago does nothing to undermine your faith. You understand it like this: that explosion is responsible for the clatter of your dish. Stardust particles traveling for millions of years landed on earth to set your dish and countless others clattering.

With this in mind, you call the woman. The one whose head was split apart by your roots. I want you. I want to hold you, suck you, be inside you where I belong. You and I, like the Buddha and the tree, wearing each other down, holding each other up. She says nothing. You may have called the wrong number. You slowly replace the receiver. And then you pack your bags and leave Angkor. For you, time is flowing backwards again.

An Interview with Kim Young-ha

Dafna Zur

Dafna Zur: It's a great pleasure to conduct this interview with you. Your stories and novels have been awarded the major literary prizes in Korea, and have been welcomed with great enthusiasm by your English-speaking readers as well. What seems striking first of all is your unconventional background both as a business major at Yonsei University and as a teacher of Korean as a foreign language. Can you tell us a bit about how you decided to become a writer, how you work, and where you get your ideas for your stories?

Kim Young-ha: Ever since I was very young, I dreamed of becoming a writer, though I wasn't sure what being a writer actually meant. I wrote my first short story when I was fifteen. It wasn't very good, but I remember how excited I felt throughout the entire process of writing it. I chose business administration as a major in college because I wasn't sure you could actually make a living just by writing. Once I became a writer, I turned to teaching Korean as a foreign language part-time because it afforded me more time to write. I am inspired and influenced mostly by books, as well as plays and film. While the countryside gives me a kind of peace of mind, I find that walking around the city and watching films stimulates and inspires me to put my ideas down on paper.

DZ: The drama in your stories seems to be enhanced by a strong visual quality; reading your stories and novels often feels like a cinematographic experience. The dynamic dialogue contributes to this aspect of your work. Is this something you develop consciously? Are there any particular stories of yours that started, say, from a visual sequence rather than an abstract idea?

KYH: I think it is more precise to say that rather than being influenced by films, my writing is less influenced by preexisting literary conventions. What concerned me most when I started to write is the economy of my sentences; I have made conscious efforts to convey my stories by using a succinct, straight-to-the-point style. Around the time I became a writer, I enjoyed reading works by authors such as Hemingway and others whose styles are concise and clear, and their influence, I think, is apparent in my own writing. Many of my works have been inspired by a single sentence, but often they are driven by a compelling story rather than my own stream of consciousness. Also, I pay attention to how people *really* talk and I'm interested in bringing this into the genre of the novel. I like to think of my writing style as a product of the negotiation between economy of storytelling and realistic dialogue.

DZ: Can you tell us a bit about each of the three stories in this volume of *Azalea*, "This Tree of Yours," "Their Last Visitor," and "My Brother's Back"? Please tell us also about your first novel that is coming out in English with Harcourt Press, *I Have the Right to Destroy Myself.*

KYH: I wrote "This Tree of Yours" when I came back from a trip to Cambodia. I was raised Catholic, and so I never felt a particular connection with the Asian tradition of Buddhism. But the trip to Angkor Wat made an immense impression on me, and for a while I became deeply immersed in that religious world and tradition. These feelings inspired this particular work.

"Their Last Visitor" was commissioned by a newspaper. I was asked to write a short story celebrating the end of the year. It started with a tale the art director working on the film *Memory of Murder* (2003) once told me. I find there's always something eerie about young workaholics. I remember I was reading a novel by Raymond Carver at the time. The story is a sort of homage to him.

In "My Brother's Back" I tried to capture what I see as the deterioration of family values in Korea today. Contemporary Korea is a battleground where the values of the older patriarchal generation clash violently with those of the younger generation, which no longer accepts patriarchy. Korea has undergone immense changes, and I see the family unit as an epitome of those changes. Some might feel that my portrayal is an exaggeration, but except for a slight comic twist, the family depicted reflects quite realistically what is happening in Korea today. The Korean family is a family in crisis, and lacks the communication skills and education necessary for confronting a new reality.

My novel *I Have the Right to Destroy Myself*, which will soon be published in English translation in the United States, is the very first full-length novel I ever wrote. Its narrator is a sort of "suicide facilitator" who carries around a catalogue designed to help people commit suicide in the most convenient way. I used this particular character to address the loves and deaths of young people living in Seoul in the 1990s. But I believe that even outside its geographic context, the message of the novel comes across because the lives depicted in it are found all over the world. I believe young people today lead very similar lives. We all suffer from issues such as high rates of unemployment, alienation, and communication difficulties, and we consume the same kind of music and food. This novel deals with the despair of young people.

DZ: Who do you like to read, or who are the writers who have impacted your work?

KYH: My favorite writers include Tolstoy, Hemingway, Kafka, Oscar Wilde, Yukio Mishima, and Rushdie. I just realized that they are all male writers.

DZ: Can you tell us about any of the current projects you are working on?

KYH: I am currently working on a new novel called *Quiz Show*. Basically, it discusses the adventures and love affairs of young people who meet one another through a "quiz."

DZ: What expectations do you have of yourself? In what directions do you wish to grow or evolve?

KYH: My goal is to produce a masterwork like Tolstoy's *War and Peace* or *Anna Karenina* that contains a rich understanding of humanity. That is what my life will be dedicated to for the next ten years.

Writer in
Focus

by Kim Young-ha
Translated by Dafna Zur

"Don't you think I should prepare *some* kind of dinner?" Yŏngsŏn called out from the kitchen, peeling off her pink rubber gloves. Between there and the living room was a walnut-colored table that barely seated two. Chŏngsu was bent over his work, his back to her.

"Don't bother. He won't be staying long."

Chŏngsu wiped the back of his gloved hand across his sweaty forehead. Yŏngsŏn dried the kitchen counter with a dishcloth. She looked over the sink out the window. Stray cats sometimes prowled along the windowsill and stared into their basement apartment. Yŏngsŏn liked to toss them scraps of leftover fish. For some reason, though, their visits had become less frequent.

Chŏngsu rinsed his narrow paintbrush in a bowl of water. Yŏngsŏn picked up the container, emptied it into the toilet, and refilled it with fresh water. "Of all days, why the hell does he have to come *today*? And at this hour?"

The television in the living room showed masses of curious spectators swarming toward Chongno to watch the ceremonial striking of the bell in the Poshin Pavilion that rings in the New Year.

"He's probably just curious."

"A pair of night owls, the two of you. This year's going to be the Year of the Monkey, isn't it?"

Yŏngsŏn brought Chŏngsu the container of water and rested her hand lightly on his shoulder. Chŏngsu was mixing colors, trying to come up with the blend he was looking for.

"You were born in the Year of the Monkey, weren't you?" she said. "Mm-hmm."

Yŏngsŏn was twenty-four. She had majored in sculpture at a prestigious art school, then married Chŏngsu, a graduate of the same school, before the ink was dry on her diploma. It happened so quickly that most of their friends thought the wedding invitations were a practical joke. She was already working as a graphic designer at an Internet firm, and a friend had gotten Chŏngsu a job as a set designer for a movie producer. Yŏngsŏn's small-scale start-up company kept her busy, but Chŏngsu was even busier. He usually worked through the night. Movies were always produced on a tight schedule. Chŏngsu basically lived with his tool belt on. He'd pound away for days constructing an elaborate set only to bash it to pieces within hours. That was life: good work went completely unnoticed while carelessness was criticized ruthlessly. He had to put up with a lot of crap. Yŏngsŏn tended to think her husband's talents were going to waste, but she kept her opinion to herself.

And then, a week earlier, Chŏngsu had brought home some materials from the art supply store.

"What's all this?" she had asked.

"They need a corpse. The director told me it was time for me to live up to my reputation."

The company had started production on a movie about a serial killer. The screenplay called for five bodies, four of which would be actors in makeup. The remaining corpse was the responsibility of Chŏngsu's unit. They were to fix up a mannequin so it looked real. Chŏngsu slaved away. He mustered his five years of art school and the skills he'd picked up on the job, and put together a dead high school girl who looked so real it was creepy. Yŏngsŏn, of course, helped when she could. The high school uniform hugging the mannequin was her own. Yŏngsŏn and Chŏngsu still felt like newlyweds, and Yŏngsŏn was grateful for the time they spent together the way they used to when they were students. Even if it *was* time spent over the mannequin of a dead girl.

"When's the director coming?"

"He just called—he'll be here any minute."

"Is he coming alone?"

"Yes."

"Isn't he married?"

"He used to be. His wife took off for New Zealand a few months ago along with their teenage daughter."

Yŏngsŏn was watching her husband's hands. His brush was tracing a thick scarlet stream from the girl's mouth down to her neck. He was alert—this part of her face would require the most delicate touch. There would surely be close-ups in the movie. Under the bright living room lights, the black lines along the throat— marks of decomposition—looked truly putrid. Yŏngsŏn chuckled— if a thief were to break in and trip over the mannequin, he'd have a heart attack.

"What's so funny?"

"Nothing. It looks almost done!"

"Look, I know this hasn't been easy for you. If it's okay with the director, how about we take a few days off starting tomorrow? Check out the hot springs?"

"Hot springs? That's for old people."

"C'mon. For the New Year."

Yŏngsŏn looked at the clock hanging on the wall. It was almost eleven. Chŏngsu examined his mannequin.

"Could you fix her right leg? It's way too straight. She's supposed to have twisted her ankle trying to escape the killer."

Yŏngsŏn bent over the mannequin and gave it a twist. It didn't bend as much as she expected. She grabbed the ankle and yanked. With a *crack* it twisted. She felt awful doing it. And then the doorbell rang. Chŏngsu paused and Yŏngsŏn went to the front door. She opened it and found herself face-to-face with a man in glasses. She recognized him from the tabloids.

"Please come in. It's getting cold, isn't it?"

"I brought a little something for the two of you." The director held up the typical housewarming gift of laundry detergent.

"Really, you shouldn't have . . ."

"I couldn't very well show up at the newlyweds' nest empty-handed, could I?"

Yŏngsŏn set the gift down beside the table. Without bothering to take off his coat, the director went straight to where Chŏngsu was working. They exchanged nods and he proceeded to examine the body as if he were a detective.

"So this is it?"

"Yes."

Yŏngsŏn caught a glimpse of Chŏngsu, who suddenly blushed like a child who'd been caught with his hand in the cookie jar. It was the same expression he wore every time he completed a piece that was to go on display. She was used to that expression. But the director clearly didn't appreciate the emotions involved.

"Not bad." The director smacked his lips.

Yŏngsŏn peeked at her husband to see if the timing was right, and turned to the director.

"Would you care for a cup of coffee?"

"That would be nice."

Yŏngsŏn led him to the small table where she and her husband shared breakfast each morning. The dead body continued to draw the director's gaze. Finally he removed his parka and sat. Chŏngsu joined him across the table.

"Unbelievable. Another year gone," the director commented, looking at the calendar hanging on the wall.

"Amazing, isn't it?" Chŏngsu stood and tore the December page off of the calendar. The wall behind it was left blank. But it was a brighter blank, shielded from months of dust.

"It looks like it wasn't easy."

"It was nothing."

"It must be your first corpse."

Chǒngsu scratched his head. "Yes, it is. It was harder than I expected."

"I'm sure it was."

"And I've heard it's your first thriller."

Instead of answering, the director straightened his suit and rubbed his face. He looked exhausted. Yǒngsǒn took the pot from the coffeemaker and poured a cup for the director and her husband. The director added a sugar cube and stirred. Yǒngsǒn stood uncomfortably for a moment, then perched on a stool between the two men.

"So . . . when's the release?" she asked awkwardly, reaching for the sugar bowl. The director's open stare was making her feel uncomfortable.

"We have to finish filming first." The director shrugged, bringing the coffee mug to his lips and sipping. Yǒngsǒn immediately understood the kind of man he was: the kind who always put on an air of bravado and mystery because he thought it was "cool." She considered his divorce. There was probably another woman . . . . She tried momentarily, without success, to come up with a convincing scenario. In the meantime, the director's eyes had returned to the mannequin lying on the living room floor. Chǒngsu and Yǒngsǒn followed his gaze, all three staring down at the bleeding girl in her high school uniform.

"It's pretty much done . . . when would you like to pick it up?" Yǒngsǒn asked.

The director turned to her; he took his time answering.

"Can't she stay here for a few days?"

"Excuse me?"

"We don't have anywhere to put her. And we won't shoot her scene for a few days. The office is so small . . . ."

Yǒngsǒn felt herself frown. The problem wasn't just that they had a body on their hands, a body bleeding from the mouth. Rather, her husband would fuss over it as long as it stayed there—he wouldn't rest. But what choice did they have? No room, he'd said.

The director emptied his cup and got up. He threw one last glance at the dead girl lying on her side, went to the front door, and picked up his shoes. He looked around briefly for a shoehorn, then wedged the shoes on unaided.

"Leaving so soon?" Yŏngsŏn asked.

"Yes, Happy New Year. You too, Chŏngsu."

Yŏngsŏn opened the door for him. "Goodbye."

"I'll be in touch."

They heard him walk up the steps to the street, slowly and deliberately. They locked the door behind him gently, so as not to make a sound. Back in the living room they stood over the mannequin. Yŏngsŏn stared at her high school uniform clinging to the doll's body. Chŏngsu returned to water down the hardening paint, preparing to get back to work.

"Oh, shit! Did you see her eyes open just now?!" Chŏngsu pointed at the corpse's face. He was always playing tricks on Yŏngsŏn, but this time the corpse's glassy stare gave her a real fright and she shuddered.

"Cut it out, will you? You're scaring me!" She scowled at him, lightly slapping his arm. Then they heard a mournful yowl. A white-striped stray was lurking on their windowsill. She walked toward the cat, looking it in the eye. She'd never seen this one before. She reached out and slammed the window shut with such force she thought the glass might shatter. At the same moment they heard the TV announcer start the countdown to the New Year.

Dong . . . dong . . . dong. . . . Thirty-three dull, weighty rings ushered in the New Year. Hundreds of thousands of people were shouting. Fireworks exploded into the city sky. Only then did Chŏngsu turn to the television. His face was blank, expressionless. Yŏngsŏn picked up the remote from the floor and turned the television off. And with that a sticky silence blanketed the newlyweds' apartment.   A new year had begun.

My Brother's Back

by Kim Young-ha

Translated by Kyong-Mi Kwon

My brother's back, with some ugly girl by his side. She had makeup on but it wasn't enough to conceal her age. Sixteen or seventeen at the most? Then she's only three or four years older than me. "We're staying here for a while," said my brother, taking off his old pointy shoes and stepping into the living room. Did they really think it'd be that easy, walking into someone else's house? The girl hesitated and tried to hide behind my brother but he pulled her by the arm and urged her to come inside too. Dad was speechless and could only stare at my brother until suddenly he shouted, "Why you little brats!" and sped out of the room with a baseball bat in his hand. A swing at my brother's thigh was a success. The bat found its target and my brother—he must've thought dad wouldn't dare and let his guard down—yelped in pain as his knee buckled. The ugly girl ducked her head and started screaming, too.

But my brother wouldn't be my brother if he just took the beating and did nothing. When dad raised his bat to strike again, my brother tackled him at the waist and knocked him off balance like a Greco-Roman wrestler. Then he grabbed the bat and pounded dad without mercy. Dad barely made it to his room and locked his door as one blow after another came down on his butt and back and legs. "Son of a bitch, you dare beat your own father? Go to hell, you son of a whore!" His rambling tirade spilled out of the room but my brother pretended not to hear him. He just marched into the other room, dragging the girl behind him. Of course, he was still holding the baseball bat.

I knew it. Dad was no match for twenty-year-old man in his prime. He's a hopeless case, that one, striking out only to get beat up by his own son. After a few kicks, even a dog hides its tail between its legs but that man, our so-called father, makes me wonder whether his IQ is lower than a mongrel's.

As for the girl that my brother brought home, she stayed with us from then on. With her yellow dyed hair and long manicured nails, she probably worked at a bar in some hick town. She talked so little that I thought she was a mute at first but I think she was just shy or nervous, because gradually, she started talking. She said, "Just call me sister" and offered me an ugly hairpin. I'd be crazy to ever call her my sister. The girl's name is the same now as then. It's "You, there." She knows I'm calling her when I call out, "You, there." "You there, can you make me some noodles?" "You there, the key's on top of the shoe case." So it went on like that.

I'll never understand what my brother saw in such an ugly girl but thanks to her, he started coming home early to hang out with her. I don't have to tell you what they do together so enough about their personal life. Besides, my undies also stopped disappearing from the washing machine since she came to live with us. What the hell was he doing with his own sister's undies anyway? Did he really think I didn't know what he was up to? He's my brother but he sure is a sorry case. I only let him get away with it because he's head of the household. Whether it's money or food, it comes out of his pocket. As for my dad . . . I hate to say it but he's a parasite.

"You just study hard and I'll take care of everything," my brother would say. He really cracks me up when he starts on one of his long-winded speeches, as if he's relieved to have at least one person to boss around. I wonder if he realizes that I'm laughing at him inside whenever he starts lecturing, at this guy who used to steal my undies every night. He simply goes on yakking with a serious

but ridiculous expression on his face. I let him off the hook only because he's less sleazy than dad and because he gives me stuff since I'm the only sister he has. I can't even begin to talk about my dad without getting red in the face. My brother's young, that's his excuse, but what can I say about my dad who's almost sixty? Why was my school uniform on his bed and not in my closet? Is this something a father should do to his own thirteen-year-old daughter? Okay, so I lost my temper but I hope you understand. Bet you wouldn't stay cool if it happened to you.

My brother, on the other hand, isn't as tolerant. He's always dying to get his hands on dad. Needless to say, dad is usually asking for it. Like that day after the girl and my brother arrived at our house. He shouldn't have behaved so childishly even if his own son *had* beaten him up with a bat. But why should I expect dad to be any better? After all, it was dad who took the first swing.

So it happened the day after they arrived. My brother came home early that day, washed his feet, and was giggling with the girl in his room. It seemed like a peaceful evening. Then, someone started banging on the door and shattered the calm. It was most likely some cop and this wouldn't be the first time, either. Although they came mostly for my dad, they also asked for my brother from time to time. I even became friends with a few of them. I wondered if they were paying their usual visit but when I opened the door and saw them, I couldn't recognize either the young man in police uniform or the old one in street clothes who was probably a detective.

"I'm looking for Kyŏng-sik Yi," the detective asked, so I nodded.

"Is he your brother?"

I said yes and turning toward the room where my brother and the girl were shacked up, I yelled, "Hey, bro!"

My brother came out of the room, pulling up his pants. The girl peeped out to see what was going on.

"Are you Kyŏng-sik Yi?"

My brother said yes and the detective asked the girl to come out too.

"What's going on?" asked my brother.

The detective glanced at the girl as she approached them. "We received a report that you're involved in the sex trafficking of a minor."

My brother scowled.

"What? Are you accusing me of having sex with a teenager? How could a twenty-year-old and a sixteen-year-old be accused of an adult-minor relationship? Besides, you have to have some money to be involved in sex trafficking. Why would I ever pay money to sleep with her? Are you crazy?"

The detective scratched his head with his pen.

"Then you must have kidnapped and seduced her. Maybe you were planning to pimp her at some bars. Anyway, you better come with us."

My brother was about to follow them out obediently when he suddenly glared at the detective and asked, as if it just occurred to him, "Who reported us?"

The detective was apathetic and didn't bother to reply. My brother still sensed something. He rushed over to dad's room and started rattling the doorknob. But the door was already locked from the inside and by locking it, my stupid dad was admitting that he was the one who reported them.

"Hey, hurry up and take the bastard away. He's a real bad piece of work for sure," Dad yelled from the other side of the door, holding onto the doorknob for dear life. Eventually, my brother and the girl went to the police station in the middle of the night and had to go through an interrogation. The charges of an adult-child sexual relationship or sex trafficking of a minor didn't make any sense because no money was exchanged between the two of them. Something like kidnapping and seducing a minor didn't work either since it was obvious that they decided to live together by mutual consent. But it didn't matter. My brother and the girl were harassed by the cops all night long before they were finally released the next morning. So, as soon as my brother came home, he charged right to dad's room with a hatchet raised high above his head. When he realized that the door was still locked, he started to smash it down. After a while, you could see inside the room through the splintered door. Dad wasn't just sitting there quietly, either. By the time my brother entered the room, he was standing on top of the bed holding one of its legs and ready to spring upon his son with a battle cry. Of course, the victory went to my brother again as he subdued dad effortlessly and wrecked every nook and cranny of the room. It looked like one of those houses in a demolished town. Dad cursed and screamed at my brother as he marched out after exacting his full revenge.

"You fucking Taliban."

My brother scoffed at him before returning to his room. So he's a Taliban now? Then what does that make my dad? A member of the Northern Alliance, maybe? Anyway, dad often bad-mouthed my brother whenever he wasn't around. He'd say a bastard like him needs to be locked up some place, like in jail or the army, and made into a human being. But my brother couldn't care less. Dad wasn't going to stop any time soon even if my brother kept reacting to his taunts.

As for the girl, she prepared dinner when my brother came back from work and sometimes dad even got a scoop of rice. She made food for me too but she was an awful cook.

I was eating pickled radish *bibimbap* in the kitchen when the girl ran in for cover after witnessing another brawl between my brother and dad. She said, "Your family really is something."

"You wimp, that's nothing." I laughed at her.

"Why you little . . ." She raised her fist as if she was going to hit me.

I thought about going a round with her but instead, I just shot back, "Remember I'm letting you off easy only because of my brother. Besides, I wouldn't talk if I were you, at least I don't pant and moan every night."

The girl's jaw dropped and I chose that moment to stick my

tongue out at her and go to my room. You see, you have to nip it in the bud when it comes to fighting.

How dare she act like a sister and meddle in my family business! All she knows at her age is sex and drooling after my brother. My brother, though, does look happy these days, maybe because of her. He and my dad were pretty quiet now because that girl at least took care of my brother's insatiable sexual appetite. Men don't seem to get their act together if their "need" isn't satisfied. They resort to fighting and drinking. It's one or the other.

My brother grew up getting beaten within an inch of his life by dad until he was fifteen. Considering what dad did to his own son in the past, it's a miracle to see them living together again. If dad wasn't satisfied just beating him up, he would throw my brother out onto the street naked. Often he got so drunk that he just fell asleep and forgot about his son in the cold. By the time I went out to bring him some clothes, he was shaking from head to toe and cursing dad: "Motherfucker, son of a bitch, fucking dickhead. I'm going to make you pay for this!"

He kept his promise when he turned fifteen. One day when dad got drunk and was about to pounce on him again, he punched dad's lights out, tied him up with a jump rope, and left home. Dad cursed his son until he collapsed on his side and fell asleep. My brother didn't come back for four years, until he turned twenty, and early that year, he returned triumphantly like an occupying army. Dad tried to attack him and screamed something like, "You bastard, how dare you come back to this house!" but one kick and he was down. Since then, my brother was the law.

If someone had to have power, better my brother than my dad. Dad had once called my brother a Taliban. Even if he's a Taliban or Osama bin Laden, he'd still be much better than his own father. Dad was indeed the sorriest excuse for a father, a "bad dad" package deal, lacking any qualification. The way I look at it, you need at least two things to be a good, or even average, parent. First of all, money. To be a parent, you have to be able to provide at least a minimum amount of support to your kids. I'm talking about money for things like uniforms, school supplies, and snacks. But this man who calls himself a father doesn't. Not only that, he even squanders the money his son earns. The second thing you need is a decent job. Don't get me wrong. I'm not bashing certain jobs. What I mean by "decent" is the sort of job you work hard at each day with a good conscience. (Wow, did I really say that?) I'd still be proud of my dad if he shined shoes at the mall and content if he dragged carts around and collected newspapers and cans on the street. But a snitch?

That's right, my dad's a professional snitch. People at the precinct office bring him gifts during holiday seasons. Mr. Pak, the public official in charge of my dad, comes groveling to see him with things like a twenty-two-pound sack of rice or a detergent gift set in his hands. I'm sure Mr. Pak has his pride too. But he's only bowing and scraping to a scumbag like my dad because he's a regular petition factory, reporting hundreds of cases a year. His specialty ranges from parking violations to dust pollution at construction sites, and even government officials' rudeness toward people as well as spelling errors and omissions on official brochures. To top it all off, he even filed a report on the city mayor's make of car and vehicle identification number. My dad is truly a new species of human created by the provincial government system. So it was understandable that Mr. Pak would come fawning to see dad during holidays and at election time. Dad would often sit Mr. Pak down and make his usual speeches about current politics and the future of local governments. I don't think Mr. Pak pays much attention. He only pretends to listen because he knows my dad can always go to customer service in the blue house or central government headquarters and spend ten days appealing his case without blinking an eye.

"You know, I try to tell myself that I should just let things go. But what can I do when things keep jumping out at me? People see injustices right in front of them and unfair things happen here, there, and everywhere. But people just walk by like they are blind.

So I decided to step forward and carry the burden of righting the wrongs I see. This is why I take pains to put together cases and make copies with my own money for high authorities even in this cold weather. The government wants to improve our society but the fish stinks from the head down. What I mean is that public officials dealing directly with small people like me have to change first. Am I right or wrong?"

Recently, a new kind of petition called a "one-man protest" was devised and it made my dad almost drop dead with glee. At the slightest incitement, he threatens government officials and clerks that he'll protest in front of the government building with a sandwich board. He's simply a pain in the butt for the local officials. Dad might think of himself as an embodiment of civil spirit fighting for social justice. I, however, find it tough to live with an alcoholic father who has a career as a snitch. If he was one of the homeless guys at Seoul Station, I could pretend that I don't have a father and live in peace with my brother. But dad will probably stick around the house, in that room with the smashed door, and torment us until the day he drops dead. I'm sure he'll live until he shits his pants, snitching on his own son.

Why did he ever have me and my brother? Maybe I should ask mom. Why would you give birth to children if you were going to neglect them like this? A few days ago, I actually went to her workplace, a temporary food joint near a construction site, to ask her. Instead of an answer, I got a ladle thrown at me.

"Stop yakking. You had to come in the morning and jinx my business for an entire day. Just be grateful that I gave birth to you and make something of yourself. My guts almost fell out trying to deliver you and now what? You're asking why I bothered? Go ask that daddy of yours, that scumbag son of a bitch!"

Mom is still much better than dad. When she's done cursing and swearing, she makes me a bowl of soup with some rice.

"Eat it, you little brat. By the way, I haven't seen your brother lately. What's he up to these days?"

"He's become a family man. He came home with some girl and settled in with her. These days he walks around grinning from ear to ear."

"Didn't your dad say anything about it?"

"He tried but his son licked him. He doesn't make a sound now but he gets meals from the girl sometimes. Give that girl enough time and she's going to act like a real daughter-in-law."

"Why, those little . . ."

Mom looked really angry. She threw her ladle in the pot and whipped off her apron. A few construction workers walked in and ordered some soup with rice but she ignored them and took off.

"Mom, what about your business?"

"Yun-jŏng's mom can take care of it."

"But where are you going?"

"You said we have a future daughter-in-law at home so I'm going to go see her myself."

"What daughter-in-law? She's a friggin' slut."

"A slut or a whore, I'm still going to see her."

This was serious. Here's how the food chain works in our family. Brother defeats dad. Dad defeats mom. But mom defeats brother. And me? I'm Thumbelina. I'm so small that no one bothers with me. It's the three of them who are always fighting. Anyway, mom heading home doesn't bode well for my brother. It's weird but he gets all soft when it comes to mom. This means his girl will also be at mom's mercy.

Mom was walking faster now so I grabbed her sleeves.

"Do you have any right to barge in after you divorced dad and left us?"

"You think I had a choice?"

"Then get rid of dad and move in with us."

Mom shut her mouth and stalked along like an angry person, tramping hard on the pavement. I pestered her like a spoiled brat.

"Okay, mom? Let's kick him out and just live by ourselves."

"What about your dad? Send him to Seoul Station?"

"He'll be fine there. He can go on reporting all the infractions of the railroad administration. And don't tell me you're staying at the food joint because you're worried about dad. Are you the epitome of a virtuous wife? Or better yet, are you an idiot?"

"Don't you feel sorry for him?"

"You feel sorry for everything in this world! What about us, do you feel sorry for us?"

"What's wrong with you today? You little brat, keep your mouth shut so you won't swallow dust. Either you shut up and come along or go your own way."

Mom pushed the old, battered gate wide open and walked boldly into our house. She acted as if she just left home that morning. (Honestly, my family members don't have a single thing to be proud of but for some reason, they are always puffed up when they come home.) Mom tossed off her slippers with the worn down heels and entered the living room where the girl was peeling green onions on the floor. When she saw mom, she froze with fear.

It was a touch-and-go situation. Tension crackled between the two women and I was alarmed by the kitchen knife the girl was clutching in her right hand. I had to intervene.

"Hey you there, introduce yourself. This is my mom. And you can put that knife down now."

She finally dropped the knife and stood up to give mom a proper bow. Her dyed hair, dry and disheveled, flopped forward on her forehead.

"How old are you?"

The girl hesitated.

"She's sixteen, mom."

"You, keep quiet."

Mom glared at the girl for a long time until finally she barked, "You, follow me."

Still, she didn't move so mom yelled again. "Hurry!"

The girl pulled on her cardigan and followed mom reluctantly. I mumbled to her back, "You're dead meat now."

Mom left home dragging the girl by her wrist that still smelled of green onions. I felt bad when I saw her leave like that. She'd said once that she didn't have anywhere else to go. And since she came, I didn't have to worry about losing my undies. She even made noodle soup for me sometimes and knew how to make good coffee since she used to work in a coffee shop. Above all, she was my plaything.

I ran to the window and peered down the narrow road squeezed between the apartment blocks but I couldn't see either mom or the girl. What the hell? I had no clue what they were up to. Even dad wasn't around—probably off making another petition—so I lay down on my stomach and started thinking about a new floor design to kill time.

Evening finally arrived and my brother got back from work. When he looked for his girl and couldn't find her, he gave me a suspicious look.

"Mom took her."

"When?"

"A while ago."

He dumped his bag on the floor and left immediately. He ran into dad in front of the house but they ignored each other and went their separate ways. My brother was probably off to the food joint so I ran after him to see what would happen. When we opened the sliding doors that had torn strips of film attached to them, there was mom, tossing onions into a pot.

"What are you two doing here?"

"Where's So-yŏn?"

"Who's that?"

"I heard you took her a while ago."

My brother scowled and glared at mom as if she had dumped the girl in the pot and boiled her.

"You brat, are you going to chew out your own mom now? Don't you glare at me and act like a lunatic. She has legs, she can go wherever she wants. Tsk-tsk, wherever did you find that pathetic-looking girl!"

My brother was on the verge of tears. He was about to say something but the girl walked through the door. She looked puzzled to see me and my brother.

"What's going on?"

We were just as shocked. The girl had changed her clothes. Gone was the old cardigan she wore when she was dragged out of the house by her wrist. Now she was wearing a pretty decent sweater. It was obviously brand new. She was also wearing a fancy check-patterned skirt with it instead of those old ugly jeans she got from some flea market near Tongdaemun. She looked like a real high school student lucky enough to have good parents.

"What are those clothes?" I asked her, pulling at her sleeves.

Mom bopped me on the head with a ladle and said, "Hey, she's three years older than you and she's also your brother's wife. Call her sister from now on."

"Sister my ass!" I started grumbling and mom swung her ladle again.

"If you're done trying them on, go change into your old clothes and come back in here."

"Okay."

The girl went off to the restroom. My brother couldn't hold his tongue any longer and blurted out, "Mom, what's going on?"

"She's no use sitting around the house all day, so I told her to come and work for me here. I'll give her a salary after I see how well she works. What's wrong, are you worried that she won't cook your meals anymore? You can eat here then."

"Where will she sleep?"

This was probably the most urgent question for my brother. He couldn't possibly let his beloved mistress sleep at the food joint where grimy construction workers come and go.

"Idiot, what would I do with her at night? Don't worry, I'll send her home when it's time. You just concentrate on making money."

"Oh, I get it. All right."

Only then was my brother ready to leave with a big grin on his face.

"And . . ."

Mom's voice seemed to grab him by the scruff of the neck and stop him in his tracks.

"Yeah?"

"I'm going home too. Today."

This time, I was stunned.

"What?"

"Your own mother is finally coming home and look at your faces, you don't even look happy at all. Rotten bastards! This is why people say children are no use. But I'm still going home."

"Where will you sleep?"

"With you, of course! Who do you think?"

This was the end of my life. Mom said she was going to stay in my room and what about my privacy? I knew her ladle would come flying my way again if I pulled a long face, so I stormed out of the joint. I found a piece of rock on my way home and kicked it as hard as I could. Damn it! She was doing well on her own. Why did she want to come back to a house so crammed it was already on the verge of exploding? If she returned, she'd start up those sickening fights with dad again. Yuck, just the thought of it made me shudder. But then, my brother has power now so dad won't be able to act like he used to.

Mom really did come home with her bundle of clothes, like she said she would. For the first time in five years. Dad nearly fell over backwards. She declared tragically but bravely like a captured guerilla leader, without even looking in dad's direction, "Let's try not to run into each other."

"How do we manage that if we're living under the same roof?"

"Leave if you don't like it."

The contest of wills stopped right there since my brother stood nearby, glaring at both of them. Mom left her stuff in my room and turned on the television. Dad looked glad to have mom back. After all, dad hasn't even gotten a glimpse of a woman since mom left five years ago. As for mom, she probably slept with some guy or other since she works at a food joint near a construction site. But who would glance twice at a penniless squealer like my dad? Maybe that's why dad called me around eleven at night.

"Don't you have someplace to go?"

"Why would I go anywhere this late at night?"

"Then tell your mom to come over."

"Don't bother. It's no use."

"Why don't you just ask her?"

When I did tell her, she only scoffed at him and turned up the volume of the television.

"Aren't you going? You know, dad hasn't had it for a pretty long time."

That got me a slap on the head.

"Watch what you say."

"It's true, anyway."

"Why don't you go to sleep?"

"I will."

I pulled the blanket all the way up to my eyebrows. I could hear on the news that the Taliban regime was about to fall. Wait, my brother is a Taliban . . . I was thinking this ridiculous thought and fidgeting around when I heard mom leaving the room. And after a while, I heard people murmuring followed by a heavy, violent reverberation. The whole floor shuddered. It was going to be noisy with a stereo blasting from now on. A low mewing sound flowed out of my brother's room as well. I don't think it's that hard to be a grown-up. First, you build enough strength to seize control from your parents. Then you barge into the house once you've found a mate. Then everything is solved. I really want to be a grown-up soon. Thumbelina in Hans Christian Andersen's fairytale was abducted by a filthy toad family. She wandered around until she met a prince exactly her size and started a family. So she received a new name. "A beautiful woman like you deserves a better name. I shall henceforth call you Maya." Oh, how romantic! My name is going to be Maya from now on. When I find my mate, I'm going to ask him to call me

Maya too. It fits me better than a lousy name like Kyŏng-sŏn.

It was Sunday, a week since mom returned home. Mom and the girl were making *kimbab* when I got up in the morning. I'd never seen anything like it in my whole life. Doesn't this happen only on television? Can it happen in reality too? I rubbed my eyes as I walked toward the living room.

"What's going on? A stranger would've thought you guys were very cozy in-laws."

"Never mind the stranger. Don't just stand there. Help us cut some pickled radish here."

"They're all sliced already."

I picked up a piece of cucumber and took a bite, looking around the living room.

"By the way mom, where did you sleep last night? I couldn't find you when I got up in the middle of the night."

The girl giggled under her breath.

"Go brush your teeth before you start chattering again."

Jeez! I went to the bathroom grumbling but dad was already in there.

"Hold on, I'm almost done shitting."

Alas, you can't expect beautiful words in a toad house! I sat outside the bathroom and waited. Soon, dad came out, pulling up his pants. I washed my face and brushed my teeth and left the bathroom in a flash but my brother was already in the living room.

"Hey, why are you up so early on Sunday?"

Instead of an answer, he said, "Come with us."

"What?"

I said "what" instead of "where" because "come with us" was completely unfamiliar to me. I'd never heard phrases like "come with us" in my house before. Words like "too" and "let us" are a dead language rarely heard at my home.

"We're going on a picnic today," said my brother while dusting some invisible dandruff off his shoulder. He must've felt awkward too.

"A picnic? All of us?"

In other words, we—a dad who's an alcoholic snitch, his son who beats him up and drives a delivery service van, the son's underage mate, a middle-aged woman from a food joint at a construction site, and that middle-aged woman's daughter who's in the eighth grade and has a school uniform that her mom's ex-husband lusts after— were all going on a picnic.

"I'm not going."

I dashed back to my room, munching on a cucumber. Mom came in after me.

"Look here missy, you want your mom to come home, right? Or do you want her to gas herself at the food joint? What's it going to be?"

"Who invited you to my room? I just don't want to go to the picnic. What the hell would I do at a picnic with dad? He'd probably get plastered and clown around until he started beating somebody up."

"Dad won't behave like he used to now that your brother's grown up."

"I don't want to go."

But the picnic turned out to be mandatory. Mom would go berserk if we didn't make it to the picnic. She just had to grill and eat meat, go to a karaoke bar, and take some family photos too. She said that a family should be like that. What the hell, mom never showed her mug around this house and was off cooking for some construction workers for the past five years. And all of a sudden, she marches into the house and insists on having a picnic! Shouldn't she at least have said a word about why she left us if she cared so much about her family? Maybe she went nuts after she snuck out of my room last night for a tumble with dad. I'm really worried about her now. As for my brother, he looked like he was scheming to enroll his mate in this family (if there ever was one!) using the picnic as a prime opportunity. Dad seemed ready to do anything that mom asked, at least for a while, and that boy-crazy girl would never object to anything my brother suggested.

And so a picnic it was. We got ready in haste and gathered at the gate. Mom wore a cheap, tacky azalea-colored *hanbok* that you'd only see at some traditional Asian festival. Dad wore the faded brown suit that he wears when he goes to the government customer service center. My brother had on the uniform he wore when he worked as a flyer distributor at a club but it could have doubled for either a school uniform or suit. And the girl wore the skirt and sweater mom bought her. Mom insisted that I wear my school uniform but after much debate, we settled on blue jeans and a jumper. We looked like a bunch of street hawkers from a circus.

We piled into the delivery service van that my brother drives at work. Unfortunately, it didn't have any windows in the cargo section.

"Let's take turns sitting in the front seat."

Dad sat in the passenger seat. The rest of us got in the back of the van, which was dark. It was an all-female cargo section. Silence. Mom must've felt awkward because she spoke up first.

"Once I get my *kyetton*, the money I lent plus the interest, you can have your marriage ceremony. Kyŏng-sik's a good kid except when he loses his temper."

"We don't need a ceremony but a wedding photo would be nice."

"A picture of that ugly face?" I barked at her and mom smacked me on the head as if playing whack-a-mole at an amusement park.

"I told you to call her sister!"

"I don't want to."

"It's okay, mother."

The girl was seriously kissing up to mom now. Okay, I got it. She's excited about getting a pretty sweater and skirt. What a bitch! I kicked hard where I thought her foot must have been. She groaned in pain and I knew I hit my target. It felt so good to see her trying to suppress a bigger yelp that I stepped hard on her instep again. This time the girl didn't just sit there and take it. She pinched my side so hard that I almost cried. So I started pinching her everywhere and the girl also started pinching my belly and thighs. It hurt so much that I almost burst into tears. "Come on, bring it on!" I grabbed her by the head and pulled out a handful of the fine hairs beneath her ears. She roughly tugged at my barrette and some hair around it. My head felt numb as if I'd suddenly gulped down a mouthful of shaved ice. Mom finally figured out what was going on and she cried, "What the hell are you guys doing?"

But we'd reached the point of no return. We were writhing like mating snakes.

"I said knock it off!"

Mom tried to pull us apart but it was no use. The van made a sharp right turn just then and we rolled off the seat and onto the floor. The girl started screaming like an animal. I realized she wasn't actually screaming but bawling really loudly.

"Why are you doing this to me? What did I ever do to you? I didn't do anything wrong but you're always mean to me. I am so, so scared and afraid. Just because it's your house, you guys boss me around, laughing at me and making fun of me all the time."

Wicked bitch! Why is she crying? Did anybody beg her to stay at our house? I ignored her and got up to bang on the driver's side of the partition.

"Hey, stop the van."

The van kept on going as if no one in the front heard us. I could hear the girl still crying. Mom was probably comforting her. Knock yourselves out, food joint C.E.O. and flunky! I got really pissed off and scrunched into a corner. What a picnic for this poor excuse of a family!

After a while, we drove into a rest stop and I changed places with dad. I was sitting next to the driver now. Dad got into the back instead. I got a bit worried about the girl. He might try to grope her in the darkness. Dad was more than capable of doing such a thing. And yet, my poor brother was grinning like an idiot. I couldn't tell whether he knew or not.

"Where are we headed?"

"Nami Island."

"Are we going to the beach?"

"No, it's an island in the river."

"Is it nice?"

"I don't know. I've never been there."

"By the way bro, that girl is really the pits."

"Why?"

"She's crying just because I pinched her a couple of times."

My brother's expression hardened.

"Why would you do that to your sister?"

"Because she kept telling me to call her sister."

"Then listen to her."

"I don't want to."

"Then I won't buy you new clothes or send you to school."

Now that's really low. It always comes back to money. In protest, I sat with my mouth clamped shut. The van purred along the Kyŏng-ch'un Highway. At least the scenery was nice. The sky was clear and the plains were golden yellow. Autumn was already gone.

When we arrived at our destination, my brother stopped the van and opened the back. Three people stepped out, shading their eyes with their hands as if blinded by the sudden burst of sunlight.

"Is this it?"

Dad squinted and looked around the riverbank.

"We have to go by boat from here."

Dad spit out a grossly huge blob of phlegm and said, "We don't need one, this place is good too. Is there any restaurant that serves spicy fish stew around here? Wait, there's one . . . a hot peppered stew with carp and mandarin fish! In this weather, there's nothing like a hot spicy stew with a shot of *soju*."

Dad, who's an alcoholic, was desperate for a drink. It was probably because of that craving that he was able to come this far, behaving himself without even complaining about sitting in the back. Mom and I didn't think it was necessary for us to go that far either so we scrambled to that shabby, run-down fish stew joint. Not many people were around by the riverside because the season was over, so the restaurant owner's face lit up with joy when he ushered us in.

"I put in an extra fish for you," said the owner as he brought over some stew.

"Can you add more flour dumplings too?" asked my brother.

"Yes, yes, of course. You can have as many dumplings as you want."

By then the owner seemed to have guessed who was going to pay the bills. Anyone can figure that out after just five minutes with my family. The owner brought out more flour dumplings and put them in the spicy stew. I don't know if it was that delicious but the girl with her puffy eyes was too busy shoveling the stew into her mouth to be bothered by her runny nose. I really wonder about her background sometimes. But my brother was looking at her sympathetically and mom was putting a piece of fish in his spoon. And dad, he was already finishing up his second bottle of *soju*. The conversation didn't flow easily so we all tried to say something about ourselves but got stuck and went right back to sticking our noses in the stew.

"So mom, are you getting back together with dad?"

The tragedy of my family is that I'm the only one who brings up issues like this. I'm the type of person who hates skating around things. Anyways, when I asked mom the question, she snatched the *soju* bottle from dad's hand and poured herself and her son a shot. Then she held hers up and said, "I'm not getting back together with your dad. Why? Because I won't give him my hard-earned money. But . . ."

She bumped her glass with her son's and continued:

"As for living arrangements, we're going to live together. Why?"

This is how mom talks. But this time, the pause was much longer than usual. She even smiled out of embarrassment.

Mom patted my head and began again:

"You know why! It's because I feel so sorry for you, my poor babies."

I knew what she really wanted to say. Wasn't it obvious? She was hungry for a man!

Dad couldn't care less what mom was saying and drank until he

knocked himself out. He ended up lying flat on the restaurant floor
and my brother had to carry him to a backroom. Then he went for
a walk along the riverbank with the girl. Only mom and I still sat at
the table, killing time by plucking out fish eyes and eating them.

"Isn't this nice?" asked mom, stripping meat off a fish bone.

"Nice my ass! I'm dying of boredom."

"Tsk, mind your temper."

Mom rapped her knuckles on my head before getting up to fetch
her son so he could carry dad back to the van. My brother pulled
four ten-thousand-*won* bills out of his wallet like a big shot. The girl
looked at my brother with adoring eyes and clung to his arm. When
we all got in the van, the restaurant owner and his wife came all the
way out to the street to see us off. That was the only thing that made
me feel good.

And so we were on our way back to Seoul when my brother
stopped the van in front of some girls' high school. Then he said we
had to get out of the van and take a family picture as a keepsake. But
how? My brother pointed to the sticker photo booth.

In the end, mom's face came out the size of a car tire because she stood right in front of the camera lens with her big mug. My brother and the girl, on the other hand, looked like two little clowns standing way in back. I looked pretty good but the girl complained that it was all due to the lighting in the photo booth. What an idiot. As if the lighting was only on me!

And my dad? He was still so drunk that he couldn't budge from the van. And he stayed that way until we got home so we just tossed him into his room with the smashed door. My brother and the girl went to their room too and mom left for her food joint to prepare breakfast. I'm alone in my room, sorry that I ate fish eyes. Shucks. Only cats eat that kind of stuff. Oh, wait, didn't the lady at the supermarket say I could have one of the five kittens that her cat just had? I should drop everything tomorrow and go get my kitten. Hey kitty cat, just one more day. Your sister's coming.

First Love

by Sung Suk-je
Translated by Ellie Y. Choi

1

D ust rose up from the ground, blossoming like a large
flower. Trucks poured out of the bread factory as full as
moon cakes. When they returned, they would be like rusk biscuits,
empty and flat. Young girls in blue school uniforms and white
scarves walked by silently. Under the tree arbors old men slept as if
already gone over to another world. Every day was the same. Like
identical loaves from a bread mold, yesterday was like today and
tomorrow would be the same. As usual, you trailed after me. You,
countless yous.

I saw Ch'unja's husband singing in front of the market. His
raggedy uniform was filthy but his shoes were sparkling. "Have you
by any chance seen my Ch'unja, my love Ch'unja? Her last name
is Kim, and her first name Ch'unja, oh my love Ch'unja." But the
people in this inferno walked by with stony expressions on their
hard-boiled faces. Soon he would grab each passing woman with
the same question, yelling "Ch'unja!!" at them, and eventually
collapse to the ground, rolling in the dirt. Writhing, his eyes rolled
up in his head, foaming at the mouth. After coming to he would
probably re-shine his shoes and begin singing again. I passed
Ch'unja's husband as I jumped over the gutter where gray sewage

water trickled past. It was the same as yesterday. As always, without fail, you trailed after me.

The children kicked a ball under Bus 287. The conductor banged on the door, "All clear, all clear."

The bus would leave the inferno for a big and mysterious other world, a destination unknown, only to return again to this hell. The soccer ball bounced against the tires with a loud pop, and shot way up into the sky.

The ever-present smoke from something burning somewhere rose into the air.

As always, you trailed after me, sometimes like the smoke, sometimes like the playing children, and at other times like the tires. At yet other times, you followed me like the ball.

You were taller than I was by the breadth of a hand. Your face was big, triangular and swarthy. Your body always gave off this strange, mysterious odor. The teachers often remarked that you looked like a bandit but I don't know where they would have seen a bandit, not that one would live in this inferno. Even the teachers didn't live here. The teachers came from another world to lecture, and left again for that faraway other world, their lunch boxes empty. When those from the other world left, darkness, dust, disturbance, and smell, charcoal gas and fat older girls were all that remained. One more thing remained. Something unbearable. Frightful human heads, countless heads, and people's faces. A place with more humans than animals. A world with more people than hairs on my own head. Hell.

The first time we met, classroom 26 in the third grade of the middle school in this hell, like the twenty-five other rooms, had some forty students who'd transferred to Seoul from the countryside. I was one of those students. Those who'd trickled in from the big town to, of all things, this infernal city, this infernal neighborhood, numbered about twenty. You were one of those. In the beginning there had not even been ten students. Those of us with questionable backgrounds had quickly established a pecking order. From number 1 to 10 all in one day. Those below tenth place fell in line at a slower pace. Soon, after only a few months, all 5,000 students had found their places in the hierarchy. The kid who'd become the boss of everyone boasted, "I hang with the toughest kids in the other school. I have high school friends, and know gangs from the other world."

I could not believe that all these kids feared you or understand why homeless punks with their knives and thugs who'd never bowed to anyone cowered before you. That's because I was just a kid from the country. I came to know that crossing the school bully was courting death. Knowing this was the only way to survive middle school in this inferno right outside the city. And the only way to escape to another world, another city, would be to graduate undamaged. But I didn't know this at first. That's because I had just transferred.

After only days at the new school the bully picked me to run a personal errand. I had no idea that he controlled everything in this hell from the elementary, middle, and high schools all the way to the vocational and weekend schools. Who could have guessed such a big-time bully would pick on pale and foolish little me: "Go get me some bread and Seven Up at the corner school. Now."

Another kid would have thought, "Nice, a chance to win some brownie points. What luck. I'm going to have to do my best getting the bread," and run off, arms pumping. I wasn't that kid though. I obviously didn't understand the way of things. I didn't know about school bullies. I was an imbecile. That's why I refused the order.

"No!"

The bully, his authority challenged, approached me with a menacing look that was dumbstruck, irked, and flabbergasted all at once. He grabbed me by the collar and dragged me from the third-floor classroom all the way back to the bathroom shed. The whole school, all 5,000 students, saw it happen but not one of them questioned it or made to help me.

So I got beat up by that gangster in the moldy area out back with the dried-up trees, broken desks and blackboards. While I was being pulverized I didn't even know that I'd missed lunch. For the first time in my life my nose bled at another's hands. So I ended up missing class and played hooky for the first time in my life. Pitifully, sadly, I didn't cry.

Instead, I decided on a different path. I decided from that point on that even if I got beaten up, even if my nose bled, or I couldn't make it to class, I would not end my life.

It was then that you first approached me. You came to me, lazily buttoning your pants.

"What do you know, someone's cutting class," you drawled, mimicking the disciplinary board, and spit in a long arc. "Who'd you fight with?"

But I hadn't fought. I'd been beaten up.

I got up and lifted my head. It doesn't matter who you are, it doesn't matter who I am, I was thinking to myself. I got ready to leave. You grabbed my shoulder, lighter and swifter than a cat or some other animal.

It was precisely then that I decided to find a new future. To escape this inferno. Grinning widely, you pushed me back down on top of the dirt and the sawdust. I did nothing but stare back at you. Because I had already decided to change the way I did things.

It was springtime. The season when African rhinos and deer from the Siberian steppes would be locking horns. From the air of this hell, where there was enough dirt to turn it mucus yellow, emanated the robust yet sour smell of bread fermenting in the factory. The sky was blue. Every day was the same. As if grabbing at something new, you lifted my chin with your fingers. The feel of your hands was soft and natural, and to me so starved for comfort from anybody, it felt like something I could not refuse.

"You look like a girl."

Glaring and glaring at you, I burst into tears. You stood there watching me while I wailed. I wasn't upset about the fight, the nosebleed, or the fact that I'd missed class. It was the way you saw me, as a girl. The fact that I didn't even have the guts to talk back and was just standing there sniffling away. It made me cry until my head felt numb. You disappeared suddenly and came back with a pail full of water. Across the pail, it said, "Soccer Division." This was the pail that except for the biggest school bullies who made up the Soccer Division, no one ever dared touch.

"Wash up."

I acted like you weren't even there. I ignored the Soccer Division and their pail. I shut out the world. I wasn't afraid of you. I was mortified.

Everyone avoided you. You looked down on those who were afraid of you. But you continued to follow me, me, who disliked you. You did not scare me. I just didn't like you. For some reason, you stopped cutting class as before. Even the teachers remarked sarcastically, "Paek Sungho, it's been a while since we've seen your face. How's it going?"

You responded with a smirk, pushing your chair way back and staring at the ceiling. You began shooting spitballs into the air one by one. The kids around me began to snicker. Her face reddening, the teacher folded the attendance roster and put it away. You changed seats, moving behind me. And used my back as a desk to write on.

"Die." I wasn't afraid of you. "Stop it! What's your problem?"

The teacher who was writing music on the board turned around, and the kids next to me and in the back sucked in their breath. Grabbing a notebook from the next desk you pretended to be writing. The teacher rapped you on the head lightly with the attendance roster and returned to the front of the room. You made a fist at her and swung it at her back. The kids laughed soundlessly. From that time on, I came to be known at school as the first kid to yell at you. I wasn't proud of this.

Every day was the same. Once in a blue moon things were different.

That day as always bread trucks were passing by. The kids playing ball in the street grabbed the rear bumpers of the trucks and ran behind them. Once in a while, the trucks would drop bread on the streets as they rattled past. That day for some reason a whole box of bread dropped right in front of my nose.

"It's bread! Bread!"

Like lightning, the kids gathered around the box. A small tent of dust rose up as they climbed over and on top of each other scrambling after the bread. I was the closest so I grabbed some bread first but before I could open the bag someone pushed my arm away and snatched it out of my hands. Numb, I stood in front of the empty box.

"Put all the bread back, you shits," you thundered, although it wasn't clear when you had appeared. The kids put all the bread back, even the half-eaten loaves.

I tried to leave.

"Hey you, you take five from here."

I ignored you. I disliked you. I didn't like you singling me out that way.

"I'm not going to eat the bread."

I knew just how delicious the bread inside the bag with the picture of a full moon would be. But to the end I refused it. I plodded home. You were waiting for me in front of the house. You pulled some bread out from inside your torn hat and handed it to me.

"Why do you single me out all the time? I'm not a beggar. I don't like bread and I certainly don't like you."

Your chin hardened. It became as angular as those chins on Greek statues I'd seen in art books. You shoved the bread toward me, screaming, "Don't you know how I feel?" And ripped up your hat. With all your strength you kicked the door and stomped off.

"What are you doing kicking the door in like that? What if the landlord hears you?" I stared at the ripped hat with the crumpled

AZALEA

First
Love:
Sung
Suk-je

bread inside it while my older sister ran over to me.

"What's this bread?" My sister began to gather up the fallen loaves.

"Throw it away. I said throw it all out."

"How could you waste food like that? The packaging's not even open. We should eat this for dinner instead."

My sister gorged on bread that night, stuffing herself like a pig. I disliked my sister. I didn't even like the lunches she packed for me. So the next day, pretending I had forgotten it, I left for school without my lunch. I was famished when school ended. So I ran hard after the bread truck. But a box of bread never fell off, not even one bag. It was the same the next day, and the day after.

Every day was the same. Once in a blue moon there were days that were different. It was the day my older sister and I had to go hungry. This was because that day the factory where she worked had not paid her. She cried and went to work, her eyes swollen. I was not as hungry as my sister because my stomach had been filled with water. That day you were waiting for me in front of the school. You dragged me into the bread store.

"I bought it for you."

You pushed a still steaming bun towards me. You also ordered milk with the big cow logo on it. I was about to faint from hunger yet still I refused to eat.

"Try it."

"Why are you treating me like this?"

"I just wanted to give it to you."

"I am not your servant."

"I don't need a servant like you."

The smell of fried food pervaded the store. I didn't like oily fried food very much. Eating fried things on an empty stomach gave me diarrhea.

"Do you want some of that?"

I nodded. You brought me a serving of it. No one in the store said anything to you. I ate the fried food like a bird, in teeny bites. You stood blinking at me anxiously like some kind dragon. I did not like you. I did not like myself. You packed some more fried food in a paper bag and gave it to me. I thought of my sister and didn't say anything. Coming out of the store I asked you, "Can I have some bread?"

You nodded. Filling a bag full of steamed buns you handed it to me. That night I ate the buns and my sister ate the fried food until our stomachs were about to burst. The next day my sister had diarrhea and could not go to the factory. Once again the days repeated themselves. Once in a blue moon a day was different.

I could not figure out why the other kids looked up to you so much. May, no, was it April, the platanus tree in front of school had begun to wear new leaves. That was during exam time. The kids shed their uniform shirts, pants, and undershirts during the physical, exposing bodies that had been scrubbed clean in a bath or kitchen the night before. There were fat kids, and kids who were white and angular like tofu. There were tall thin bodies and plump flat ones. Pressing their nails into their backs the kids tickled each other and giggled. Then all of a sudden, silence. You had just appeared.

You had something we didn't have, or had only a little bit of: hair, which we yanked on thinking it was string, hair that had started to give off a strange, foreign, adult odor. Underarm hair, and hair that was rippling from your chest and stomach all the way down to your groin, disappearing into your underwear. Hundreds of eyes focused on you, scattered, and then refocused, all on you. Even the strongest kid was rendered speechless by the sight of your hair. Were you the oldest amongst us? I didn't know. Were you more mature? I had no idea. Your thoughts and actions were like those of the other kids. But it was the tufts of hair on your body that got you all that respect.

You lifted your strange hairy body onto the scale. I was next. You gave me a quick look as I got on, as if to ask, "How do you like me?"

I stayed silent. It had nothing to do with me. You seemed to find it strange that I had no respect for you or your tufts of hair. Maybe that's why you tried to show them to me. That thing, which others could only dream about.

I went to the study room and registered to work there for a month during summer break. I'd decided that the only way to escape this hell was to study. I devoted myself to studying, studying, studying, and still more studying, and even tried my hand at the high school textbooks. The owner gave me special permission to work in the high schoolers' room, encouraging me to study harder alongside the older "brothers" preparing for college entrance exams. One day you appeared. You'd purchased a half-month's pass.

I worked with the older kids studying for college, and you hung out with your followers. There was nothing to learn in the middle schoolers' room except how to make ramen with chopsticks and an empty powdered milk tin wired with electrical cord. I no longer had any reason to go back there. If I hadn't gone to the study room rooftop one night at 3 A.M., I would not have run into you at all that summer.

There was a public bath on the first floor of the building next to the study room. The scent of flesh and soap wafted all the way into the nostrils of the middle schoolers in their room as well as the high schoolers. At dawn on Sundays after rolling up the study hall shutters on our way home, we would run into young girls and women, faces flushed and hair still wet, walking with their bath pails. Their bodies and hearts puffy from the hot water, they giggled nonstop as if their mouths were overflowing with soapsuds.

From the study hall rooftop all that was visible was its twin on the other side. There was a small room on top and on top of that was an electrical tower looming over like a giant with arms akimbo. The dawn moon had long since passed beyond the bread factory chimney that was still spitting out smoke without a break. It had been a while since stars were visible in this hell's sky anyway. The lights in the rooftop room where the girl lived were off. She had a habit of sleeping with the lights on. Only the older kids who hadn't yet gotten into college knew this secret. They had placed a padlock on the stairs leading up to the rooftop. Only they and the manager knew the combination. I'd eavesdropped on the older students and somehow gotten the combination. After confirming that the older kids were sleeping, I'd opened the combination lock and come up. Sure I was only a middle schooler in study hall. But even middle school students in this hell had to grow up sometime. And growing up meant sneaking a peek into the girl's room when the lights were still on. In order to do this, I had to get onto the rooftop. The girl was a precious princess who lived in some sexual fantasy the boys had made up. She worked in the factory and supposedly had the habit of singing and brushing her hair in the nude. As if every princess held captive by an evil stepmom in a tower in hell did this. Though I didn't want them to, my hands started trembling in the direction of the dark window and I cursed at them. The sound of a stretched rope being snapped came out of nowhere. I couldn't figure out when you'd come up to the rooftop or how long you'd been watching me. You were standing there like an electrical pole, smoking a cigarette.

"It's been a long time." You flicked your cigarette in my direction. I knew you were just trying to mask your nervousness.

I asked, "What are you doing here?" As if you were the one who'd come up first and I was the one interrupting what you were doing. You didn't call me on this though.

"I came to see you."

"What for?"

"I took a train and traveled around everywhere. It made me miss you."

With that you relocked the padlock on the rooftop door. Now I was a virtual prisoner on the roof. This is why I indulged you your attempts to engage me in conversation. It was also true that I was a middle school student who'd never been on a train before.

"Where did you go?"

"I went all the way to Ŭnchŏk. I got off at every train station from here to Ŭnchŏk, and visited every station from Ŭnchŏk and back."

"You idiot, aren't those stations one and the same?" It was nothing to laugh about but laughter flowed out of me anyway. You also laughed awkwardly.

"Who lives in that room over there?"

"I don't know."

I returned to being the cold middle school student. I started to move away. Someone could have come by. If the college exam crammers had found me out, I would've been beaten half to death and forced back to the middle school room. When I tried to pass you, you grabbed my arm stupidly.

"You're just going to leave?"

The feel of your hands gave me goose bumps. They were amazingly strong. It was something only someone in love could feel.

"Yes."

I wasn't a middle school student stupid enough to fall in love so easily. I pushed you away coldly. You begged me hotly.

"Let's talk a bit."

"I don't have a thing to say to you."

We struggled a bit.

In the midst of it all, you panted out, "You want to see a girl that much?"

"What?"

"I know why you're up on the rooftop."

I was embarrassed. I was also mad at you.

"I can give you a peek."

"Forget it."

"When the bathhouse opens, come to the back. There's a narrow alley between the building and the wall. There."

"I'm not coming."

I knew the place. Behind the building was a wall so high that you couldn't touch it with your hand. It had pieces of glass sticking up on top and looked as if it might topple over. The wall and the glass discouraged those who might be tempted to try to look into the bathhouse.

"At 5 o'clock."

You left saying just that.

I washed my hands. Washed them over and over again. I promised myself I wouldn't go. I fell asleep on my stomach, draped over my desk. Or rather tried to sleep.

At the crack of dawn at 5 o'clock, just when the steam began to rise again from the bathhouse, I found myself under the wall behind that building which looked like it would topple over.

"You came."

You were there early. You moved the blackboard under the wall. Underneath the board were some bricks you'd piled up. So that we could step on the bricks and climb over the wall.

"Climb up. I'll help you."

You were about a handbreadth taller than I was. And you were about two times stronger. It would work if you boosted me up. The more trustworthy and earnest you looked, the more awkward and embarrassed I became. So I looked for excuses.

"There are glass spikes on top of the wall."

The bathhouse window was higher than the wall. You had to stand on the wall to look into the window but there was that glass embedded on top. I wasn't about to risk having my rear end ripped open just to satisfy my curiosity.

"I removed all the glass."

This was true. You'd gotten there earlier, climbed on top of the wall, and smashed away enough glass so there was room for one person to sit. In the time I was wondering why you'd done such a thing, how hard you must have tried not to make any noise, not to get caught, you had already flung my leg up. Flustered, I ended up climbing and got on top.

"Can you see?" you asked from below.

72

I couldn't see a thing. The bathhouse was full of steam. I couldn't distinguish human bodies from lumps of meat in all that steam. Even if there was a person there, I couldn't tell if it was a man or a woman. And even if I could, I couldn't tell if the person was getting dressed or undressed. Watching me shaking my head you got anxious and also boosted yourself up. Seeing that steam shooting out of the bathhouse window like a canon, you apologized, "Next time will be better. We had no luck today."

I was about to tell you, you who'd somehow managed to settle your large butt atop a narrow shard of glass, that I was okay. I was about to tell you that you had no reason to be sorry. I was going to tell you that I would never again climb a wall like this to sit sparrow-like next to you.

But before I had the chance, I heard "You, you, you rascals!"

Screaming, someone ran out of the bathhouse. Someone emerged in the faint dawn light, brandishing a hammer. Frozen, I dropped my shoes.

"My shoes!"

The shoes my older sister had gotten me. They were worn right through but I owned only one pair. You pushed me off the wall. Even while jumping down, I yelled, "My shoes, my shoes!"

You were falling over the other side of the wall, but I ran off, limping. You ripped your butt cheeks on the glass. Your shins got clobbered with the hammer. But you did not fall like my shoes. Instead you jumped off. While the owner grabbed you by the waist and slapped your face, cursing triumphantly at you, you'd found my shoe, and pushed the owner so he stumbled. You brought the shoe all the way to my house.

"Sorry," you mumbled.

Thinking back, I had never once apologized to you. Apologizing was your territory. I took back my one shoe and didn't even thank you. I only said one thing.

"What about you?"

You wordlessly folded your pants up to your knees to show me your legs. They were bruised from your ankles to your knees, your hairy legs. I turned around, and the words "I'm sorry" stumbled out of my mouth.

"Next time I'll show you something cooler." Those were the words from your mouth.

2

Yesterday's yesterday was the same as yesterday's today. At ten, steam started to pour from the bread factory. Mixed in with it was the robust and sour smell of baking bread. The scent traveled through the sky like a kite, intensifying right before lunchtime when it entered the classrooms, teasing the famished students. They came to consider bread their sworn enemy. Whenever they saw any they went crazy trying to devour it.

"You know the bread shop girl, right?"

The bread shop girl you were talking about was actually not a girl but a young woman who'd stayed to help out at home after finishing middle school. There wasn't anyone who didn't know her. If she'd stayed in school she'd probably be in the tenth grade. She was slim and beautiful with full breasts, and detested the fact that the middle school kids took such an interest in her. Even the biggest bullies fell silent in front of her, wordlessly stuffing their faces until their stomachs were about to explode with bread. Eyes so cold they could freeze the kids in an instant, an expression filled with disdain and tedium, and sharp and cold hands. Even despite all this, none of the kids were able to walk by the store without looking in. The graffiti on the bathroom wall was a testament to her beauty. She was like a secret bread delivery, one that even the first graders, unfamiliar with lust or her legendary cruelty, couldn't resist.

"I have no interest in girls," I said. Half of this was a lie but there was also some truth to it. The music teacher, also a main character in those same bathroom stories, was the only other person I was interested in at the time.

"I've had a piece of her."

A lie. The girl who made the air around her cold as dry ice. If kids lingered in front of the store or dared to look inside, a stream of expletives exploded from her mouth like lava. Before or after this string of curses she would utter: "And the blood isn't even dry on your heads yet!" It was the same thing every day. So you had a piece of that shrew-like ass, huh?

When fall came, as if from another world, the wind swept through the place where you and I had met. Near the house on the site of the old orchard, several small cheeky pears ripened on a tree that was no more than a few stumps. Soon the tree and its pears would be sullied by trash. You trailed after me. You were always hanging around me.

"Do you like her?"

I didn't know the girl very well. I didn't feel things like jealousy. She had nothing to do with me.

Still you boasted, "I'm not that into her but she keeps chasing me. Did you know her underclothes are all holey? If you want, I can get one for you."

I looked down on you every time you said such things. The rotten pear fell off. When I tried to leave, you became frustrated.

"Do you want to watch me getting a piece of her?"

I looked straight into your eyes.

"Whatever."

You looked crestfallen. Yet you muttered, not giving up.

"Can you come to the boulder after your exam's done?"

I went home and washed my hands. I didn't pay attention to your words. So why did I go to the boulder after the exam? It was in a secluded place behind the school where lovers were rumored to do unmentionable things. I didn't get any sleep the night before. I tried to pull an all-nighter preparing for my test in order to regain my position as first in class. Winning first place would get me out of this hell. You followed me around, me the stellar student, though you weren't good in school at all, though you had no desire to study hard, though you didn't even understand why you should study. You were like an adult but you liked me, me who was more or less a child. If you had one thing going for you that I had to give you credit for, it would have been your blind devotion and what I owed it. Of course, of course, of course, of course, I had to graduate from this hell.

I got to the top of the boulder still carrying my schoolbag, but you weren't there. The girl wasn't there either. I lay on top of the boulder and wondered why you would have come all the way out here. I came here at the risk of scratching up the only pair of shoes I owned, the pair my sister had bought me with her first paycheck. I had listened to you. There underneath the autumn light in hell, I laughed all by myself. My debt was cancelled out now that I'd been duped by you. The slate was wiped clean by the fact that I'd actually come. I got up to leave, but was stopped by murmuring. I flattened myself on the boulder. At the time, it seemed to be the right thing to do. I couldn't tell if the murmurs were coming from you or from someone else. When I heard a male voice too thick to be comprehensible followed by a female voice saying "I'm cold," my clamoring heart clashed violently with another heart contained within me. I finally heard a sound I was able to discern. Even though it was my very first time, I knew it was the sound of the most fragile parts of a man's body and a woman's rubbing and grinding against each other.

Uuum, the pulling sound.

Swish swish, the steady rocking.

Oooo, the sound of something being pulled.

I grabbed my chest to keep from making a sound.

Then nothing.

All of a sudden a smell accosted me, a smell akin to the bread, yet dirty like sewage water, and not unlike the steam from the bathhouse. From the top of the boulder the schoolyard looked too quiet. The platanus trees stood at attention like toy soldiers, and someone was singing in the distance. I wanted the people below the boulder to leave so I could leave. Then I could stand in an empty part of the schoolyard and listen to the music teacher's singing. Something welled up from within me, as if my throat would close. I thrust my head out, getting ready to leave if no one was there.

But something was moving at the foot of the boulder. Someone's butt. Were they your buttocks? I never asked you. In the same way you never asked if I had come to the boulder. I just remember underneath the butt were two smooth long legs stretched out. I couldn't tear my eyes away from the blinding sun reflected on those two legs stretched out below me. I tried not to be dragged from behind although it felt like someone was tugging my feet. I tried not to be dragged forward although it felt like someone was pulling me down from the front. It felt like I was going to fall so I held on to my hat. The shape of the legs changed during that time. Their owner raised her head. It was the bread shop girl with her eyes closed. The girl with disheveled hair. Her legs began to shake like her tightly clenched lips. A burnt smell came out of my mouth as if a high voltage light had switched on.

I wasn't sure. Not sure. When the girl had opened her eyes. How long her eyes had been closed before they met mine.

Oooooh! When a pebble rolled down and I was caught watching, I ran several hundred meters downhill, without caring that I had startled them apart, without fear of falling, or of being scratched and ripped. Her eyes followed me home, into my dreams and to the first day I slept with a girl, in my twenties. They still follow me sometimes. Follow me. Those eyes.

I had fallen in love. I had fallen into the girl's eyes. Eyes wide open, shooting out bullets of shock, anger, confusion. Eyes whose boundary between black and white was so pronounced I could still draw it in my head. Round eyes. Eyes, opened so suddenly.

After that, every day was the same. I ignored you and she ignored the middle schoolers. We were like planets traveling our separate orbits. You, lost to sorrow, did as you liked, and I, mired in

unhappiness, did likewise. You got expelled from school, and I took
the last exam which would deliver me from this hell. When you
disappeared so did that girl.

Before graduation, we all received numbers on pieces of paper.
Those lottery numbers determined which school you ended up
at. Those still going to a technical high school for engineering or
trade school in this hell didn't even bother with the paper scraps.
Of course, those who'd failed didn't have pieces of paper either.
So it was strange that you, who'd dropped out without taking the
official exam, who had no interest in engineering or trade schools,
appeared that day in the very place where the scraps were being
distributed. As soon as I got my piece of paper I ran out of the
school onto the athletic field, fat like my sister with the complacency
of freedom and two handbreadths taller. I barely stopped when I
passed the bread store, singing some song about being resigned to
the laws of love.

That's when I saw you walking toward me in the sunlight. You were wearing a large thick coat and a rakish hat, like some rich dandy from the other world, like a government official, a sailor, a pilot, or an alien.

"Where're you headed?"

"What about you?"

We stopped in front of each other on the athletic field. You approached slowly. How did I know this was the last time? The yellow light radiating off your face seemed as if from a better world where I would soon be as well. With your back to the sun, the shadow jutting from you was both thick and short.

"Let me give you a hug."

"Okay."

I opened myself to you for the first time.

You shifted the arm that was holding me and undid your coat buttons.

"So you're never coming back."

"Nope."

You opened your coat. One final time I went into your embrace.

"I love you."

You embraced me with your whole body.

"Me too."

The other kids passed us by and looked at us askance.

In hell, trucks were pouring out of the factory while in another world whales were jumping out of the sea. It was then that I realized for the first time that I had become a man.

AZALEA

To Bury a Treasure Map at the U-turn

by Yoon Sung-Hee

Translated by Ji-Eun Lee

1

Father said he smoked his way through a whole pack of cigarettes outside the delivery room. The TV was showing a street scene as the year neared its end. Snowflakes were scattering in the wind. Mother was in labor for eight hours. Father mumbled, "Wait, wait a little," looking at his watch. He wanted his child to be the first newborn of the year. He thought all the luck in the world would rush toward him if that happened. His store had been in the red for several months. Winter was far from over, but there were only a few charcoal briquettes left. The hospital announced that they would offer free pediatric care to the country's first newborn if it were born in their obstetric clinic. My sister was born on December 31st at 11:34 P.M. "Would've been great if she'd been born thirty minutes later . . . ," father told the nurse. "Don't worry. There's one more to come," she replied. Upon hearing this, father shouted "A little quicker!" checking his watch. I was born on January 1st at 0:31 A.M. "Would've been great if it had been born thirty minutes earlier, wouldn't it?" This time it was the nurse who said this to father.

Mother was transferred to the intensive care unit immediately. Father sat beside her while she was wearing an oxygen mask and told her about his childhood. Grandfather was the owner of a rather

To
Bury a
Treasure
Map at
the U-
turn:
Yoon
Sung-
Hee

popular nightclub in the city of D. He pushed only one virtue in raising his children: mental fortitude! He was also once a judo athlete who had made city D proud. Father learned judo, taekwondo, and kendo, according to his father's wishes. For father, who was born premature at eight months and grew up sickly, sports were really beyond his ability. As they became more intense, father's stammering got worse. "It's strange. I can't talk when I see my father's face. But I said these last words just fine: 'I'm leaving home. I won't come back.' I didn't stutter at all." Father continued stroking mother's hair.

Mother was never able to hold in her arms the two daughters she delivered. After the funeral, father returned to his hometown with my sister on his back and me on his chest. Ten years had passed since he left. Grandfather still owned the nightclub. "I will work hard," father said without stammering. Grandfather held his young granddaughters, one on each knee. My sister and I immediately pooped and started crying at the same time. Grandfather, who especially hated the sound of babies crying, handed over the keys to an apartment he had bought for a bar owner he was dating, and said, "Go live on your own with your babies." Grandfather never could tell my sister and me apart until the day he died.

Father was always busy. He had to report the previous day's profits to grandfather, and every time, his father railed at him: "Bastard!" His half-brothers each had their cut and so business at the nightclub did not fare well. Father had seven half-brothers, each from a different mother. One of them manufactured fake foreign booze and sold it at the club. Another cooked up cheap snacks and sold them there for a fivefold profit. Yet another got commissions for recruiting singers for the nightclub. Whenever someone said anything bad about his brothers, father would never forget that he was the responsible one, the eldest of all the sons. But his brothers didn't care. Each was the eldest son of his mother.

It was Nurungji Granny who raised us. She had lived next

door and she loved the scorched and dried rice from the bottom of the pot—*nurungji*—so my sister named her Nurungji Granny. Nurungji Granny's eldest son ran off in the middle of the night to avoid paying a debt of several billion won ($1 million). Granny was away seeing the spring flowers with her neighborhood friends that day. She was carrying bananas she bought for her grandson. She rang our doorbell instead of her own. And she fed us the bananas instead. Nurungji Granny often dozed off: while eating, while watching TV, and even while sitting on the toilet. So we learned to play silently. We threw out toys that made loud noises. My sister was my toy, and I was hers. When people asked, "Who is older?" we replied in one voice, "I." When asked again, "Then, who's younger?" we pointed to the other with a finger: "She is." When my sister walked, I walked behind her mimicking her. When I drew, she sat next to me and drew the same picture. We called this "shadow play." Nurungji Granny handed us sugar-coated *nurungji* and said, "It's confusing, so confusing."

Nurungji Granny caressed our cheeks and murmured her grandson's name. She repeated "confusing" so many times that her memory seemed all tangled up. We stopped playing the game when she was around. But her mistakes didn't stop. She coated *nurungji* with salt instead of sugar, and put vinegar in the soup instead of soy sauce. Her food wasn't tasty, so we drank milk instead. We drank a liter of milk a day, and grew up tall.

There was a big rug rolled out in the living room. It had patterns of circles, squares, and triangles. We had our own rules when walking on this rug. My sister must not step on the red, and I must not step on the green. It was difficult to walk on the carpet without stepping on the red or the green. We couldn't help falling over when walking on tiptoe. Father didn't know the rules to our game and took us to a traditional doctor. "My children cannot walk straight. Do they have anemia?" We drew a line in the middle of the wall and put stickers on either side. If my sister stepped on the red, a sticker was added on my side, and when I stepped on the green, a sticker

AZALEA

To

Bury a

Treasure

Map at

the U-

turn:

Yoon

Sung-

Hee

was added on her side. We promised that when we turned ten, the one with more stickers on her side would become the *ŏnni*—the older one. When people asked about the stickers we told them, "We add one for each good deed." Then adults patted our heads and said, "You girls grew up so well despite the loss of your mother."

Once when I stepped on a dandelion, my sister hit me on the back lightly and said, "One sticker." We laughed, looking at the squished dandelion. From that day on, we also played the game walking on the road. Father must have been very shocked seeing us laughing at a dead plant. He phoned and consulted with an expert in child psychology. The answer was simple: "Love them unconditionally. That kind of behavior stems from lack of love." Father started hugging us tightly at least once a day, no matter what.

New stones were laid on the sidewalk in front of the bus stop. Of all colors, they chose red bricks. Sister was careful not to step on the red bricks when walking along that road. She looked like a gymnast when she walked on the edge of the sidewalk with both of her arms stretched out for balance. Her arms were stretched out like that when a Chinese delivery motorcycle couldn't slow down and rushed toward her. I was alone when I started elementary school. Father hugged me tightly twice a day. I still didn't step on a green color when walking down the street. If I did so by accident, I'd put a sticker on my sister's side when I came back home. Nurungji Granny often called out my sister's name. Granny's gaze was always directed somewhere in back of me. Granny and I were the only ones who knew that my sister stood behind me. When Father sent Granny to the hospital, I was the only one left who knew it.

Grandfather passed away when I was in my first year of high school. Dog parasites grew in his body and ate into his eyes and brain. The cause of death was known only to the immediate family. It was not a death befitting the person who opened the first nightclub in the city of D. So in the newspaper obituary, Father said it was a "heart attack." Grandfather raised five dogs in his later years. Although he had never warmly embraced his children, he would sleep with his dogs in his arms. His sons, who thought they were less loved than even the dogs, cooked up all five and ate them.

Grandfather's last word as he lay in the hospital bed was "There." His sons had asked Grandfather, who was short of breath, "Where is your will? Where did you put it?" Grandfather pointed to the hospital ceiling and said, "There . . . ," and could not continue. While Father attended the funeral, the other seven sons searched Grandfather's house. No will was to be found. The sons sued one another. None of them called Father "hyŏng"—older brother. Father summoned the seven brothers home. "I am not the least bit interested in the inheritance." As he finished the sentence, his brothers' eyes narrowed with distrust. "Really?" asked the oldest of them, who had been born within several months of Father. "Really. But on one condition. I will forego my portion on condition that I slap each of you in the face." The brothers went into the smaller room to talk it over. They came back, stood in line and stuck out their right cheeks. Father hit them one by one.

At dawn the next morning Father left home. A letter said, "I will wire you money on the twenty-fifth of every month. Take care." I stuck his note on the fridge door. During sleepless nights I rolled out all the quilts from the armoire and walked on them. I skipped the red pattern on one night, the yellow on another, and the blue on yet another. Time flew by rapidly. I graduated from high school and got a job at a travel agency. I didn't want Father's help so I closed the bank account. As I was looking at the cancelled bankbook, I had a feeling that I would not see my father again.

2

Father passed away on the train. A train ticket to Pusan aboard the Saemaǔl Express and four ten-thousand-won ($10) bills were all they found in his pocket. I quit the travel agency. In five years of work I hadn't once taken a trip. For those five years I sat on a broken

AZALEA

To
Bury a
Treasure
Map at
the U-
turn:
Yoon
Sung-
Hee

chair with a crooked back and smiled at the faces of customers who were excited at the prospect of leaving. When I quit the travel agency, I got myself a train ticket to Pusan on the Saemaŭl Express, fifth train, seat number 25. That was where Father sat and closed his eyes. Between Seoul where he got on the train and Pusan where his body was found, I tried to conjecture where his heart would have stopped while riding the train between Seoul and Pusan.

I met Q on my seventh round trip between Seoul and Pusan. He was sitting in my reserved seat number 25. "Hey!" I shook his shoulder. "This is my seat." Q didn't open his eyes for a long time. He was humming some kind of tune, his hand beating the rhythm in his lap. I lowered my gaze to look at his hand. All the knuckles had hard-worn calluses on them. "Hey, I know you're not sleeping. Let me have my seat, quick." Hearing this, Q let out a faint laugh. He blushed, something you don't expect a big guy to do. We bought a pack of four hard-boiled eggs, split it in two, and ate them. Q drank a soda and let out a burp. When I told him I never burped in front of people, Q handed me the soda and said, "Drink this and try." I finished it off and let out a long burp. The man sitting in front of me turned around and stared at me. It was refreshing. I became friends with Q.

Q had been working as a driver for the subway. He really wanted to be a locomotive engineer but this was the closest job he could find. Q's father, who lost a leg in a train accident, threw a big party for the villagers when Q became a subway driver. The villagers smiled and said that trains and subways are almost the same. They drank more than Q's monthly salary could cover. Q went through more than a pack of chewing gum everyday at work. His heart shrank and he felt claustrophobic passing through the narrow dark tunnels. Many people attempted suicide on the subway rails as the economy staggered. A woman threw herself off the subway platform around the time he hit the one-year mark at his job. She was wearing a blue blouse and black skirt. Q's eyes met the woman's for a split second before she jumped. "I will never be able to forget her eyes. I see them so vividly whenever I close mine." Q's pupils grew in anxiety and before I knew it, I was holding his hands to calm him down.

I got off at Q's stop. "No luggage?" I smiled and showed him my empty hands. "I have nothing." Then I remembered that I hadn't locked the front door of the house in city D. But there was nothing to worry about even if a thief came. Things at home would stay as they were for several months and then eventually start to lose their colors. Q hired me as an assistant to the chef in a Chinese restaurant. His cousin had entrusted Q with the restaurant when he left to go abroad. I tend not to cry easily, so I was fine skinning onions. The chef, who'd worked in Chinese restaurants from the age of fifteen, cried like a baby when he peeled them.

After work, we sat in the kitchen and drank half a bottle of *soju*— the clear strong spirit. All we had for munchies was leftover broth from spicy Chinese noodles. Q suffered from insomnia. I advised him to not to stare at the customers with his red eyes. "We don't have many customers to start with, and you'd scare them away." At this, the chef looked at me askance. He seemed to know that the lack of customers was a direct consequence of his bad food. On rainy days, Q made *mandu* dumplings for me. Q's dumplings with meat were really tasty. Q had been a crybaby when he was little, but would stop crying when he heard the word *mandu*. "They are really delicious. You would make a good business with these," I told him as I swallowed the hot dumpling that almost burned the inside of my mouth. He smiled forlornly. "These are nothing compared to the *mandu* my mother made for me for over twenty years."

I used a *jjimjilbang*—public bathhouse and sauna—as my home base. They gave a twenty percent discount if you paid one month's fee in advance. Every day I slept tight after taking a bath. I didn't desire anything that didn't fit into my locker at the bathhouse. New appliances didn't tempt me, or pretty clothes.

One day I stepped on someone's foot while walking out of the bath. "I'm sorry!" She nodded as if to say she was okay, and she continued wiping off the floor. The next day, I sat on her leg while

To

Bury a

Treasure

Map at

the U-

turn:

Yoon

Sung-

Hee

she was folding towels. "I'm sorry. I didn't see," I apologized again. I collided with her the next day as she opened the door and emerged from the bath. We lay side by side on the floor clutching our throbbing foreheads. Someone ran a towel under cold water and brought it out to us. "Are you okay?" I asked her while putting the cold wet towel on her forehead. "I'm fine. It happens all the time." She smiled faintly.

Her name was W. She showed me countless bruises on her body. "I bump into people several dozen times every day. People tell me 'Sorry, I didn't see you' when they step on my foot as I'm standing still. I may really be invisible to others." Like W said, I didn't feel her presence before I collided with her. "How long was she there?" was all I could think after I bumped into her.

W's nickname in school was Ghost. Once her homeroom teacher didn't count her present at a roll call on a field trip. W's classmate who sat next to her didn't remember W's name until the term was over. W once fell from the second floor while cleaning the windows because her classmate didn't see her wiping off the dirt from the window and closed it. Her boyfriend of more than a year broke up with her saying "I'm scared of you. Please don't follow me around from now on!"

W's mother was quite a famous actress. She first got some notice playing the role of a depressed housewife struggling to protect her ruined family from her husband's infidelity. W told me that she was born before her mother became an actress. She smiled, twitching the corners of her lips, and said that no one knows of her existence except her mother and grandmother. "No, now that my grandmother passed away, so long as my mother keeps her mouth shut, nobody knows I exist!" she murmured, as if to herself, looking into the empty distance. W and the actress don't look at all alike. "Her father may have been ugly," I conjectured while listening to W talk. As her mother became more famous, W became more ghost-like. On the day her mother won an award for acting two years ago, W was walking on the street and was startled to realize that her shadow had disappeared.

W and I paid frequent visits to *naengmyŏn* noodle places. We soaked our bodies for about thirty minutes in the hot tub, then we went out with dishevelled wet hair to look for a cold and spicy noodle place. W could eat spicy food well. "These hot foods clear my head completely." W put a steady stream of chewy noodles into her mouth. W told me that she felt alive when spicy food slipped down her esophagus. W always carried super-spicy hot sauce that she made herself. When *naengmyŏn* was served, she added her sauce to the noodles before eating them. I started to add W's hot sauce too. We breathed with our burning tongues stuck out. I lost a bit of weight too, so it might be true what they say, that pepper powder helps you diet.

On days when the restaurant was closed, Q came to the *jjimjilbang*. While W was at work, Q and I learned yoga and jazz dance. We bought and drank *sikhye* rice drinks when we were thirsty. They were too sweet, but cleared up the chest when they were chilled until slightly frozen. As the number of families visiting the *jjimjilbang* increased, they added a room for various games. When W finished work, the three of us went there and played word games. We also played the game where people had to guess the number of fruits, or the one where you had to catch the running pig. Customers sat at the round table and rolled dice. When the blocks were knocked down, people cheered: "Wow!" Toy hammers made sounds here and there as they hit an object. Q said that he doesn't like games that don't involve betting. So we bet one thousand won per game. I lost thirty thousand won in one day. The person who won most of the money at the end of the day bought seaweed soup for all. "Why do people sell seaweed soup at bathhouses?" I asked the woman who ran the kiosk, but she didn't give me an answer. After finishing the seaweed soup, we went our separate ways and had a relaxing nap. We were not interested in the weather outside. We never watched a weather forecast. Q stepped on W's ankle when she was lying down,

To

Bury a

Treasure

Map at

the U-

turn:

Yoon

Sung-

Hee

injuring her ligament, but W just made her usual indifferent face.

One day when we were playing the Go-stop Flower card game, a young girl about high school age approached. "May I play with you?" Q grumbled and said that one person had to sell *kwang* cards in a four-person game. W was the one who most often ended up selling *kwang*. Q, who never loses money playing Go-stop, lost one game after another to the girl. Finally, when the whole ten-thousand-won ($10) bill in his wallet had to be handed over, Q became angry. "Tell us the truth. You're a high school student, correct? Is a high school student allowed to gamble?" Spittle flew from Q's mouth as he railed at her. The high school girl put her arms around W's and my shoulders and spoke very softly. "I will tell you a secret. I have a treasure map. Are you up for going and finding treasure with me?" A runaway high school girl would lie in the blink of an eye, Q said. The girl took out her wallet and produced a carefully folded sheet of paper. "My father stored this map in his vault for the last ten years. Shouldn't there be a reason?" The girl looked around to make sure no one else overheard. The more I listened to her, the more real the treasure felt. Why else would she have taken only the map when running away from home? We couldn't sleep all night. The next day I concluded, "The world doesn't collapse just because you believe in a lie." Q's thought was, "If we indeed find the treasure, we divide it equally in fours." W took a long look into Q's face and mine: "All three of us are very bored right now."

Q said we had to know how to drive just in case. Seizing upon his advice, W and I learned how to drive. It took two whole months to get a driver's license. Meanwhile, every morning we climbed up the hill behind the village. According to the map we'd seen, the treasure was buried on top of a mountain. It would require physical strength to carry the treasure down on our backs, we thought. At first, we could go only as far as the mineral water spring, but several days later we could reach the top without being short of breath. I realized, after getting up early in the mornings, that early mornings are more invigorating than I had imagined. While we climbed the hill and learned to drive, the high school girl took up the task of finding out which mountain was described on the map. Q bought a used truck through his old friend from middle school. It had four seats. We went to the mountaineering store and bought four backpacks. Q said that he always wanted to have a sleeping bag, so we bought him one as a present. Q went to the hill that night and did not come back. "This sleeping bag is really warm." Next morning when Q came back from the hill, there were scores of mosquito bites on his face. At the end of the long rainy season, we finally left, loaded down with two shovels and two pickaxes.

3

The truck stank of tobacco smoke. The air conditioning wasn't working. When we rolled the window down, bugs swarmed in. Q stuck his head out the window and spat. "Do you want me to take over?" W asked. Q nodded and pulled the truck over to the side of the road. When W was about to move to the driver's seat, the girl asked, "By the way, didn't you two get second-class driver's licenses for passenger cars?" W and I answered in one voice "Yes, we were told that was the easiest to get. Is there a problem?" Upon hearing this, Q started swearing into the air: "Stupid!!"

After turning off the highway, the high school girl started navigating. "Turn right. Go straight for a while, and there will be a Y-shaped fork in the road." Q turned right, following the directions. But the Y-shaped fork never appeared, however long we drove up the road. The girl ordered Q to stop the car and ran to the streetlight because the interior light in the truck would not turn on. The girl came back after a while said with a smile, "I'm sorry. We had to make a left turn at the last three-way junction." Q stuck out his head out the window and swore, "You stupid . . . !"

The truck traveled along the unpaved road for a long while. Every time it rattled, W got a hacking cough. When she was about

To
Bury a
Treasure
Map at
the U-
turn:
Yoon
Sung-
Hee

to spit phlegm out the window, the truck stopped. The noisy engine fell dead silent. "Be honest with me. How much did you pay for the truck?" I asked while kicking the tire. "Eight hundred thousand won ($800) . . . ," answered Q, running both hands over his face as if scrubbing it. According to the girl's map, we'd reach the foot of the hill in about ten kilometers. We each grabbed either a shovel or a pickaxe and started walking in the dark. Q was swearing privately at his friend who sold him the truck. "I didn't pay back a two-million-won ($1,000) debt so you took vengeance on me, you bastard!" Upon hearing this, we all started blaming Q in unison. A whistling sound came from the mountain, chilling us to the bone. "It's a bird. Really. I saw it on TV once," whispered W, and she whistled in reply.

We reached the foot of the hill as the sky started to brighten. We prayed as we watched the sun rising between the peaks. I felt red-hot energy welling up from inside my chest. I was never so thrilled in my life. At that moment, the high school girl who stood next to me asked, "Why is your face so red?" We hid our shovels and pickaxes under the leaf litter and went to a nearby village. One must eat well before starting work. We knocked on the door of a restaurant that advertised "free-range chicken." A man in pajamas opened the door. "If you can fix a chicken dish in an hour, we'll pay double." We made this absurd deal because Q has temper tantrums when he gets hungry. The restaurant owner went out to grab some chickens, and his wife started to set the table without even washing her face or combing her hair. The food was brought out exactly fifty-six minutes from the time we placed the order. We ate the two chickens in ten minutes flat.

The hill was steep. The pickaxes were too heavy, and the long handles were bothersome when were climbing. "You know, wouldn't shovels be enough? The ground isn't that hard . . ." We abandoned the two pickaxes halfway up the hill. Just in case, we hid them under some leaves and marked the location with a red handkerchief tied to a tree. The girl made a note in her book: halfway up, red handkerchief on a tree, three meters east.

W found a telescope. When she heard a bird sing, W stopped walking and took out the telescope. She started searching for the tree where the chirping was coming from. Because of W, our uphill journey became even slower. The girl found a hat hanging on a branch, high up out of reach. She borrowed W's telescope to examine the hat and said, "It's the brand I like." We picked up rocks and threw them at the hat. It almost seemed to fall from the branch several times, but didn't. Only after we promised to buy her the same hat when we returned home did the girl give up.

Finally, we found the three big rocks near the summit that were drawn on the map. "Now, let's smoke a cigarette to celebrate." The girl produced a pack of cigarettes from her backpack. We sat on the rocks in a circle and smoked. We—W, Q, and I—had never smoked before. W, Q, and I were each sitting on one of the three rocks, and then we got up and took one, two, three, four equal steps toward the center. The girl drew a circle where the three of us met. "Let's dig!"

Digging wasn't easy. W and I dug first. Blisters quickly appeared on our palms. We dug down to knee height but found nothing. We were out of breath. Between the two of us, we finished one and a half liters of water in one sitting. While Q and the girl dug, W and I had fun looking through the telescope. "There's something out there." W pointed at a spot about 100 meters in front of us. It was hidden by leaves so it was difficult to make out any details. Downhill was steep going, but we slowly descended by holding onto branches. I slid and stepped on an orange flower. Startled bees buzzed around. What was hidden under the leaves was a mountaineering shoe. Not far from the shoe, we also found a pair of sunglasses. "How are they? Do they look good on me?" I looked up wearing the sunglasses. "They look great!" W applauded.

A big rock appeared after we had dug down about a meter. It was entangled in tree roots. I threw the newly found shoe and the sunglasses into the hole we dug. W tossed the telescope in. The girl laid down the pack of cigarettes and the lighter. Then she took out the notepad, ripped out the page where she had written down the

To

Bury a

Treasure

Map at

the U-

turn:

Yoon

Sung-

Hee

location of the pickaxe, and put it in the cigarette package. Q threw in the key for the truck. We filled in the hole. On the way back home on the express bus, none of us spoke. Instead, we slept. The girl went to the biggest bookstore in town and slipped the treasure map in between the pages of a map book.

While we were off searching for the treasure, the chef ran away from the Chinese restaurant. He disappeared with all the serving dishes from the kitchen, a fridge full of ingredients, and the delivery motorcycle. Q collapsed on the kitchen floor and cried like a little kid. "Cry all you want!" I patted his back. W went out and phoned somewhere. Four servings of *naengmyŏn* noodles were delivered. "Situations like this call for spicy food." W took the hot sauce out of her bag. "You're right. It's less embarrassing to say that you cried because the food was too hot than because you were sad." The high school girl said this while mixing the sauce into the noodles. We sat on the floor in the empty kitchen and ate the super-spicy noodles. W made a point of putting a generous amount of her sauce on Q's noodles. At that moment, a thought struck like an arrow: "Yes, this is it!" I cried, pumping my fists in the air.

I suggested we open a dumpling shop at the place once known as Q's Chinese restaurant. The menu would be *mandu* dumplings and *jjolmyŏn* spicy noodles. Q would make the dumplings and W would make the noodles. "This girl and I can take the orders and serve the food," I said, tapping her lightly on the head. The high school girl said, "Thank you for counting me in," and started sobbing. "I'm crying because this is too hot. Don't take me wrong." She gulped down the noodles without chewing.

I chipped in with the money I earned working at the travel agency, and W contributed her income from working part time at the bathhouse. We painted the walls and laid non-slip tiles on the floor. We found an expired lottery ticket at the bottom of the safe. The four of us gathered together around and scratched it. First, we verified the winning money. One hundred thousand won ($100). The winning number was 5. W moved the coin slowly over the surface. The number 5 slowly revealed itself. "What a pity! If only it hadn't expired," the girl said over and over again. Q stuck the lottery ticket on the wall next to the cash register. "This will bring us good luck."

The high school girl took a bite of Q's dumplings and gave him a word of advice. "They would be better with thinner skin. Thinner but chewy skin would be perfect." Q didn't leave the kitchen for three days after hearing this. He mixed more than five big bags of flour to produce a thinner skin. The girl commented on W's noodles. "Our selling point is the spiciness. How about we sell not just one kind, but different kinds of noodles rated by the degrees of spiciness?" We accepted her advice and came up with four different kinds of noodles: not spicy, slightly spicy, very spicy, and crazy spicy. The girl came up with the name "crazy spicy."

People lined up to eat the dumplings. Those who tasted the spicy noodles left their comments: "I've never had anything this spicy." Once in a while, there were people who ordered crazy spicy noodles. We advertised that the food would be free for those who could eat more than two servings of crazy spicy noodles. Several have tried, but so far no one has succeeded. We did not let the high school girl work in the evenings. Instead, we sent her to a school to get her high school equivalency. She finished the entire high school program in a year and entered college the following year. "She got her brains from me," W, Q, and I each claimed. The three of us collected money to pay her tuition. Dumpling shops mimicking ours began to spring up. But at no place else did they taste like ours. When the girl graduated from college, our assets increased to four small apartments and four small cars.

When the nights felt long, I'd go driving out on the highway. My only hobby was to drive for a while, pick a rest stop that attracted me, and order an *ŏmuk*—fish cake soup. I put up a map of the whole country in my room and circled in red the rest stops that had good fish cake soup. Once, while driving at night, I went back to my hometown of D despite myself. Children's clothes were hung out on the veranda of the apartment I used to live in. I looked up at the lit living room for a long time. I was glad I'd left the door open. Houses are supposed to be lived in, no matter who does so. Grandfather's nightclub wasn't there anymore. Instead, there was a multiplex theater. "When did the nightclub disappear?" I asked the vendor across the street. "A long time ago. Don't start with me. The sons fought one another and made a big fuss." The vendor blurted out the whole story without being asked. The son that received the smallest inheritance set a fire at the nightclub. The cases of several of the sons were still pending.

On New Year's Eve, I drove out on the Yŏngdong Highway. The road was jammed with people heading east to see the sunrise. I followed the taillights in front of me. The clock read 11:34 P.M. "Happy birthday, Sister." I whispered softly. "If you had lived a few years longer, I would have gained more stickers. Then I could have become ŏnni—the older one. It's unfair!" My voice was drowned out by the music from the radio. I bought a bowl of fish cake soup at the Yŏju rest stop. I paused while drinking the broth to tell myself, "Happy birthday." The clock on the wall was turning from 12:30 A.M. to 12:31 A.M. People were heading east to see the sunrise. I made a U-turn at the next tollbooth exit and drove home thinking, "Should I drive out along the west coast tomorrow? I wonder which rest stops have tasty fish cakes?"

Five Poems from
A Glass of Red Mirror (2004)

by Kim Hyesoon
Translated by Don Mee Choi

BOILING

You who fly deep into the night sky

I detect your heat while I sleep

A cruise missile launched!

The heat of explosion far above the sky!

Soon the water in a pot boils

I can't sleep, so I might as well have a cup of coffee

I almost dip my hand into the boiling water

for the boiling water looks so cold

Instead I dip my head inside the pot and say something

Are thousands of layers of ear membranes boiling?

Or are they a metaphor for birth and death?

Thousands of Morse codes undulate in the evaporating boiling
     water

It is like Mass at a cathedral

The condor shoots up high against the harsh air streams

slowly circles, then rapidly descends

and with its distant gaze looks down at the boiling water

Maybe someone has hidden a helicopter in the forest

From faraway the sound of the trees boiling

The thousands of red soldiers on the front lines pinned to the body's
    interior
begin to emit electricity to the inside, inside
this is not just a feeling but an ultrasonic, a hydro-current
my inside can get electrocuted when I place my hand in it
this time I begin to boil like an electric pot
this isn't love but an electricity detector, a missile
Hear a boiling sound from the ear
Swish, swish, I escape from my body
All the water evaporates

You may be able to swallow the entire world
but you can never swallow this
the most delicious thing
my tongue

Tonight our two pages of tongue
face each other in the dark

The black moon inside me
My tongue bloated like a balloon
The moon was in the middle of an eclipse
The owls that only open their eyes at night
inside the black moon cried

We set out wine and each of us
typed away at all kinds of words in the air
but in reality our monitors didn't save any words
Our monitors were facing one another

With my long tongue I will suck your breast-milk dry
and lick your brain

All night the two pages of tongue
whimpered like death
Without bodies
we stuck out our tongues

SPRING RAIN

I missed my stop from thinking of you

Rain fell as I pressed the bell stop, Please let me off

People in the street walked slantwise

Their screams as I jumped into the rain

The birds that talk inside the throats of the people running peeked out

Each of them shouted, I don't want to live inside someone else

A man followed a woman and a woman followed a woman and

a woman ran, following the previous man

Mr. who got off the same bus behind me followed, calling me, Sis, Sis

The handkerchief in front of his chest flapped like a flower with a

    broken stem

The sky with a damaged immune system coughed away

Dark spots below the thighs were spreading

All the clock hands attached to the rooftops slanted to the right

A previously frozen lump of clay began to melt

Ugly faces fell and splashed down onto the ground and rolled about

The birds that live inside other people's bodies flew up all together

They spat as they kept shouting

My head that used to think about you spreads to the rest of the street

I came to find a peach in this life
I came to find the red stain, the stain from the bite
of the peach you spat out as you departed
They say you are sick in the world of ghosts
but I am in the frozen mountain valley of a snowy night
I think I must have flowed down the field of snow
Where am I?
They say when you circle the entire field, red baby
becomes white grandma and white grandma becomes red baby
Peach blossom flurries, flurries of snow
fall and keep falling again
and yet the endless white paper
The footprints of my life are erased as soon as they are made
The bloodshot eye stays open somewhere deep in the ground
The hot thing that popped out from my vagina
The pencil breaks, I have a lot of homework
But where is it really?
It seems as if the peach scent is coming from somewhere

Naturally, rain fell from the sky

(However, she didn't get wet)

She took a bus to her house

(She didn't have a home)

All the passengers on the bus had a home

(However she didn't have a home)

The windows of the bus are segmented like a cartoon

(The cliffs with numbers attached to them honked and sped up)

The bus soon arrived at the terminal

(However, in truth the bus didn't have a terminal)

She stopped in front of her house

(Her house shook as though hanging from a swing)

She quietly bent down and put her face between her two legs

(She didn't have legs)

Was her house hiding inside her body?

(The house grabbed her by the throat)

Everywhere I step is my home—did she believe this?

(There was no floor to spread a blanket out on in her house)

Was the road a home for her?

(She just stood there holding her house)

Ripples continuously spread above the roof

(Her house didn't have a roof)

Her house flowed down from the crown of her head like blood

(Who pulled out the house?)

Doors fell

(However, in truth her house didn't have any doors)

The doors flowed downstream

(The river was crammed with her doors)

Her house that quietly crumbles into the river

(Where have you been your whole life?)

A lifetime of rain from the sky
(However she didn't get wet)
Her house that she can't even live in
(Her house that is draped with her eyes)

AZALEA

Five Poems from

Someday I'll Be Sitting in a Dingy Bar (1998)

by Hwang Jiwoo

Translated by Scott Swaner & Young-Jun Lee

CONTOUR LINES OF THE RAIN 1

1

I've lived my life like a waterfall, no, I can't say that but
couldn't I have lived like a water droplet flying around a waterfall?
A rainbow suspends a droplet, defying gravity—
When a droplet floats, the membrane around the void is so sweet it
    seems to shudder.

"I'm going out," she slams the door, is gone.
"No, this room needs the sound of your breathing"
mutters the man, some time after she's already left.

2

Standing for a moment on the road back, my résumé submitted,
"The world, it doesn't want me" is what I thought.
Couldn't my life's mass, weighed on a butcher's scale, always be
    more
than its true weight, like the exaggerated square footage of my
    apartment?

My life has remained just as it is, the children grow up recklessly
    before I know it,
the water level has risen now to right under my nose—
I've always been at the limit,
in fact I myself am the limit.
Somewhere on my person, I don't even know where,
I must have had some deformity
that others clearly saw and they just couldn't bear to tell me.
When I'm exhausted because someone is keeping me waiting, sitting
    in a coffee shop,
looking outside, I realize how cramped it is in here.

3

Each time I start feeling how cramped it is in here
I think about India.
The Ganges where corpses burn—
I think of the Indian boy who swooned to see
a bird's shadow huge upon the water
pulling nirvana in its wake
because the world is too beautiful.
Each time I start feeling how cramped it is in here
I think of a traveler gone as far as the Himalayas,
who is pulled along the shadow of the mountains
never ever to return.

I trust you're well. Another year has passed.
At the railing of the Tongjak Bridge I stand
looking out lazily over the golden river.
The water rushing westward
as if it would linger here a little longer
leaves behind
a surface quivering all by itself
like the fringes of a Turkish rug.
That light, if only I had compared it to
your narrow scowling eyes, I thought.

I only now received the postcard
you sent from Machu Picchu.
If I could set my life aside for a time
in that citadel floating in the middle of the sky
where breathing itself is difficult, then
the desire to live would rise again, but
avoiding year-ends and new years, I want to find someplace
desolate and remain there, in a continuous daze,
so my life would flow, be filled with questions
like a lazy bird,
its head tilted as it peers down into the water.

A Flash

The lightning bolt is a whip that strikes my medieval garden—
the violet flash welding heaven and earth into one,
a moment with nothing but the outlines of paradise, then nothing
    at all.
It will be a solitary instance of enlightenment
in which this fool, taken in by dreamy ignorance,
will spend an entire lifetime without ever realizing it.

Shortly afterward the sound of thunder, or possibly anxiety?
Someone stamping their feet on the floor of heaven—
all the flowers and branches that saw the flash of light turn to
ash and torrential rains pour down
transforming the garden into heaps
of coal—could it still be paradise?

My Lotus Pond, My Sanatorium

When I take off my clothes at the public bathhouse
there is something that makes me want to take off more.
I can feel it from within myself,
the old Indian lilac dreaming of reincarnation
of changing its body into a life different from this one,

standing there, a bit hunched over,
at the edge of the lotus pond
like bodies old and bent, about to enter the tub,
a stand of three-hundred-year-old Indian lilacs.

August in full bloom and the Indian lilacs
face me like the glowing edges
of fanned coals, growing brighter bit by bit,
I want to strip, slide into that pool of the Buddhist sublime,
exchange my life and then emerge.
Donning my crown of ember-like petals
I will laugh when my friends come from Seoul
I will say "It is the wounded who decorate this world,"
then when they are about to leave
I will make them turn and look once more
as I take these flowers full of heat
and thrust them into their eyes!

STONE BUDDHA LEANING AGAINST A WALL
IN THE SUBWAY

On the stairway down to the subway—
the Seated Bodhisattvas crouch there at the entrance
selling dried squid, fresh corn, *kimbap*, and rice cakes wrapped in
    cellophane,
a leper who once stood in the Unju Temple valley—one stone Buddha,
stands dozing off halfway down the steps.
The stairs run busily down to the subway,
run over by the stairs coming up from the subway,
the make-up advertisement depicting an orgasm,
and as if it were Holy Communion itself, a vending machine offers a
    fluorescent pack of Mild Sevens.

Young man's voice: Me, sonnofabitch, I'm gonna die. (He mumbles the
    same sentence over and over.) They'll find me under that scaly old
    tree at Sin'gal Reservoir.
Middle-aged woman's voice: Oh god! I left without locking the door!
Middle-aged man's voice: Look how old I am and I haven't
    accomplished anything. When am I going to get in to see the dentist?
    How's mother doing? (Harsh sound of phlegm being coughed up.)
Young woman's voice: Everywhere I go there's always at least one
    person who hates me. What should I do? No, I'd rather not drink
    coffee from a vending machine.
Old woman's voice: You think it's raining at the Pyŏkche Public
    Cemetery too? God, I keep thinking about that grove that appears
    only on misty days. I should go soon.
Different young man's voice: Those bastards don't know who I am yet,
    dude, I nod my head once and the cosmos spins around. I say one
    word, and you guys are dead.
Man's voice, scratchy: I really oughta quit smoking . . .
Woman's voice, choking back tears: It was all a lie.

110

Different middle-aged man's voice: If my finances don't square this time, I'm history. How can I dodge my bills . . .

Yet another middle-aged man's voice: Where do I get off for the Seoul National University Hospital? In any event, what am I supposed to say to a cancer patient who is terminal? The guy should already have a very clear idea . . .

Different middle-aged woman's voice: Honey, do you think we're going to survive this audit?

Yet another young man's voice: All day long I can't think about anything but sex, I feel like my brain's gonna melt!

Old man's voice: Me, I am just a victim.

Yet another middle-aged woman's voice: You don't think the subway tunnels could collapse?

Different old man's voice: Yep, our house is in Pyongyang. It's an old-style four-room place, traditional tile-roof, up by the Pot'ong Gate. Yep, that's what I said, I gave the address and a map to my son. (As if it were his last will and testament.)

Different young woman's voice: I just wanna suck some red throbbing cock.

Yet another middle-aged man's voice: You crook, wait 'til I get my hands on you! (Shouting)

Little boy's voice: School is scary.

Young girl's voice: It's like weird. Like that actress, Sin Aera, on the soap opera *Love in Your Heart*, like she came out wearing a green sweater, and then, like, I was all wearing a green sweater too. Then I'm all holding a ballpoint pen, and like, she's on TV holding a pen too! It's like, sooo weird!

Some aging youth's voice: It's way too constricting here. A moment ago when I was looking out the diner window, that's when I felt it. I'm leaving for India. I'm leaving and I'm not coming back.

The train approaches, finally, pushing the wind before it.
On the windshield of the train from Sindorim, station of trees,
leaves wet with rain are plastered all over like stickers.

Azalea

The Silver Trout Fishing Network

by Yun Dae Nyeong
Translated by Young-Jun Lee

*T*he day I was born, July 12, 1964, my father had gone silver
trout fishing at the Wangp'i River in Ulchin. He went
freshwater fishing every summer, sometimes at the Wangp'i, and other
times at the Kagok River in Hosan, or even the Namdae River in
Yangyang. So my mother ended up giving birth to me one sweltering
July day, sweating alone in labor.

My father had luck in the waters that day, returning home with a
bucketful of silver trout.

"I'll take him trout fishing when he's old enough," he said, gazing
down at me swaddled in a blanket.

I awoke and began to cry at these words.

I grew big like a "forced" vegetable and soon began to tag along
with my father on fishing trips. The silver trout rose to the bait we
cast out on the water when we went fly-fishing, or when we trolled,
using live trout as decoys. We'd fish all the way up to the month of
September, when the silver trout would head downstream to spawn by
the river's mouth.

Just as the silver trout would return from the ocean each spring
and swim upstream, I, too, would go back upriver every summer.

AZALEA

*The Silver
Trout
Fishing
Network:
Yun Dae
Nyeong*

The first time I received their bulletin was late one Wednesday night. It had been placed in my apartment mailbox. That rainy autumn evening I had just come back from Lawson's, a 24-hour convenience store. I was carrying some quick-fix food items— bread, V8, cans of beer, coffee filters, things of that sort. In the faint glow from the streetlight, I cast a long and rather lonely shadow. Stepping over my own shadow as I entered the foyer of my apartment building, I found a sky-blue envelope tucked into my orange mailbox.

In the left corner was printed "The Silver Trout Fishing Network." The sender's name, address, or telephone number were nowhere to be found. I thought for a second it had been delivered to the wrong place but my name and address were printed on the bottom right in the same font.

I stood at the entrance to the building wondering where the envelope had come from while the security guard, taking a break from the 9 o'clock news, shot a sullen glance at me through his window.

I threw my wet clothes into the washer, ate dinner, and took a shower. Then I turned on Billie Holiday and sipped a beer alone on the sofa in the dim living room, which seemed to cry out for a visitor. Billie Holiday had been unable to escape the depressing cycle of alcohol and drugs. She had crooned melancholy lyrics right up to her death at the age of forty-four in 1958. On lonesome and gloomy evenings I often drank beer and listened to her sad words. Why would someone with such a great gift take her own life? I listened to the lonely voice of a black singer who had died before I was even born, and shuddered at the realization that I had somehow arrived at the loneliest place in the world.

The phone suddenly rang, rattling the dead air in the room. I glanced over at the darkness gathering beyond the windowsill, and waited for five rings before picking up. It was rare for someone to call me so late at night.

I said hello, but for a while there was no answer. I almost hung up thinking it was a wrong number, but then I heard a faint, faraway voice, "Um. . . ." I felt something wasn't right and brought the phone closer to my ear, waiting for the caller to say something. After about ten seconds, a thin, unfamiliar female voice spoke.

"You are listening to Billie Holiday."

"! . . . ."

I felt as if someone had pricked my nerves with a sharp needle. As if someone had somehow snuck into my locked room. I held my breath tightly. When faced with unexpected encounters I usually try to relax and proceed calmly. I never just charge ahead because there have been times when I made myself vulnerable to counterattack that way.

"You must be surprised by my calling so late. I am phoning because . . ."

Now her voice was really raspy.

". . . I was wondering if you'd received the invitation from our Silver Trout Fishing Network?"

"Silver Trout Fishing Network?"

She didn't respond to my question, as if waiting for my reaction. Is she about my age? She sounded single. She must be calling alone, talking to me from an empty room. I was old enough to sense things like this. I grabbed the unopened sky-blue envelope and asked her.

"If you hadn't called, I would never have thought to look inside. What is it anyway?"

"It's an invitation from the Silver Trout Fishing Network."

I glanced at the clock on the wall. A call from a fishing club at 11 P.M. and it wasn't even fishing season. What's more, I'd long since quit fishing, and had never been a member of a fishing club.

"Do you recall writing a newspaper article about silver trout fishing last summer? Our club read it, and we followed your advice and went to the Puk River in Kansŏng and the Wangp'i River in Ulchin for some mountain stream fishing. Anyway, we want to invite you to join our club."

AZALEA

The Silver
Trout
Fishing
Network:
Yun Dae
Nyeong

"Sure, I'll read the invitation then."

"You'll find the time and location written on it. We'd really love for you to come. I have to hang up now, but I think side A on your record is done."

She hung up the phone before I had a chance to respond, like a postman who quickly vanishes after delivering the mail. I disliked such late night calls. They disrupted the fragile emotional rhythm and balance I was just barely maintaining. I decided to let this one go though. She knew Billie Holiday. That was a good enough reason for me to put up with it.

I calmly cut the edge of the envelope with scissors from the desk, and took out the contents.

Inside was a postcard with a xeroxed picture. It was, to my surprise, a piece by the American frontier photographer Edward Curtis called *Hopi Indians*. I couldn't imagine where they found this image. I was both delighted and shocked at the same time. I had once owned a collection of Curtis photographs called *The North American Indian*, but after I lost it I never imagined I'd run into a photograph of his again.

"Something is about to happen . . . this doesn't feel like a normal invite," I muttered to myself, sitting back on the sofa.

I sat bolt upright. Reading the machine-engraved letters on the back of the postcard, I started to feel increasingly tense. Finally, I felt as if I were being seized against my will by some police force.

The Silver Trout Fishing Network 930911

After reading the article on silver trout fishing you published last summer, we decided to have you present at our club meeting. You might recall meeting and parting with a woman several years ago. We cannot reveal to you who this is, but you might guess to whom we are referring. If you happen to remember and want to meet her, please come to our meeting at the time and date specified on the bottom of this letter.

One more thing: we are an anonymous underground network that operates through secret word exchanges, using "silver trout" as our code. However, thanks to your outstanding fishing article, we were actually able to try silver trout fishing this past summer. From now on we are planning to go fishing every summer. If you were to join us in this endeavor, it would truly be a great honor. I would like to suggest to you once again that we are intimately linked by our pasts, even aside from this recent shared interest in fishing.

The third Saturday of September (18th) 18:00, Café Telephone at the Old Kwanghwa Gate
P.S. Please burn this correspondence after you've read it.

I looked down at this strange postcard, smoking one cigarette after another. My head slowly began to throb, the blood started coursing faster through my veins, and the pulse in my temple beat hard against my eardrums. I reread the postcard more closely while polishing off some leftover beer from the fridge. Who sent this postcard that was more like a subpoena than an invitation? The third Saturday was this week. Telephone just happened to be a café I frequent near the Old Kwanghwa Gate, believe it or not. These people clearly know who I am. Damn. Who is this woman I've supposedly dated and parted from in the past? Who remembers their exes' names anyway? I lay on the sofa and stared hard again at the postcard of Curtis's *Hopi Indians*. Billie Holiday's record was still rotating soundlessly on the turntable.

The fishing article they were referring to was one I'd serialized in the *Daily News* the previous spring and summer entitled "Following the Road, Following the Water." It was part of a weekly feature series published in the "Life and Leisure" column as a useful reference for fishermen. The press team had traveled all over the country to take pictures of the best fishing grounds, gathering information on nearby lodgings and strategies for navigating local traffic. I had to travel around the country myself for five straight months examining

AZALEA

The Silver
Trout
Fishing
Network:
Yun Dae
Nyeong

each of these famous fishing spots as these articles became more and more popular with readers. It had been a good opportunity that came my way through a connection at a newspaper publishing company. I'd been bored at the time working as an ad photographer after years of struggling in creative photography. This meant officially working as a pressman, and taking as many landscape photos as I wanted. By then, I had grown sick and tired of doing commercial photography for firms and ad agencies, so I jumped at the chance to do something different. Since I was a ten-year veteran of fishing, the series was almost guaranteed to be a success.

My mind descended into greater chaos as I lay in bed, restless and unable to fall asleep. The postcard image I'd left on top of the dining table refused to disappear from my eyes.

So *Hopi Indians* had been unexpectedly delivered one day by an underground group operating under the guise of "The Silver Trout Fishing Network." I could not begin to fathom the presumed "intimate" relationship between me and this group. Maybe I slept with one of them in the past. After all, they were insisting that I had.

Was it about two in the morning? Like a sleepwalker I slowly climbed out of bed and picked up the postcard.

I *did* remember in the deepest recesses of my heart. Moments from a time so dark that they had been transformed into transparencies and discarded. I had given the Curtis photography collection to "her" long ago as a present.

She was the one who'd called me . . . , that's right. As part of some anonymous group. Who could have guessed that she still existed somewhere in Seoul?

That was three years before. Enough time for someone like me to have gone through countless relationships. Anyhow, she was the one who in the fall of that year had simply vanished like the closing scene in a movie. Speaking of movies, she had been an actress and commercial model. She studied acting in college and had some B-movie roles but never got much exposure. When I first met her, she had been shooting a TV commercial for some clothing company. We were both twenty-seven at the time, and both coincidently had July birthdays. She was already too old to make it as an actress. Knowing this, she continued working as a commercial model just to eke out a living. She'd started out as an underwear model but by the time we were going out, she was modeling for small business catalogues. An opportunity had just opened up for her to be in a swimsuit commercial for a larger corporation. I had been working as a photographer for an ad agency at the time, and had gone to Cheju Island to shoot the swimsuit commercial. That was where we met.

Ch'ongmi Kim. I'd always wondered if her name meant fresh rice or fresh beauty. But I never asked. I just liked to wonder about things like that silently.

The commercial was scheduled to come out during the summer, and the early spring beach shoot was tough on the staff as well as the models. The girls had to go in and out of the icy seawater again and again during retakes, and shoot scenes four or five times including revisions and alternatives, holding the same pose no matter how exhausted they were, until the executive producer was satisfied. The TV commercial was going to air for a long time and needed to be flawless.

The sea felt dry, almost like a desert. Behind us was a field of yellow rape flowers, symbol of Cheju Island, but we did not have time to enjoy the scenery. The models had to smile like cheap dolls in the cold, enduring the abrasive language the staff hurled at them for days on end. The agency, moreover, was trying to keep within budget and had booked the cheapest inn, making the stay even more uncomfortable. Following the shoot the staff went out for drinks downtown, and on top of everything, they forced the models to serve them like hostess girls.

The very last night of the four-day stay, I left the party to rest alone at the inn for a while. Around midnight I decided to get some fresh air along the beach. Night after night of heavy drinking had left my body feeling as if it were disintegrating like grains of

Azalea

The Silver
Trout
Fishing
Network:
Yun Dae
Nyeong

sand. The wind was cold but the giant full moon tacitly swayed and floated like a flying saucer over the cobalt-colored sea. It was then that I discovered her crouching in a field of blossoms. I approached thinking I would console her, thinking of all the humiliation she'd had to endure from the drunken staff every night.

"I left because I was getting nauseous. I can't drink with people like that anymore. This whole thing just makes me want to throw up. It makes me realize that people are just the same everywhere."

Her face was swollen and feverish-looking. Blowing cigarette smoke toward the sea, she coughed several times. Her sadness kept her calm despite her exhaustion. She shuddered with cold from time to time. My eyes rested for a while on a flock of birds flying over the horizon.

"Are those geese or seagulls?" she asked me, pointing at the horizon with her cigarette butt, while I regretted not bringing along a camera. There was a sparkle in her voice.

But the birds were so far away that I couldn't quite pinpoint what they were. They couldn't have been geese though.

"Geese would have left already."

"Yes, they would have, huh?"

Instead of responding I simply nodded my head. Pausing she turned to me and asked, "Do you think they're homing birds or migratory ones?"

She was inquisitive. Her heart was as pure as a river sprite's or she would not have been asking all these questions.

"Well, they look migratory like swallows. As for homing animals, you're thinking of pigeons, honeybees, salmon, trout, and silver trout."

"Ah, I see."

"They use the sun as their compass during their mass migration so their destination is always determined by the sun's position."

"Where did you learn all that?" she asked me again, looking up trustingly with her river sprite face. River sprite—I pictured kids in the summer frolicking naked in the water, and let out a tiny

120

chuckle. The river sprite, an imaginary creature that looks human and sounds like a crying child.

She had asked the question while I was preoccupied with that absurd image.

"It's not as if I know that much about it, but I used to fish a bit when I was young. Silver trout always return home to their river of origin."

"Ah, silver trout."

"Yes, right about now the silver trout would be swimming against the current from the ocean back to the river. When the cherry blossoms are in bloom and the days are warmed by a southern wind. Then in the autumn they return to the river mouth where they were born and die after spawning their eggs. They're similar to marine salmon, which also swim upstream to their birthplace."

"Wow, I didn't know that."

After this pleasant exchange I began to ramble on about my experiences fishing for silver trout. She listened to my words, quietly nodding her head. The yellow blossoms behind me were rustling, busily chattering away as well.

"I started silver trout fishing with my father when I was five."

"Fascinating. So where did you go to fish?"

"You name it, the Milyang River, the Sŏmchin, as well as Kangwŏndo streams like Namdaechŏn, Pukchŏn, Maŭpchŏn, Chusuchŏn, Nakp'ungchŏn, Wangp'ichŏn."

"Wangp'ichŏn? Isn't that in Ulchin?"

"How did you know that?"

I asked because I really wondered. Then she responded, almost parroting me.

"It's not as if I know anything about it, but I have passed by it several times."

"What do you mean, you've passed by it?"

"I lived in Kyŏngju for a while when I was little, and sometimes I would get on a bus to Samchŏk going along the eastern seaboard, and then back. Not for any special occasion, but because the

Azalea

The Silver
Trout
Fishing
Network:
Yun Dae
Nyeong

ocean view from Samch'ŏk to P'ohang was so glorious. It's the most beautiful road in our country. But I've never heard of silver trout making their homes in Ulchin's Wangp'ich'ŏn. Anyway, in retrospect, I think I took that bus whenever I needed to get away."

Sensing the sudden awkwardness she lowered her head and cracked a shy smile. Not that it was something to smile about. After my father's death, I too had visited Kyŏngju a couple of times to take in the beautiful coastline, usually after one of my solitary trout fishing trips to Wangp'ich'ŏn. Of course I also went to Kyŏngju to see the Sŏkkuram Buddhist statue.

I gazed at her warmly.

"That means we could have bumped into each other on a bus or something."

Not understanding, she raised questioning eyes at me. I tried another route.

"We must share some kind of karma or something then."

At this my heart overflowed with sorrow and yearning. I started imagining the two of us traveling the coast. She must have been thinking the same thing because when our eyes met she immediately lowered hers and played with the sand for a while. My mind was deeply immersed in thoughts of silver trout.

All of a sudden I felt myself blacking out as if I had a huge hangover. My whole body went limp, and I found myself gazing numbly into the swaying ocean moonlight, my jaw fallen practically to my knees. I could not figure out how much time had passed.

Then, she slowly ran her hand down my shoulder. Like an unexpected guest knocking on the window.

In our clumsiness and awkwardness she and I started pushing through the transparent space that had isolated us, and brought our mouths together limply. I quivered to realize at that moment how longing could produce desire. All of a sudden she was nestled in my arms like a baby. Everything happened so quickly that I had to try numbly to take deep breaths. I had no idea what to do next. She clasped my neck tightly, shaking, and said, "Hold me."

She and I became one in that sea of yellow blossoms, free of regret or promises. As the moonlight faded so did we, slowly floating away like the ebbing tide.

A week after I came back to Seoul, I saw her again at a café in Insadong. Her face was pale that day as if she'd been suffering from some emotional distress. We sat in silence as she chain-smoked and sipped beer. She seemed to be struggling with something, but I didn't know how to begin to help. When midnight drew near she rose unsteadily from her seat and asked me to let her rest. I took her to the nearest inn. We watched television in silence for a while, and without planning to, I undressed her and climbed into bed.

She closed her eyes and lay there like a mummy. It was only after we had begun to have sex that I realized this was not what she'd wanted. The "act" ended uneventfully. Then she opened her eyes slowly, and listlessly mumbled.

"Everything's become scary. Even this."

I continued to see her for a couple of months afterward. We usually had fried pork cutlets or beefsteak for dinner, drank some beer, got intoxicated and had mediocre sex. It was always the same. Fried pork cutlet, beer, sex, beefsteak, beer, sex, fried pork cutlet, beer, sex . . . we weren't that into the sex, but did it anyway like people stranded on an island with nothing else to do.

I waited for her one autumn day in front of a downtown theater.

I remember waiting for a pretty long time, not questioning why she might have asked to meet me at a theater. Dressed in a purple Burberry coat, she snuck in the back way twenty minutes after the movie had begun. She took me into the dark movie theater, just as I was getting over the unfamiliarity and discomfort of not being able to recognize her right away. We kept our eyes glued to the screen until the very end of the movie, like complete strangers. Time passed awkwardly until the bell rang and the lights came on. Bleary-eyed, the rest of the audience rose from their seats to leave. Suddenly she blurted out, "Man stranded in a desert."

Azalea

The Silver
Trout
Fishing
Network:
Yun Dae
Nyeong

I looked up at her. That was when I realized that her words were aimed at me. Her face was pale and stiff as usual.

"A man addicted to his wounds."

She repeated this as if her eyes were drilling a hole in the snowy screen. I listened to her, frozen in place.

"Pretends to be vulnerable emotionally but is inconsiderate and cold. A terminator."

"....!?"

"A scary man."

With this her head drooped as if her neck had broken and she began sobbing. She continued crying quietly until a couple came to claim their seats for the next show.

We came out of the theater, passed by Ŭljiro Boulevard and Paek Hospital, and crossed the walkway toward Myŏngdong Cathedral, all in utter silence. The longer we walked, the more acutely I felt the distance between us, as if with each step we were growing further and further apart. I approached the hill that led to the cathedral and realized I could not possibly catch up with her. But this was what she wanted. With this revelation I paused in the middle of the street in the midst of a sea of people making their descent. She never stopped to wait for me though, and soon buried herself among the throngs without bothering to look back, not even once. She became smaller and smaller, like a single letter inscribed in a book, and vanished completely from my sight.

When I returned home that night I donned my fisherman's outfit—a pair of polarized glasses, tights, yellow boots, and a landing net at my waist—and stood in front of the mirror scrutinizing myself.

After that, I would see her occasionally on TV or in magazines, but did not feel it would be possible to see her in person again. It was as if she had completely disappeared from my life. The Cheju Island commercial stopped airing after a season, and she disappeared from the media about a year after that.

I sat waiting, staring at the autumn rain streaming down the window that Saturday evening. Telephone was booming with people who'd been drinking since the early afternoon. The manager shot me dirty looks for only ordering a beer and occupying a whole window seat. He was normally gracious but today his severe glances were unwelcoming. Five minutes before six. Still smoking, I looked at my watch. I only had to wait another five minutes.

Sitting on my living room sofa that very morning I had burned, in an ashtray, the postcard they had sent. It was tucked between the pages of a book so no one would have found it, but it seemed to be calling out to me, "I told you to burn me!" The "Disappearing Tribe"—the *Hopi Indians*—disappeared quite literally in my ashtray.

Then something unexpected happened. Until that morning I had been ambivalent about going out to the Telephone Café, but staring at the ashes I began to miss "her." I'd developed a sudden urge to go out and meet her.

I began feeling antsy as the clock struck six. I thought I'd order another beer but instead glanced toward the window and decided to wait a bit longer. Just then I heard someone calling my name. It was the phone. I walked up to the counter and answered. It was a familiar voice.

"It's so loud where you are. Come out to the parking lot behind Sejong Cultural Center. I'll be in a red sports car, waiting for you."

It was the woman who'd called me Wednesday. After I hung up the phone, I walked out of the café, and crossed over to the parking lot across the street.

A woman with long hair and sunglasses sat smoking inside a red sports car. I paused for a moment during my approach and studied her, ignoring the raindrops starting to fall. The door swung open silently. "Get in," the woman coughed out. I got into the car as if sucked inside.

I sat awkwardly looking out at the raindrops splattering the window, until she had finished her cigarette. Outside, people were floating in the night's misty darkness. I found myself inhaling the perfume of the woman sitting next to me.

Azalea

The Silver
Trout
Fishing
Network:
Yun Dae
Nyeong

"I've never had a frozen corpse in my car before."

She initiated the conversation with a dry remark yet her tone was gracious. Or maybe her attempt at a joke created an air of friendliness. To tell the truth, I really was frozen stiff.

"This is the first time I've ridden in a red hearse," I shot right back at her.

"This hearse . . . , there are times it accelerates as if trying to escape death. Drunk with speed."

". . . if it accelerates to the speed of light, time would stop and we would escape death."

"Then space itself would bend out of shape."

"If we were to go even faster than light . . ."

"Then, we'd return . . . to the place we must go to."

She turned on the engine. As the windshield wipers clicked on, I felt as if my brief conversation with her had been a dream. She maneuvered the car expertly past the Koreana Hotel and slid into the lane toward Grand West Gate. Jane Birkin's "Yesterday Yes a Day" played quietly on the car stereo. Was it the theme song from *Madame Claude*? It had been more than ten years since I'd heard it. . . . At any rate, one thing seemed certain, I seemed to be revisiting the past, maybe even spiraling into it.

"Are you usually this quiet?" she shot at me, watching the road ahead.

"I tend to be a slow and clumsy speaker. They say this is typical of men born in the Year of the Dragon."

"I already knew you were born in the Year of the Dragon. Should I take a stab at your birthday as well?"

Doubting she'd guess right, I looked at her indifferently.

"July twelfth, 1964."

I felt my blood curdle as goose bumps rose all over my body. The suspicions I'd temporarily pushed aside all resurfaced. Who were these people and why did they know so much about me? I shot her a fierce look but she remained unperturbed. Laughing casually, she said, "It was only a guess, but was I right?" Her face, framed by hair that flowed down to her chin, was actually quite beautiful, but at the moment she looked as frightful as a ghost. Those sunglasses of hers were even more mesmerizing. But I didn't want to be drawn in by her so easily.

"You must work at the local office, right? Don't you have more important things to remember than my profile?"

"We were all born in the same year. July 1964, to be precise. Are you starting to get it?"

What did she mean "we"? All born in the same year and the same month! Unable to stand any more suspense I was about to yell at her to stop the car, but we ended up stopping anyway because of the horrific traffic jam in front of the Donga Daily News building. My nerves tightened, and I began to feel flushed.

"You might want to try and relax. If I were to tell you that we were all born in Seoul, I'm afraid you'd try to jump out the window."

Charcoal-colored cigarette smoke filled the air. Suddenly my head began to ache and an indescribable fatigue came over me.

"I'm getting carsick. Can you at least crack open the window a bit?"

"Sure. It's understandable that thinking about the past is making you nauseous."

I felt better when gentle raindrops cooled my face. But my heart was still racing. There was no sign of the traffic clearing on Mapo Bridge.

"Where are you taking me?" I turned and asked her, "and how about letting me see your face. I don't like being kidnapped like this. You have to give me something to go on, anything at all."

She remained quiet for a time. The sound of the rain grew louder. After rain the autumn leaves would be a deeper crimson. The car proceeded about ten more yards and then stopped again. "Tell me," I said again. She appeared to think hard about where to begin.

"Have you ever heard of the famous artist, Arnulf Rainer?"

Her voice became deep and throaty. She didn't really seem to expect a response so I didn't answer.

AZALEA

*The Silver
Trout
Fishing
Network:
Yun Dae
Nyeong*

"Then do you know what body painting is?"

Yes, I remembered it from some art magazine. I'd seen pictures of men and women covered with paint, walking down a path or lying in a park.

"It's an elevated form of art that disregards social taboos and expresses freedom in life. I'll quiz you a bit now. If you get it right, I'll put a star up for you tonight."

The car turned left at the Kongdŏktong rotary and headed toward Sŏgang University. The rain and fog descended so heavily it felt as if we were swimming through a black sea.

"This car contains things that were killed because they dissented, things deformed by pain, frustrated ambitions, and other things of that sort. Are you beginning to catch on?"

"So now this funeral hearse is some sort of a racing cemetery?"

"Yes, a cemetery, but one dreaming of rebirth."

"Okay."

"We have our own constitution, so to speak."

"Sure," I responded blankly.

"Article 1 Clause 1 of Eluard's poem 'Freedom,' Clause 2 in Schweigger's novel *Wake Up and Face the Sorrow*, Clause 3 from Jarmusch's film *Stranger than Paradise*, Clause 4 Mozart, Clause 5 Van Gogh and Munch, Article 2 Clause 1 marijuana, Clause 2 camera and free sex, Clause 3 spaceships, Clause 4 India and Tibet, Article 3 Clause 1 beer cans and sandy beaches, Clause 2 Maria Callas and Mike Oldfield, Clause 3 Roland Barthes and Pascal Resnais . . ."

She unemotionally rattled off a list, enunciating each word as if reading from some menu.

"You must know that some of those things are illegal," I commented in a low voice.

"Hmph, haven't you heard of the phrase 'vanished without a trace'? Look here. We won't even know when and where we'll meet again. Do you understand?"

Vanished without a trace. . . . I repeated this to myself, thinking

128

of the Hopi Indians. Wondering if these people would also vanish into the depths of an abyss.

"Okay, now let me start the questions."

Suddenly she became more animated and stepped on the accelerator. We glided swiftly down the road ignoring every traffic light. The sports car zigzagged between rows of automobiles like a beetle high on some phosphorescent drug. I wiped the cold sweat off my forehead.

"Would you ever have thought that all these articles from our constitution are on this car?"

"On this car?"

"Yes. On this very car."

For the first time, I sensed a strange anxiety come over her face. Her movements became more abrupt, and the air around us suddenly chilled. Without a word I pretended to look around inside the car. It was the kind of question that could only be answered by the questioner. So I sat there, blindly staring ahead without even bothering to come up with a response. The car stopped at a light, and she started to try to explain in that same lackluster voice.

"I . . . painted them all over the car, on this car. Then I painted everything over with red. Just as in body painting."

I stared at her blankly.

"You mean this very car?"

"Yes, so that they would no longer be suppressed or managed, yet protected from further attack or damage. It's analogous to the structure of our underground network. We are finding ways to recover within a state of unboundedness."

A state of unboundedness. . . . It was within this state of unbounded consciousness that I was moving toward an unknown state. Yet there was no way to escape. I could only move forward.

Were we going in the direction of Hongik University? She muttered, "We're here," as the car disappeared into a narrow alley in the café area. It had all happened so quickly, I began to feel myself getting agitated again.

AZALEA

The Silver
Trout
Fishing
Network:
Yun Dae
Nyeong

As we had near the Old Kanghwa Palace, we stayed inside the car for a while. She turned off the radio, the headlights, and the engine, and started smoking again. Her face disappeared and reappeared each time she exhaled and inhaled. Though I was tempted to say it had been an awesome drive, now wasn't the time for levity. I was trapped inside this car like a captive in a holding cell. There was one last thing I wanted to ask her. But the time never seemed right, and the waiting only grew more painful. I wasn't the first to break the silence. She took off her sunglasses and looked directly into my eyes. For a brief moment, she took my breath away. Her eyes resembled those of Monica Vitti in the film *L'Eclisse*. They were soft and luminous. Somewhere I heard a distant sound like a water jug rolling around.

"You have traveled back to July 1964 in a time machine. You will not be able to leave until tomorrow morning. You must promise no matter what happens that you will not try to leave."

"I promise. But there's something I need to know. It's the reason I came all the way here."

The sound of the rolling water jug stopped, drowned out by street noise. She nodded as if telling me to proceed.

"Tell me if she's here. This is very important to me."

"She's here," she confirmed.

"Let me explain. Our very first meeting was two springs ago. An unknown actress at the time, she began to meet with a group of fellow magazine writers, college lecturers, and artists at a café in Sinch'on. This grew into what we have today. They all had different reasons for joining but all the members had been rejected by life in some way. They sought out others like themselves, and the meetings became more and more secretive. As time passed, architects, doctors, underground singers, and poets joined the group, but membership was eventually restricted to those born in July of 1964 as a way to strengthen club solidarity. Of course to the outside world, all these people continue to lead normal lives. But all the members are unable to find any grounding in that existence.

We meet in secret once or twice a month. In a way we are leading a double life, unable to accept the real world. So we live as people who've built an entirely different community underground. This is why we decided to use the coded language of silver trout among ourselves. It is here that we practice over and over again strategies for survival."

I looked through the dim window and took stock of the world we had just passed through. I was not sure whether I belonged here or there. "Okay, let's go," she said as she unfastened her seat belt. I was jolted from my numbness. Then she got out of the car.

Unfamiliar concrete roads stretching on and on. Eaves of roofs connecting in all directions, and between them, dark, cramped alleys. The rhythmic sound of her walking in front of me, blocking my way. Finally the sudden hazy silhouette of a stairway. Icy darkness pressed down on my back and chilled my heart.

I was roused out of my stupor by the heavy sound of a knock and turned to look at the wooden door of the underground shed in front of me. My rain-soaked body started to shake. I noticed that her silhouette was also trembling before me, standing a dark distance away.

I was overcome by a sudden desire to stand there all night in that exact position. Carried away by a strange excitement, I just wanted to stay with her in front of that unopened door. But I heard footsteps from within, scraping toward the door. I was overwhelmed all of a sudden by an intense urge to hug her. How could I have explained this unstemmable tide of longing sweeping over me?

I was afraid. I'd never really met people that different from myself. It was really beyond my realm of experience. But before the hand I had reached out could make contact with her I heard her talking to someone inside.

The door opened with a creak.

"It's raining," a man said in a scratchy voice. His face was occluded by a strange darkness. There was a stream of blue light

AZALEA

The Silver
Trout
Fishing
Network:
Yun Dae
Nyeong

along the path he had just taken. I was surprised by the warmth of his hand, which I shook. He remained silent as I followed him along a corridor. I began to feel numb again as I took in the scent of wood and another unfamiliar odor, sour and vinegary. Maybe it was the smell of burning candles, but I couldn't be sure. I was barely able to keep my balance. The hall felt so much longer than it really was.

Eventually, I heard people talking. The fading blue light revealed the texture of the wooden floor, and the smell of alcohol assaulted my nostrils along with the smell of burning plants. I saw lit candles arranged in a circle. Then my consciousness dropped away like a lizard's tail. I meant less than a single candle. I was nothing more than clothing draped over empty air. All the commotion in that airtight place stopped when I entered, and once-scattered eyes focused on the very space of my existence. There were about ten people there. Some were lying around holding cups of wine, some were half naked and holding each other in the corner, still others were strumming guitars, reading by candlelight, or drinking coffee. All these scenes were channeled into my pupils. I stood alone in a corner of the room, confused as to how I should act. When the tension dissipated, I realized that their looks were signs of approval. They only wanted to confirm that I wasn't a threat. One of them mumbled without even looking at me, "The world is divided into two groups: our side or their side. You have just crossed over to our side."

I sat uncomfortably on the corner of a cabinet that held some books. Had I really come to the other side of the world? The woman who'd brought me disappeared briefly and returned in a different outfit, carrying a green bottle of alcohol. It could have been wine, but there was no way I could even register its taste. She poured some into a cup, and I gulped down two glasses quickly.

"Stay here. Until someone comes for you."

She left me then to join the others.

From that point on, no one gave me a second glance or even tried to talk to me. They just sat around as before, occasionally clinking their glasses in the midst of incessant chatter. I found my whole existence again reduced to that of a burnt-out candle, and apprehensively tried to keep track of time. I couldn't find any traces of "her" although they said she was here. I wondered who would come for me, and when?

My mind wandered again, thinking about the Hopis, that tragic tribe standing on a windy mesa waiting for eternal oblivion. I thought of them and the woman who had left me long ago.

I waited and waited some more, until I forgot the meaning of patience. I could do nothing else. I finished the bottle of alcohol and passed the time listening to the chatter around me. Nothing happened. They turned their backs on me, engrossed in their own business. I wasn't being neglected, just excluded.

I hadn't noticed that they had all begun to gather in a circle. They had stopped chattering. I watched them closely, expecting something to happen.

They sat bent over, as if about to throw up, chuckling quietly and chanting, "Peace, peace." Even though I had never seen such a thing, I knew intuitively what they were doing. The smell of burning marijuana rose slowly and clung to my nostrils. My guard went up instinctively, but my body became lethargic as my pulse slowed.

Right then, someone tapped me on the shoulder. I was stunned and couldn't turn around at first.

. . . My body recognized that hand, though. Its size, shape, weight, and feeling as it touched my shoulder. It was then that I realized how much I had missed that very familiar hand. I also knew I was in no position to indulge in such a reverie.

The hand took my own silently and pulled me to an unknown place beyond a door behind the cabinet.

"I have been spiraling down ever since that time," she said.

What did she meant by "that time"? I could only see three chairs in the room where we were sitting. It felt like a small dank café. A candle burned dimly on the table, but the interior was dark,

AZALEA

*The Silver
Trout
Fishing
Network:
Yun Dae
Nyeong*

mysterious, and cold. Here I was, seeing her again after all these years, in a basement cellar that looked like a defunct bar. She sat, motionless, on a chair in the corner. Her face was pale and drawn, like a frozen face scribbled on a white sketchpad. Her skinny bare feet peeking out from underneath her skirt were the only proof she was alive. The words we exchanged seemed surreal. I was barely holding on between reality and illusion.

I had returned to that original place.

From inside the sketchpad her voice droned forth. I felt tormented by its tenacity. Her dessicated look was empty. I shook my head and stared at the cold darkness of the floor.

"You, too, are now beginning your return. Until now you have been straying far, far from here. You might have forgotten the way back forever."

I did feel as if I had drifted too far from where I belonged, as if I had existed in isolation all this time. In a desert outside existence.

"I want to return now," I said, painfully.

For a moment her face swayed like a water plant in the candlelight. I recalled the night I first met her, on Cheju Beach. Spring, the yellow blossoms, the geese, silver trout, the moon, the *river sprite* . . . , all those things. The girl I had met in that beautiful mythical place. Thinking such thoughts, I found courage and made a declaration: I would cast off all ambition, deceit, and vanity, as well as this sleepless age.

No, you need to go back further. You need to come back to the place you once were. She repeated this again and again, and I felt my heart grow sicker.

I told her I was back at the Wangp'i River in Ulchin. I knew I had to talk this way.

". . . Come, a little more," she said.

Then I sensed shaking and agitation in her once expressionless face. In the midst of it all I realized that our time together had scarred her in incurable ways.

She stood there with her mouth open, trembling like a silver trout spawning its eggs. Staring at me like this, she slid against the wall, whimpering softly.

I knew that to return to my distant origin, the place where I belonged, I would need many more days and nights.

I drew closer to her and firmly grabbed hold of her icy hand, which felt drained of human warmth.

I held her hand until morning, and threw away thirty years of my life to return upstream to that place where I belonged.

931122.

I received a second envelope from them on the first snowy night back in Seoul.

Inuk the Inventor

by Kim Jung-Hyuk
Translated by Jenny Wang Medina

The Interview

The most amazing inventors in the world? And there are six of
them? Of course I'd do the shoot; that decision was simple. I only
remembered the five other photo shoots I had scheduled after I
confirmed. Shoots that were already overdue. I have no idea why I
agreed to do it. It's just that when the reporter from *SciFi Magazine*
said the word "inventor," I was suddenly transported back to my
childhood. They say that nine out of ten little boys want to be
inventors when they grow up, and true to form, I was one of them.
My math and science scores didn't reflect the aptitude of a kid who
wants to become an inventor, though, so I soon gave up on my
dream. The years passed, but even now, ten years later, just hearing
the word "inventor" always makes my heart race. In-ven-tor. It
just sounds like someone who does great things. It even sounds
good when you're only talking about the person who invented the
portable electric fan.

The feature was titled "The Six Most Amazing Inventors of Our
Time." It would be a while before the actual shoot, so I did a lot of
advance preparation. I looked at foreign magazines, drew diagrams
of possible shot compositions that would suit the inventors, and
even watched several movies about inventions. All the machines in

the movies were beautiful. The cold metallic images that looked like they could cut flesh, the exquisite structure of the joints connecting machine to machine, I thought it all so beautiful. I thought that if I could somehow create an arrangement of what I imagined were the piercing gazes of these people with the intensity of focus to create images like the ones I saw in the movies, I would have an absolutely stunning photograph. But my dreams became nightmares as soon as the shoot started. I was definitely operating under some huge misconceptions about the whole situation.

The bickering started the moment we decided where the inventors would stand in order to shoot the cover photo. "A scoundrel like you is no kind of inventor, get in the back . . . don't make me laugh, the only original idea you ever came up with was to copy someone else . . . what the hell, who do you think you're calling a copycat . . . shit, why don't you prove it . . . yeah, stealing is better than making something stupid . . . ooh you bastard, I'm gonna . . ." Listening to them from a distance you'd think they'd already come to blows, but there wasn't much physical action besides shoving each other with their shoulders. All of them were holding their own inventions for the portrait, so apart from their shoulders, they had no other way to restrain their opponents. They could only make a loud fuss, and not one of them was willing to set his invention on the ground. I don't know whether it was that the confrontation wasn't worth setting the inventions down to really fight, or that they didn't have the nerve to get into it, but it was a good thing as far as I was concerned. In the end, I had no choice but to give up my innocent plan to have three inventors stand in the back row and three in the front.

If I said, "Excuse me sir, yes, the one with the radio; can you give me a little smile?" I'd get a scowl and, "It's not a radio, it's a combination radio and microwave oven." If I asked the inventor holding five inventions if he really had to hold up that stick, I got, "It's not a stick, it's an eight-layered folding umbrella," as he suddenly popped it open, startling the person next to him into dropping one of his own inventions and getting angry, and then the commotion would get louder again . . . in any case, it was that sort of affair. The shoot was becoming chaotic. Suyŏn, the lead author of the feature, didn't know what to do, and she just stood quietly by my side, not saying a word. She would dart anxious sideways glances at me once in a while, but all they told me was that she wanted the shoot to be over already.

"Okay, I'm just going to take a few more shots. You all know the title of the article, right? It's called 'The Six Most Amazing, Mind-Blowing Inventors of Our Time,' so you all need to give me your best 'inventor' faces. You understand what I mean, right? No, please don't scowl at me like that, try to smile, smile and give me your best . . ."

I clicked the shutter without confidence. And they wanted this to be on the cover of the magazine? Would I be able to salvage it with all the inventors looking like that? No, that would be a feat far beyond my capabilities. It looked like I'd have to be satisfied with a shot that had all of them with their eyes open.

"Excuse me, but I'll just be leaving now," the inventor standing in the far left corner suddenly piped up as he moved toward the front. The displeasure on his face was clear, but he had been the quietest person during the entire shoot. I knew exactly how he felt, and wanted to tell him to please go ahead and leave, you can all just leave. I was going to try to take a few more but it don't think it's going to get any better, so please, just go, but I couldn't. All of the other inventors could only stare at him aghast. Suyŏn the reporter, who was still standing quietly off to the side, suddenly darted after him as he headed toward the door. The inventor and the reporter had a long exchange. She seemed to be pleading with him, but he smacked his right fist into his left palm, visibly irritated. Finally, it was the reporter who sighed, and the inventor remained impassive. Then the reporter approached me.

"He said he has to go after all. What should we do?"

"What can we do? If he has to go, then he has to go. Did he say whether he brought his invention with him? I have to take a quick picture of that, at least. I didn't see him holding anything before. . . ."

"Oh, we got something from him a few days ago. But Mr. Kim, do you think we'll be still be able to get a cover shot out of this?"

"Maybe we can do without a cover this time. It just makes the magazine heavier, doesn't it? You just get the copy ready and we can say it's a special issue of *SciFi Magazine*: we got rid of the cover for this issue out of concern for your physical well-being, dear readers."

"Are you serious?"

"No, I'm just frustrated too. What can we do? I guess we'll just have to use the pictures of the inventions for the cover. Just make it sound good to the editor."

Shooting the inventions wasn't easy either. The inventors ignored my request that they leave their inventions and go home. Instead, they waited as I took the pictures. When I started shooting, each inventor would sidle up to me and start explaining his work. "So, the core of this invention is the fusion of a radio and a microwave oven. It seems strange at first glance, doesn't it? Of all the machines in the world, why would you combine a radio and a microwave? That's where you can see my own personal philosophy coming into play. A microwave oven warms food, right? But a radio, now that's something that warms our hearts. Therefore, through the convergence of a microwave oven and a radio, I tried to combine food with sound. So you need to take the picture in a way that shows the concept of sound and food at the same time."

I'm very sorry, but you can go ahead and tell the reporter all that crap. I take pictures however I feel like taking them, I thought, as I bit my tongue trying to ignore him, but then he tried to give me advice on how I should angle the camera. "As I see it, that invention won't look good from a rho angle. I know because I used to dabble in photography too. . . ."

It went on and on like this. It was a steady stream of prattle, but it wasn't just one of them; all five were armchair photography experts. Suyǒn had told me before that we would only do the photo shoot here and that she'd do the actual interviews over the phone, but she didn't take the inventors home. Instead, she started doing the interviews on the sofa in the corner, but the interviews were just as bad as the photo shoot. Two or three of the inventors started reviewing and criticizing each other's creations and the studio suddenly turned into a local flea market. They sounded like they were haggling over prices as they explained the qualities of their products. I wouldn't even call them inventors; they were more like street vendors hawking their cheap wares. The shoot, which started at ten in the morning, wasn't over until five in the afternoon. Even after all the inventors were gone, the studio seemed to echo with the sound of their voices. Words like "convergence," "new product," "new idea," and "innovation" continued to reverberate in the now empty space, as if the door might open at any second and the inventors would return. Suyŏn and I collapsed on the sofa, exhausted. Our bodies sank into the soft cushions like they were sucking us in.

"Let's tell the editor never to do a special issue on inventors again," I said, leaning my head back against the sofa and staring up at the ceiling.

"I'll quit if he says we have to do this again. Aren't you hungry?"

I realized that we hadn't had time to have lunch. How was it that out of six inventors, not one of them had thought to invent some food?

The Design

After some dumpling hotpot, I felt the strength coming back to my arms and legs. We ordered a hot pepper pancake and a bottle of *soju* to supplement the meal. I thought my nerves would settle after I got a little liquor in me. Suyŏn, who hadn't said a word while she plowed through the hotpot, scraped her rice bowl clean and set her chopsticks and spoon down with a sigh. She looked like a drowning swimmer who'd just been given mouth-to-mouth.

"I think I might survive now."

"Tell me about it. I'm telling you, there's no greater invention than rice."

She nodded, stretching her arms behind her.

"Do you really think we can just put the inventions on the cover? We've never done that before. . . . We've always had the inventors on the cover in the past. Who's to say that the editor won't make us do the shoot all over again when we tell him what happened?'

"Don't worry about it. You're forgetting who you're dealing with here. I got the cover shot earlier."

"Really? When did you take it? Didn't all the pictures turn out funny?"

"Remember when that one inventor said he was going home? All the other inventors were looking at him right then, and it looked okay, so I just went click, and snapped the shutter. I checked it out before we left, and it turned out well. The one guy was standing there looking feisty, and the rest were holding their inventions, gaping at him in shock or amazement. . . . We'll probably be able to use it for the cover. That's the great thing about digital photography."

"What a relief. But then that man will probably stand out on the cover."

"There's nothing we can do about that. He had the most inventor-ish look about him anyway. Why did he say he had to leave right in the middle of the shoot?"

"I don't know. He just said he had to go all of a sudden. He said had something he had to take care of. He's supposedly a friend of the editor, but all I've heard is that he's really eccentric. He even has an unusual name. It's like Inuk, or something. Oh, I almost forgot to give you this at the shoot."

She reached into her bag and pulled out a crumpled, folded up piece of paper. It was Inuk the inventor's creation. I could see some scratchy writing in ballpoint pen on an A4 sheet that had been folded about ten times. It was poorly preserved, and a lot of the writing looked indecipherable too. There was a drawing of a structure that looked like it could be a boat, or a plane, or even a giant robot, with tiny sesame-seed-size numbers and symbols drawn next to it. It looked like it might be a design, but it could also be a page of random doodles.

"That's all there is? You call this is an invention?"

"No matter how much I pestered him, he said that's all he could give me. He told me he didn't even have any actual inventions; that he was a *conceptual inventor* or something like that, but I didn't really know what he meant. You can ask the editor about it . . . when he gave it to me, he acted like he was entrusting me with something really important and told me to be careful not to lose it."

"What kind of design is this, anyway?"

"He said it's a flying boat, but you'd probably have to hear a detailed explanation of it to understand. Well, just get a good, comprehensive shot of it somehow, okay?"

"Now look here, little Miss Reporter. Those are the most frightening words you can say to a photographer: 'good,' 'comprehensive,' and 'somehow.' But the main thing is always the 'good' part."

"That's your specialty, isn't it? I don't know. In any case, I trust you."

Our conversation ended when the hot pepper pancake arrived. I put the sketch in my back pocket and scooted closer to the table. We both concentrated on the table to clear a precise space for the round plate to land, like we were welcoming a UFO from another world. The pancake was incredibly tasty. We parted amicably after sharing two bottles of *soju* and two pepper pancakes. Actually, I don't really remember leaving. We probably only had one bottle of *soju*, but I don't remember how I got back to the studio or how I got home after that. All I know is that I woke up alone.

When Suyŏn called me a few days later, I wanted to curse myself. Dammit! Not only had I not photographed the inventor's design, I couldn't even remember where I'd put that piece of paper. I wanted to say that I'd been busy doing shoots for several different magazine interviews, and that I was traveling to on-location shoots for a different book I was working on, but those were all just excuses, so I dodged the issue by saying that I'd taken the pictures, but hadn't finished processing them yet.

"The inventor wants us to give him his design back soon, but I'm going nuts with these deadlines. Do you think you could messenger it back to him for me? I'll take you out for a bite after I'm done with all this."

I still needed time to take the pictures, so I had no choice but to agree.

"Oh, the design team wants you to send over the photos right away," Suyŏn added before she hung up. Maybe it was because she was stressed about her deadlines, but there was absolutely no warmth in her voice. It sounded like she might go off at any second, like a bomb with a lit fuse. I doubt I'd still be alive now if I'd told her that I hadn't even taken the photos yet. I started searching my apartment as soon as I got off the phone, but with absolutely no recollection of what happened that night after we drank together, finding a single slip of paper was no small task.

It wasn't in the back pocket of my pants. That means I took it out and put it somewhere, but it wasn't on the desk either. If it wasn't on the desk, then I probably didn't work on the computer that night . . . then maybe the futon? Not there either. Did I try to photograph it while I was drunk? No, it wasn't on the product set either. I turned the studio upside-down looking in every nook and cranny, but it was nowhere to be found. I sat on the futon and tried to retrace my steps that night, but no matter how hard I tried, all I could remember was the perfect red and green symmetry of that hot pepper pancake.

I called the younger photographer who shared the studio with me. "Hmm, a piece of paper? Like a receipt? Not a receipt . . . oh, like a sketch, you mean? A sketch . . . I'm sure if I saw something like that I'd put it somewhere safe. Then I'm sure it's there somewhere. You didn't wash your pants yet, did you? Yeah,

I guess you wouldn't have done that. Well, I'm sure it'll turn up as long as it didn't get wet. I'm in the middle of a shoot, though," he said and hung up. Right, as long as it didn't get wet, it must be laying face down somewhere, holding its breath. It's probably laying somewhere, trembling with little sobs, hoping that someone will find it someday. The only problem is that someday has to be now. I walked over to the sink in the corner, the only spot in the whole studio with water. There was an impressive pile of dishes, cups, and pots in the sink that would make the trash heaps at the city dump green with envy. That's right, the pots . . . oh no, the sketch was pressed between them. It was all wet and plastered to the bottom of a pot. It all started coming back to me. When I got back from drinking, I took everything out of my pockets and put it on the desk. I made myself some ramen, and must have used the design as a trivet for the pot.

I pulled the paper out of the water and tried to spread it flat, but it was so wet that calling it "paper" would be a joke; a dishrag was probably more like it. And actually, rather than "spread it flat," it might be more accurate to say that I peeled it apart, one fold at a time. I launched a full-scale rescue mission with a hairdryer, iron, and a dry towel, but it wasn't like I could crumple it up, plant it in the ground, and have it sprout like a tree, with the design already transformed into its original form. The good thing, well, if you could call it a good thing, was that since I hadn't done the dishes yet, I had avoided turning the design into mush. If that had been the case, my last known whereabouts would probably remain a mystery forever. . . . Come to think of it, disappearing might actually be better. Cold sweat dripped down my back.

The Workshop

I only had one option, no matter how hard I thought about it. I'd have to go find that inventor Inuk, or whatever his name was. I got his address from Suyŏn and stuffed my camera into my bag. I scanned the studio to see if there was anything that would work as a gift, but the only thing worth giving him was the print I'd made of the shot of the six inventors. I thought about giving him a few photo set props, but that didn't seem like the kind of thing you give an inventor. Anyway, would a present really mollify him? I remembered what Suyŏn said about him being a huge eccentric. If he was really that strange, there was no way of knowing if he would tear up the picture right in front of me, throw my camera out the window, then even pick me up and throw me out the window. But that would only happen in a comic book. Most of the time, people who are described as eccentrics either have an aversion to people, or are just unusually absorbed in their work. I'd met a lot of people like that doing photo shoots for feature interviews. There were comic book authors who yelled at everyone including the photographer when they got upset, and novelists who chased fact-checkers out of their workrooms just because they didn't like the look of them. But then, those extreme cases are so often blown out of proportion by rumors that when you actually meet them, a lot of them are so nice that you almost want to ask them to get mad at you. Once in a while there are people who are really defensive and have a wall built around them, but they usually let down their guards after I talk to them for a half hour or so, and a lot of them tear down their emotional walls completely after a few hours with me. When I think about it, I realize they must be very lonely people.

At some point I got to a place where I'm not afraid to meet people, but I haven't been this nervous in a long time. Even if he's a complete pussycat, I'm presenting him with a situation to which there is no other response but anger. What do I say if he asks for his design? Do I say I lost it, or tell him that it got wet? Or should I just go in there and tell him that I ripped it to pieces and storm out? No, that's too dangerous. Should I get down on my knees and apologize? I tried to clear my head by looking out the bus window. It was a crisp fall day. Maybe it was because the sky was so clear and high, but people looked taller, and the buildings looked higher too. Gazing up at the lofty sky, I thought to myself that destroying one little piece of paper wasn't such a big deal. It's a big world and there's lots of paper, isn't there? The soft strains of Bach's *Goldberg Variations* floated toward me over the bus's speakers. What a perfect day.

I rang the doorbell at the inventor's house, but there was no answer. I tried again at least a dozen times, but the house remained completely still, so I followed the fence and circled around the back of the house. The entire building was painted blue and the roof was a bit round, but aside from that, it was a pretty unremarkable single-family house. I went back to the front door and rang the bell again. I couldn't go back home now. I pulled my camera out of my bag and started taking pictures of the house. If my plans didn't amount to anything, I thought that at the very least, they could use pictures of the inventor's house in the magazine instead of the invention. They'd probably caption it with something like, "The unassuming home of an inventor. Inside, the world is created anew." I composed a shot centered on the front door that showed off the house, the surrounding trees, and the sky nicely, and pressed the shutter. You could see the blue of the sky behind the blue of the roof. I went around the house, taking pictures at regular intervals. I circled the house again, taking almost identically composed pictures, and returned to my starting point. I set the camera on the tripod and continued taking pictures of the front of the house. I took several pictures with the same composition at different shutter speeds and exposures. I kept pressing the shutter like I might be able to capture the wind blowing on film.

Just then, someone came into the viewfinder. It was a short, matronly woman. She appeared at the right side of the screen, glared, and slowly walked toward me.

"What do you think you're doing there?"

"I'm just taking a few pictures, ma'am."

"Do you have permission to do that?"

"No, I don't. I came to pay a visit to the famed inventor who lives here, but he doesn't seem to be at home. I'm sorry, should I have gotten permission before taking the pictures?"

The words "famed inventor" flew out of my mouth before I knew what was happening. In hindsight, I couldn't have said anything more awkward.

"Ah, you've come to see the professor? Please come with me."

The lady strode toward the door and unlocked the front gate. There wasn't a single plant in the spacious garden, just random piles of scrap iron and bricks here and there. The woman entered the vestibule and pushed the buzzer on the intercom. Through the receiver, I heard her say something in a low voice. "Please tell him that I'm a photographer, but I'm here about his design." She repeated my words into the intercom. "He says to leave it and go," the lady said, repeating the inventor's instructions, but I told her that I had something to tell him in person. She asked what I wanted to say to him. "I'd like to discuss it with him myself," I said, and she scowled and gestured dismissively at me. I told her that it's just that I had a lot of questions for him that would be difficult to ask in this manner, and she turned back to speak into the intercom. "He says to go on down." Finally, I had managed to get past one barrier.

"It's that way," the lady instructed me. "The professor's workshop is in the basement, you see," she explained before going back into the house. The inventor's name "Inuk" was written on the doorway leading to the basement. I pulled out my camera and took a picture of the wooden door. But aside from his name, there was nothing special about the door.

The stairway was deep and long. I don't think I would've believed it if anyone had told me they made basements this deep. I wondered how much dirt they'd have to dig up to make a basement like this. The staircase was made of wood, so a long plaintive creaking noise greeted every step I took. I felt like I was entering a beast, not walking into a basement. It was like walking into the belly of an elephant that had swallowed a huge wooden staircase, or maybe a humpback whale that had accidentally swallowed a

148

carpenter who was especially good at building stairs. Halfway down I thought to myself that I should have counted to see how many steps there were, but by then I'd already gone too far to go back up. A long hallway started at the bottom of the stairs. I took my camera out of my bag again and took a shot of the staircase. I doubted that the shot would even turn out though, because my hands were shaking with anxiety over being in such a dark place. I turned and snapped the hallway as well. The hallway was made of wood too. I couldn't judge how big or deep down the basement was, but it was obviously huge. I continued along the hallway, which was only lit by a few small lights placed here and there, and was extremely dark. The creaking continued, gradually getting louder. I even started holding my breath as I crept along because it seem like every step I took shook the entire basement.

A huge workroom appeared when I turned the corner of the hallway. The walls in the workroom were all made of wood, and there were several enormous machines situated in the center of the room. The room was very quiet because all the machines were still. Vivaldi's *The Four Seasons* floated softly out of one corner of the room.

"Ah, so you've come?"

The inventor turned his head and looked at me with an expression that was very different from the one he wore at the photo shoot the other day. He greeted me cheerfully, as though he had invited me there himself. I bowed quickly in greeting. He was wrapped in a long, blue cape-like thing with a drooping, dirt-blackened hem that looked like it had been dragging around on the floor for some time. He pulled out a chair and invited me to take a seat.

"I've heard that messengers and delivery services are really fast these days. But you came all the way here in person. I'm actually quite shy about this place," he chuckled.

"Why is that, sir? It's extremely impressive. I was really taken aback by how remarkable the entryway is."

"Oh, really? Do you think so? I chose all the wood myself, you know."

The inventor, who had been covering his mouth with his hand, was all smiles. The moment I saw his smile, I suddenly felt my heart sink. I had no idea how I was going to tell him. He looked to be about ten years older than me, but his smiling face reminded me of someone's kid brother. My mind was in chaos. Telling him that I wanted to give him the cover shot as a gift seemed too transparent, and I didn't have the heart to explain the actual situation to him. So I didn't say a word, and he remained silent as well. The silence held for quite a while, until he suddenly opened his mouth.

"Isn't this bit nice? Da da da, da da dum."

"Excuse me?"

"It's the Fabio Biondi performance—my favorite. It's summer now, and the leaves are fluttering, fluttering, and then boom! Here comes the typhoon. That's what the violin is imitating, isn't it?"

"Oh, I see. You mean in the music."

I sat still and listened carefully to the piece. He closed his eyes and nodded along. It was a brisk and aggressive performance. The volume of the music was low, but somehow every single tone and vibration penetrated my ears. It seemed like the basement had been built to very precise, exacting specifications. I made up my mind as I listened to the Vivaldi.

"I brought this for you, sir. It's the photo we took the other day. . . ."

I handed him the picture, and his eyes widened appreciatively as he looked at it.

"Wow, you really captured them."

"Pardon me?"

"You really captured all the people in the photograph. My pictures never turn out like this. You have to grab the image like this, but it passes so quickly, doesn't it?"

"Yes, that's true. It does go by pretty fast."

He took the print over to a desk in the corner of the room, made six circles of tape that he stuck to the back, and very earnestly fixed it to the wall. After smoothing it down a few times, he stood back and admired it with satisfaction. This was the first time anyone had ever treated one of my photographs with such care. Watching his actions, I was moved. And it wasn't just because it was my own work; there was something very solemn and sacred about the deliberation of his actions.

There were countless pieces of paper posted above his desk, hundreds of little memos that looked like the design I had destroyed. All of them were covered with writing. I went over to the desk.

"These must be your notes for all the inventions you make, right?"

"No, no, I'm not very good at making things, actually."

He shook his head with all his might. I suddenly remembered what Suyŏn had said the other day: he called himself a conceptual inventor. I thought I might know what that meant now.

"Then you didn't make those machines yourself?"

"No, I made them, but I didn't invent them. I needed them at the time, and I ended up depending on them after a while. Necessity is the mother of invention, or so they say, but now we've run out of need."

"Isn't that the truth," was all I could think of to say. He wasn't wrong, but there was something unsettling about what he said.

"Your name is quite unusual, isn't it?" I said, trying to lighten the mood. Ever since I first heard the name, I thought there must be some special story behind it.

"That's something I invented," he chuckled. "The word is actually 'Inuuk,' but I shortened it to Inuk. My last name is Yi, so it works perfectly as my full name—Yi Nuk."

"Inuuk, sir?"

"Inuuk is a revered Eskimo shaman. It's not that people worship me, but I think it would be nice to become a person like that someday. A long time ago, the Eskimos were being persecuted, so Inuuk gathered his people and some animals and created an island.

But this island was no ordinary island; it was a floating island, like the *fumdis* that the Nagamis tribe in India live on. So Inuuk made this island, and . . . oh! You know about Noah's Ark, don't you? Inuuk made an island like Noah's Ark, and they lived on that island, floating all over the world. If you'll recall, the earth had just been destroyed."

I listened very intently to what he said, but I had no idea what he was talking about. There was no logic to his words; it seemed like he was just stringing together words he plucked out of the air as they floated by. It reminded me of a DJ mixing songs. I could only nod my head.

"Invention is imitation, after all. No, I guess everything is imitation. Maybe it's dependency, and not imitation? It's invention when you make something that didn't exist before, but everything already exists. So the island that Inuuk created wasn't actually an invention, but I'm presenting it somehow as an invention. Given that the island is the only thing that survives when the world disappears, is it a future invention, or has it already been invented? If everything is wiped out, then everything that appeared or was created after that would be an invention, right?"

He phrased his last remark as a question, but didn't seem to want an answer from me. I gazed at him steadily. He wasn't looking at anything in particular. I thought then that his eyes weren't like clear windowpanes that looked out on the world, but rather mirrors that reflected back in on himself.

My cell phone rang. It was Suyŏn. I answered as I walked into the workroom. She started shouting as soon as I said hello. "Why haven't you sent me the images? I told you there was no time!" I could hear the panic in her voice, so I had no choice but to tell her that I'd lost the design, and then let her know I was at Inuk the inventor's workshop. I told her that the workshop was so cool that I thought it would be much better to put a shot of it in the magazine instead of the design. She sighed. "You should have told me before," she said. "I made a photocopy of the design. . . ." The violence had gone out of her voice, and she asked if his workshop was really that special. When I said it was like a secret underground fortress, I could almost hear her journalistic instincts perking up and making a mental note that we'd have to use that workshop interview idea next time. I'd lost the original design, but at least there was no need for me to throw myself out a window since there was a copy of it. I told Suyŏn that I would send her my pictures of the workshop as soon as I got back to my studio, and hung up. Inuk, unable to sit still while I was on the phone, was drawing something on a big blackboard. From the back, with his blue cape draped around him, he looked like a character from a graphic novel, but there was a tragic air about him. I pointed the camera around my neck toward Inuk and said loudly, "Would it be alright if I took a few pictures in here?"

He snapped his head around and stared at me in alarm.

"I don't mean I'd have to take any pictures of you, sir, I just thought I could shoot the notes on the wall over here . . ."

"I'm sorry, but that won't do at all."

He raised both arms and shook them violently, his face severely contorted. It was a completely different face from the bashful one he'd shown me until now. It shouted how dare you try to photograph this place. I quickly bowed my head in apology for my transgression.

"Would you mind terribly if I just had a look around?"

He nodded tersely, but his expression told me that it was not acceptable. I had suddenly become an unwelcome intruder. I had to tell him about the design, but the situation was steadily deteriorating. I tried to regroup as I looked around the workshop. There had to be something I could do.

There was nothing special about the interior space of the workshop. Aside from the huge machines whose purpose I couldn't even guess at, there was nothing but wooden walls. There were hundreds of slips of paper on them too. I went closer to the wall and read what was written on a few of the slips of paper.

i-3123412: What if there was a fountain pen that you could sharpen like a pencil? What about sharpening ballpoint pens or markers? Wouldn't it reduce the number of pens used?

i-3123413: Population limiter. Set a fixed number for the entire population, and when a baby is born, the oldest person would automatically die. People might stop trying so hard to live longer.

i-3123414: Unmanned confessional booths. Wouldn't need priests—a machine could listen to your sins. Would that increase or decrease people's sins? How much would it cost to use?

The memos went on forever. What if his numbering system really started from 1? That would mean that there were more than three million of these ideas. I looked again at the millions of slips of paper stuck to the wood wall. They didn't look like paper to me anymore; they were mounds of eggs waiting for incubation, but there was no way of knowing what would hatch from them. As soon as the clusters of paper on the wall turned into mounds of eggs for me, I started to feel queasy and I wanted to vomit. What the hell was this Inuk person thinking? I could feel his eyes on me as I read the abstracts, casting sidelong glances at me as he continued to work. He was watching me like a mother hen guarding her eggs. Inuk came toward me.

"I need to eat before I get back to work."

At first I thought he was inviting me to eat with him, but when I saw the look on his face, I knew that he was asking me to leave. His expression was frigid. He was pushing me out of this place using some mysterious force. I could be overreacting, but there was clearly murder in his eyes. As soon as I saw that look in his eyes, I hopped to it, got my things together, and slipped out with a hurried bow. It wasn't until after I passed through the long, creaky hallway, went up the creaky wooden stairs, and was out in the yard that I realized that I hadn't told him about the design. I must have completely blocked out the fact that I had to recover the design for him in the wake of his wrath, but I couldn't go back down into the workshop now. It was probably for the best anyway. I could just have the copy of the design messengered to him and have done with it. My heart was racing like I had just run a gauntlet, and it didn't settle until I opened the front gate and walked out into the street.

Need

There was nothing else I could do. Except for the pictures I took of the house, I had nothing worth sending her. I wasn't able to take a single shot inside the workshop, and to send the shots of the staircase or the hallway was something I just couldn't do. Of course the spread would look strange because all the other inventors' pages have an image of their invention and only Inuk's would have a picture of his house, but there was nothing I could do. I helpfully suggested scanning the design and putting that in there, but my suggestion was met with silence. Suyŏn said that the other inventions are actual physical objects, and this one is just too . . . two-dimensional. On top of that, the copy was crumpled and didn't have an air of authenticity about it. She justified all this by saying that the editor thought that using the shot of the house would be better too. She tried to get me to tell her why I hadn't been able to get a shot of the workshop, but I had no way of explaining it to her. I tried to say that the mass of papers seemed like a cocoon and Inuk was the giant larvae, but I knew I wouldn't be able to give her a sense of what my real impressions were. I was curious about the interview with Mr. Inuk, though.

"There wasn't much to it. It was just typical inventor-speak. Why? Did he say anything peculiar to you? Well, it's too late for that anyway. The manuscript's already been squared away."

Maybe it was because she met her deadline, but her voice was much more forceful.

"Now that I think about it, he did seem a bit odd. We did the interview by phone, and whenever I asked him a question, his responses were so fluid and unrestrained that I almost felt like I was talking to some sort of machine. Why, what did he say to you?"

"It's not that. He didn't say anything . . . it's just that he seemed like such a unique character that I was a little curious. . . ."

"That's what's so strange about it. He's supposed to be really eccentric, but he seemed perfectly normal to me."

"He probably seems different depending on who you talk to. How were you able to include him in the article when he was the only inventor without an actual invention, anyway? You wrote another work of fiction, didn't you?" I teased.

"He had an invention too. It was 'need.' Isn't that just like a conceptual inventor? He said that in order to invent things, there has to be need, and right now all the need has disappeared from the world. So all he's going to do is invent need. It's kind of opaque, isn't it? The truth is, I wrote the article and I still don't really get it. Anyway, he said that's why he doesn't invent physical objects or products."

"What was that design he gave us? Didn't you say it was a flying boat or something?"

"I wouldn't stop pestering him for an invention, so he probably just sent me any old thing. It was a sketch he said he did when he was really young of a boat that floated around in the sky. He said that he often dreamed that he would get on the boat and fly off into space. Everyone imagines stuff like that, though, don't they? It's nothing special."

"Hey, the editor didn't say anything about the cover shot did he?"

"You know, that cover shot saved our lives. He said it was really good."

"Well, that's fortunate."

After I got off the phone, I went online and did a search for the Fabio Biondi performance of Vivaldi's *The Four Seasons*. I couldn't find the whole piece, but luckily there was a site where you could listen to the "Summer" part for free. I wanted to listen to that piece very carefully again. The strange thing was, no matter how high I turned up the volume, I couldn't hear all the sounds in the piece the way I could in Inuk's workshop. In the workshop I could hear every sound that came from the violin, including every breath the performer took. When I listened to that music, I actually thought I could hear a typhoon approaching me from afar. It was like standing in the middle of a vast ocean, listening to the sound of the waves crashing in from the west. I could feel the passionate and melancholy vibrations of the violin through my skin. It almost seemed like someone was performing it from the other side of that wooden wall. I don't know if he invented something somewhere for that. I remembered what he said when he saw my print. "You have to capture it this way, but it passes so quickly, doesn't it?" I don't know, maybe he wanted to capture sound in space the same way he saw people captured in photographs.

I printed the shot I took of the front of Inuk's house and put it up over my desk. I taped it up with the exact same care that he did when he put my photo up over his desk. The texture of the wood on the domed roof of the house was beautiful. I crossed my arms behind my head, leaned back in my chair and admired the picture with satisfaction. It was a beautiful house and a beautiful sky. Looking at the gorgeous scene, it seemed like time had stopped.

Photographs don't just capture people, they capture time as well. No, you can't catch hold of time. You can only think you catch time. Time keeps moving forward, and we stop as we look at the image. It occurred to me that maybe the reason pictures exist is so we can constantly lag behind in the race with time. I contemplated a lot of things as I looked at Mr. Inuk's house. It would be great if I invented a camera that could penetrate any object, and even take pictures of basements with low visibility. That was too bad, I thought. The image of the giant basement that I couldn't see appeared before my eyes.

There was something strange about it, though. As the image of the basement appeared before me, the house didn't look like a house anymore. It looked just like a huge ark, and the house seemed

like it was just the top part of the ark. I opened all the image files
I saved on my computer and took a closer look. I tried to connect
the pictures I took at regular intervals around the perimeter of the
house in my head. It was definitely an ark. Then I remembered his
design. I only saw it once, but now that I thought about it, it was
definitely a drawing of an ark. I remembered the ridiculously long
staircase and hallway. Did that mean this house could fly through
the air? I called Suyŏn. Luckily, she still had the photocopy of the
design. She said she had just called the messenger service. I asked
her to do me a favor and fax a copy of the design to me. "Um, aren't
you a little obsessed with this? This is some kind of joke, right?" I
hung up without so much as an explanation. On second thought,
maybe it wasn't such a big deal after all. So what if the house was
a flying ark, or just a wooden box? Would it matter? I was really
worked up about it for some reason, though. I felt as excited as
someone who had uncovered a huge secret, or had just discovered
the fundamental principles of the universe. I mean, it was almost as
if I had invented that ark. I was like a little child, standing in front
of the fax machine and waiting fretfully for it to ring.

Five Poems by Huh Su-gyung

Translated by David R. McCann
& Young-Jun Lee

Evening Soaks into Us and

As the light floods, leaves lush under evening light, drops of water under the tender flowers' flesh, as evening soaks into us, dear friends roast the meat, glass in hand,

When once I heard the sound of evening, it seemed evening was being gathered up, as if all the neighborhood bars in the world were opening their doors all at once and gathering up the harvest,

Now, we sit, glass in hand, roasting the meat. In the marinade, the meat has grown easy and soft, the green peppers are crisp, and the evening soaks into us,

Like kind-hearted mist as a circle of mind releases itself, we are released to draw the evening soaking into us into our embrace,

One friend has lost his son, one friend has lost his house, one has lost everything but survives, and we are roasting the meat, we sit by the fire sweating, with chopsticks lifting a piece of meat up onto the fire,

 Under the light, the leaves lush under evening light, under the light soaking evening, evening soaks into us.

THAT TIME

A child brought up on some unknown street
entered my dream

The child had a gun, was wearing a soldier's uniform,
asked me to put a handful of peppermint candy in his pocket

The child brought up on some unknown street
as the sky was quietly receiving the sun is right there
entered my dream

I thought about the city destroyed in the earthquake
or about the city I can no longer visit because of war
a day I stayed on too long in the library

A day I might have spent
looking into onion production figures written out in cuneiform

When that child in the street holding a gun
struck dumb stood looking at all the yearned-for faces in the world
disappearing off in the distance
like the animals vanishing from the burning forest of New Zealand

Tonight somewhere airplanes fly and on the streets
children still do not forget where they were born

While no one yet has prepared the coffins
for those old people, the ones turning the lamb over with hands still
bloodstained,
roasting the lamb as they build the fire

While women were out on the street, their faces wholly uncovered,
womanly men wept, pounding their breasts

YŏNGBYŏN, LEAVES OF REED

On the day a new sanctuary was set up
at the tavern for right-wing extremists

On the day the gods of the old sanctuary
who had delivered the wine all at once disappeared

On the day the sun solemnly rose
like the dawn in the city
where the massacre was to begin

The day a priest who had lost speech and held his tongue aloft
as he wept by the trash at the roadside

Don't cry, child born peacefully,
don't cry, don't cry

Listen to the light
as mother sister distant Yŏngbyŏn,
the sound of water fallen on the reed leaves
open their flesh

Sound of Trees Swaying

When we listen to the sound of trees swaying in the forest
like, say, hearing the news of the world by embracing electric waves

In the forest dead birds and squirrels decompose beside the moss
and bracken,
while alongside, a small brook runs the world like an electric wave

When all the tribe of dying people yearn for the time they lived and
open their eyes wanting to see the world again and the sound of
trees swaying strikes the ear as if it were the end of the world

The sound of trees swaying even in the hearts of all those who pick
up their weapons again to aim at the eye of someone else as they
live on through the moment when all the tribes of the earth have
perished from the earth,

O that sound, the sound of the cosmos entering into the body of
what we call the human tribe

Thus laughing days continued, foreigners riding big blue birds came along, and children carried bombs in their pockets, everywhere a donkey passed black oil overflowed, from the black oil people who had disappeared long ago appeared covered in sticky oil and asked about houses torn down long ago then flowers bloomed on that river side, red or white, and when the wind blew, the flowers fell and left their seeds, which were each like the eye of the weeping woman, when the seed was eaten, suddenly all sadness accumulated in the heart disappeared, they wanted to laugh themselves crazy, so they went to the riverside and laughed, the bombs carried in their pockets blew up and the children were blown into the air, so the laughing days went on, the seed resembling the weeping woman's eye kept watching us,

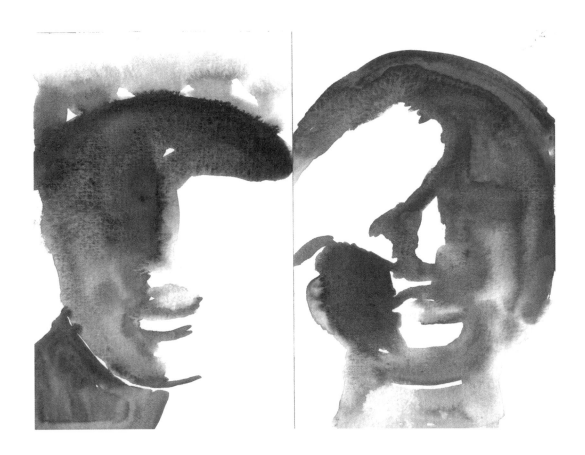

Five Poems from *Distance* (1996)

by Lee Si-Young
Translated by Brother Anthony of Taizé
& Yoo Hui-sok (Yu Hŭi-Sŏk)

A DRIED FISH

There's been something wrong with you lately.
What on earth have you done with your body?
This morning you brazenly failed to turn up in time for a meeting,
didn't even have your glasses on.

What?
We should live with one side of our souls totally emptied out?
That's the only way we can hear the birds singing
and the angry voice of last night's spirits?

Why, indeed.
Just so,
maybe you're right.
But what are you up to, now?
Where's your body?
That once so nimble, dried-up soul?

PARALLEL

One morning after I'd dreamed a dreamless dream
heavy snow had fallen:
a couple of early-morning magpies seem to have already walked there,
two pale blue lines of silk-like footprints leading endlessly away.

DISTANCE

The drizzling rain soaks the roadside trees.
An old man was crossing the street, holding up
an oiled-paper umbrella, just like in the old days.
Desolation.

RISKY ABODE

A few sparrows alight on one trifling branch.
Bending, the tree finds the earth's center anew.
An armful of wind comes blowing past; the branch trembles.
The sparrows' little eyes shift briskly
and dark night soon descends on them.

EVENING HOURS

Once I used to think that I ought to take responsibility for the
whole world in some area or other. That was how it was in those
days. There were battles and struggles in solidarity, day in and day
out; wounds spread across our angry brows. I am sorry, but that's
how my youth flowed away.

But nowadays, across the park where cicadas are singing shrilly,
I find myself standing in a time of shadows where I eat lunch
alone and supper alone. Nowadays no one talks of the beauties
of solidarity, and nobody says he'll take responsibility for this
complicated world.

Evening hours come to me so quietly.

Blooms of Mold

by Ha Seong-nan

Translated by Janet Hong

From the fifth floor, the playground looks like a small pond because of all the rain that has collected there. The heavy downpour from two days before has created muddy puddles that refuse to dry up. There are pools of rainwater everywhere—under the opposite end of the seesaw that the woman straddles, even under the monkey bars that the child hangs from.

The woman is shelling beans. Every time the shells are twisted open, speckled kidney beans peep out, nestled neatly in a row. The smell of tender greens is strong on her fingers. If a bean pops out of the shell onto the sand, the woman reaches to pick it up, raising her bottom in the air. Her end of the seesaw rises up to find its balance point.

The child's entire weight hangs from his right hand that is gripping the monkey bar. He is catching his breath before swinging from the third bar to the fourth. If he wants to land safely on dry ground without getting his feet wet, he has no choice but to go all the way across. His pants are slipping down and his shirt, pulled out by his right arm, rides up to reveal a blinding patch of ivory skin.

The woman is sitting with her back toward the man. From his vantage point all he can see is her hunched frame and her plastic container on the sand. Soon the container is brimming with beans.

So are you planning to cook rice with beans tonight? The man tosses the question in her direction but she doesn't respond. His voice doesn't reach her. *How can anyone ever forget that taste? Nothing beats the way it crunches between your teeth. Could I have some?* Standing by the balcony window, the man keeps smacking his lips. He can imagine it all—everything from the texture of the downy fuzz that covers the shells down to the very fibers that get stuck in your thumbnails from snapping open the beans. Luckily the woman still hasn't noticed the man who's been watching her all this while. She is entirely absorbed in snapping beans. She is deep in concentration, like a student solving a math problem. The child still hasn't crossed the monkey bars. With his teeth clenched, he continues to hang onto the bar.

The man takes out a little notepad from his back pocket. It is completely bent from having been pressed against his rear end. Bits of food have dried between the pages; they stick together when he tries to turn them.

Bean shells, seesaw, monkey bars, boy, puddles.

The man writes down a few words that will help him recall the woman. Later, the shells she chucks will become the only clue in identifying her garbage bag from all the others. The man doesn't know what suite she lives in. Luckily there's only one apartment building, but with ninety families living inside.

On the news that morning, the weather person gave the forecast in a yellow raincoat while holding up a yellow umbrella. A low pressure system was moving in and continuing to develop across the western coast and all of Kyŏnggi Province. Scattered spring showers were expected all week. The forecaster remembered to add that this early summer heat wave in April was the result of El Niño. If the heat and humidity continue, the man's work will become more difficult.

The man wakes to the sound of a woman shrieking. It's a little past two in the morning. Glass shatters and crashes to the ground. Frantic footsteps echo throughout the apartment. The woman—a young woman's voice—keeps screaming at the top of her lungs, but he can't make out her words. The man's wardrobe and stereo system are placed against the wall; this wall is all that separates his room from suite 507. The man gets up from his bed, walks over to the wardrobe and puts his ear to it. The front door of 507 opens and crashes into a wall. Whoever got shoved out the front door slips and falls with a dull thud as a pot lid is thrown out into the hallway. It rattles noisily until it eventually stops.

Don't you ever come near me again! The woman yells. The door slams and the bolt turns sharply.

The man tiptoes towards the front door and looks out the peephole. The dark corridor looks as gloomy as a cavern. Soon it will be time for the newspaper boy to come charging in with the morning paper. After the woman's door has been shut for at least half an hour, footsteps finally start to descend the stairs. It sounds like the person's shoes are not on properly. They sound like clogs. The man waits until the footsteps have gone down the stairs and out into the parking lot.

When the man steps into his storage closet a bit less than twenty square feet, his shoulders get wedged between the walls. The sickening smell hits him full force; the humidity was already making his garbage rot. He takes a plastic bucket down from the shelf. Having put on rubber gloves, he creeps quietly down the stairs with the bucket. To avoid attracting attention, he purposely doesn't turn on the light in the landing. Even in the dark the stairs are familiar. The L-shaped stairway has a total of seventy-two steps; eight steps and then a landing. It continues in this pattern all the way down. He knows these stairs like the back of his hand—so well that he doesn't need to test his footing. The second step going down from the third to the second floor is higher than the others. At first this step caused him a lot of trouble. He even sprained his ankle once but now when he comes to this spot, he automatically adjusts his footing.

Large rubber trash bins the size of tiny bathtubs line the flowerbed outside the apartment building. Shadows fall across the maple leaves that light from the streetlamps doesn't reach. There's no one in sight. The man pushes off the trash lid and steps up on the ledge of the flowerbed to look into the bin. There's hardly anything inside. The bin comes almost up to his chest, so he has to bend all the way down to reach for the trash bag. The liquid from the garbage bag has collected at the bottom of the rubber bin; the smell turns his stomach. There is only one bag in the bin since the garbage truck from the district office had just collected the garbage that morning. The man's bucket barely holds twenty liters. In the beginning he had carried the garbage up to his suite without using the bucket. The next day on his way to work he discovered that the liquid had leaked from the garbage and there was a trail leading up the stairs and ending at his front door. The garbage bag is heavy. Even though he lifts up the bag with care, putrid stuff drips onto his slippers.

It's a good thing that he didn't get rid of the small bathtub when he renovated his bathroom. When he first moved into this run-down, fifteen-year-old apartment, he repapered the walls, redid the floors and replaced the sink. The porcelain tub and toilet were full of chips and cracks. Even the navy blue tiles were chipped; there wasn't a single piece of tile left intact. There was mildew between the cracks and there were tiles that had fallen off completely. One night after he washed his face and pulled the stopper to drain the water from the sink, the dirty water that should have drained down the pipe poured onto his feet. There was a leak in the water pipe. While the plumber replaced the sink with a lightweight plastic basin that wouldn't get dirty so easily, he advised the man to get rid of the bathtub. The plumber kept pestering him: why did he insist on keeping a bathtub in this tiny bathroom, now that more and more people were opting for showers these days? However, the man ignored the plumber's advice and kept the tub. But that night after the plumber went home the man regretted his decision. The bathtub was so tiny that even though he was average height, water would slosh around his hips and overflow whenever he took a bath. The tub was so short that soaking his whole body in hot water was out of the question. If he tried to soak his shoulders, he had to stick his feet out of the tub and place them on the taps. If he tried to soak his legs, he had to hang his rear end out of the tub. Before the man started this whole business, the bathtub was a real headache, just as the plumber warned.

He puts the garbage bag he carried up to his suite into the bathtub. The garbage is already starting to give off a different smell. When summer comes he won't be able to continue this work anymore. Even though he washed and disinfected everything with bleach and sprayed the room with lemon-scented air freshener, his 525-square-foot apartment still reeks of soggy fish that wasn't dried properly. Garbage spews out of a rip in the overstuffed bag. The bag is knotted tightly. He tries to untie the stubborn knot, bending all the way into the tub. He straightens out and massages his sore back. *Whoever tied this damn knot sure did a good job.* Taking off his rubber gloves, he tries to undo the knot with his bare fingers but it still doesn't untie. He can't blame somebody for tying a garbage bag so tightly that it doesn't easily come undone. People never think that the garbage they throw out might be opened by someone. He used to think the same way until he started this work.

The waste management program that required everyone to use standard plastic garbage bags started on January 1, 1995. The man was in bed all day after a drinking binge the night before. The doorbell rang. He wasn't expecting anyone. After a few seconds, the doorbell rang again. He looked through the peephole, but it was an old building, and the lens was so cloudy that he was forced to open the front door. The women who identified themselves as members of the apartment council crowded in front of his door. There were over ten of them. Those who couldn't fit into the narrow space spilled out into the stairway that led down to the fourth floor.

An older woman with age spots blooming on her face nudged a young woman beside her, causing the younger one to blurt out, *Are you by any chance learning acupuncture?*

It was only then that he recalled the unopened box he had placed on top of his wardrobe. After purchasing the box of acupuncture tools and manual from a pushy salesman who had come to his office, he hadn't opened it even once. How was it possible that these strangers knew about his acupuncture set? The young woman stood staring at him, her gaze unflinching. He did receive a monthly newsletter from the acupuncture association. . . .

Have you been snooping through my mail? The man flared up in anger.

We've finally found the culprit! the women shouted in unison. *See? I told you it'd pay off sooner or later. We haven't seen him before, though.* The women started to whisper amongst themselves.

Pushing aside the young woman, the one with the age spots stepped up. *So they say it's the guilty dog that barks the loudest. I guess we're looking at one right now.*

A heavy garbage bag was passed from person to person up the stairs until it reached Age Spots. Once she received it, Age Spots threw the bag at the man's feet. It burst open. Through the rip, he saw patches of the phrase "Market delivery available" written in red. At once he realized that it was his garbage—the garbage he'd thrown out two days before. There was no doubt about it.

Do you know how much trouble we had to go through to find you? We had to comb through every piece of trash like we were picking out lice. They are right about persistence being rewarded in the end because we finally came across this garbage bag. Age Spots held up an envelope and shook it in front of the man's nose. The words *Acupuncture Association* were written on the envelope in Chinese characters. In the bottom right-hand corner the man's name and address were neatly typed. The envelope was dirty, as if flecks of kimchi had been stuck all over it. *Pretending you didn't know that you had to use proper garbage bags isn't going to get you out of this.*

Then a shout came from down the stairs. *It's because of people like you that this country has come to such a state.*

Enraged, Age Spots spoke with a trembling voice. *Ever since I*

*crossed the Taedong River with my father, I've been through all kinds
of hell, but never, in my whole life, have I dug through someone else's
trash.* She then let out a deep sigh.

The man vaguely recalled hearing about the waste management
program.

Don't let this happen again.

One by one, the women filed down the stairs.

The young woman, having fallen behind, started to follow the
rest of the group down, but stopped and turned to look at the man.
*You live alone, right? Try to understand. It's not just once or twice that
something like this has happened. I mean, how much can garbage
bags cost that people are dumping their garbage secretly at night? Even
garbage trucks refuse to collect something like this.*

Age Spots shouted from a few stairs down. *What are you doing?
Hurry up and come down. We have to go through the other bags.*

The young woman spoke as she went down the stairs. *The fine is
a hundred thousand wŏn. We're going to let it go just this once. That
lady has arthritis. If you make her climb five flights of stairs again,
you're really going to be in for it.*

Garbage continued to spew steadily from the rip. A trail of
putrid discharge had leaked from the bag, dotting up the stairs all
the way to the man's front door. He put on rubber gloves in order to
pick up the garbage strewn about his front entrance. Rice covered
with green mold and rotten potatoes crumbled in his hands as he
picked them up. The smell made him gag repeatedly. Although
it was definitely his own garbage, it seemed alien to him. As he
picked up the trash, he discovered crumpled-up letters. They were
already somewhat flattened out. It was clear that the women had
already gotten to them. As he pictured them sniggering while they
passed around his letters, anger surged through him. Even his own
handwriting seemed alien.

". . . The man you are planning to marry is not right for you.
I knew him long before you knew him. I have often witnessed a
hidden side to him that you are not aware of. However you haven't

177

taken my advice and have now gone ahead and decided on the wedding date. Today at work I saw you two standing side by side, handing out wedding invitations around the office. Why can't you see him for who he is? Is it like what you say—that love is blind? It's not too late. I love you more than life itself . . . ."

There wasn't a single letter that was finished. Completely drunk, the man had written letter after letter until early morning. In the end he couldn't send any of them. As soon as he picked up the garbage bag, a *soju* bottle cap fell out of a tear and bounced off the ground. The noodles he had boiled to have with his *soju* had gone straight into the trash untouched; they were swollen and stuck to another unfinished letter.

The knot in the garbage bag finally loosens. As soon as the bag is untied, a fistful of trash spills out into the tub. Strands of hair are tangled up in dust and cigarette butts. The man brings a folding chair, sets it up in front of the tub and sits down. He puts on his rubber gloves again and begins to pore over every piece of trash. He recently replaced the fluorescent lights in the bathroom with a 100-watt bulb. It's blinding. The length of the hair is easily over twenty centimeters. Pulling the strands taut, the man holds them under the light and slowly examines them. He picks up a cigarette butt burned right down to the filter. On the tip of the filter are teeth marks. Looking at the garbage spread out in the tub, he crosses his legs and opens his notepad on his knees.

April 23. OB Lager bottle cap, Pulmuone bean sprouts, Shin Ramen, Coca-Cola, Chamnamu Soju . . .

The man's notepad is crammed with writing. The list looks like a series of items to be searched for in an *I Spy* picture riddle book. He works more earnestly than a watch repairman removing a part from a broken watch with his tweezers. Looking through every single thing meticulously, he stops occasionally to scrawl something in his book. Kool menthol cigarettes. His writing is barely legible; he's holding the pen by its end so he doesn't get his notepad dirty. Two instant noodle containers are stacked together. It's instant udon, the kind that comes with all-in-one soup mix and freeze-dried shrimp. Ottogi Vermont Curry. He also finds the peels from the potatoes and onions that would have been used in the curry.

When he dumps out a twenty-liter garbage bag, the tub fills up halfway. The slimy cabbage leaves and potato peels slip through the fingers of his rubber gloves. Foods rich in protein smell the worst. The foul stench of fish heads, entrails, and chicken bones is unbearable. A pink rubber glove surfaces with a chicken bone stuck to it. It's a right-handed rubber glove with the words "Mommy's Helping Hand" impressed on the wrist. The man flips through the pages of his notepad and finds the page that has a record of a left-handed rubber glove he had fished out a couple of days ago. March 23. Cheiljedang Beat laundry detergent (750 g), Kool cigarettes, Coca-Cola, Nongshim Big Bowl Noodle (shrimp flavor), Mommy's Helping Hand rubber glove (pink, left hand). The brand and even the color are the same. When everything fits like this, there's no question about it. The garbage is from the same household.

She enjoys drinking OB Lager and Coke, smokes Kool cigarettes, and likes to eat shrimp-flavored instant noodles. She is also left-handed and has long hair, but it might not even be a woman. It could be a long-haired man. Making some inferences is easy. Since things like diapers, chocolate, and candy wrappers haven't turned up, it's safe to assume there's no child in the household at present.

From last winter to now the man has gone through over a hundred garbage bags. While rummaging through them, he gradually learned the different tastes and lifestyles of the ninety families living in the building, although what he learned doesn't amount to much. Two kinds of people live in these cramped 525-square-foot suites: young married couples and single people like himself; and elderly couples who have married off all their children and sold their big house. It's always the younger people who get sucked into buying the newest products advertised on TV. They are more open to trying new things. Without any hesitation, they buy things with flashy packaging and beverages like punch made with exotic tropical fruits. They are the ones who also buy items that are quite expensive, considering their quantity or size. There were times when he compiled statistics from the data he gathered. The women in this building use a higher grade of dishwashing soap with aloe that is gentle on the hands, and perhaps it's because many of them are career women on the go that they use two-in-one shampoo and conditioners. They also tend to use sanitary napkins with wings.

With his gloved hands, the man sweeps the garbage strewn about the tub back into the bag. There is less garbage now that the liquid has drained. After he reties the bag, he carries it back down to the ground floor and puts it into the trash bin. He takes his cigarettes out of his pocket and sticks one in his mouth. Only if he could have looked through *her* garbage, he could have discovered what she was really like. If so, he could have learned of her weakness for the color cobalt and that she was attracted to articulate men who dressed neatly.

She quit her job when she got married. To see her one last time, the man went to the newlyweds' housewarming party, even though he didn't feel like it. Sporting an apron and her hair in a ponytail, she squeezed in beside him as if it was the most natural thing to do.

As drinks started to flow, someone questioned her. *Miss Kim, no, I guess we have to call you Mrs. Park now, how did you end up falling for Mr. Park?*

Giggling, she replied that it was because of the cobalt-colored dress shirt he was wearing.

Park, two years his junior, had graduated from the same university. Park didn't change a bit, even after marrying. He still holds the same position in the accounts department. The man, however, moved up fast and now sits right behind Park, at a much-coveted location that provides him with a view of the whole office. Every time he looks up and sees Park's shirt, stiff as if it were starched, and his suit, neat and wrinkle-free, he remembers her long, white fingers hitting the keyboard. He'd hear Park entertaining their co-workers with stories by the vending machine.

Damn, she's always buying me cobalt-colored shirts. Now, I shudder if I even hear the word "cobalt."

He even caught Park coming out of a restaurant with a new member of the female staff. Even now, the woman has no idea what kind of man she has married.

As he is going up to his apartment, he bumps into the paper boy who is rushing down the stairs after having delivered the morning paper. The boy pinches his nose in disgust as he moves away. In the dim fluorescent light he eyes the man's gloved hands curiously. He is also wearing a red rubber glove on his free hand. You can get a rash from constantly rubbing the inside of your wrist against the metal mail slot when you slip your hand in and out. To prevent this, milkmen and newspaper boys have started to wear rubber gloves. With his long legs the boy bounds down the corridor. Even though the man uses a lot of bleach to rinse his bathtub and tiled floor, he can't seem to rid his apartment of the smell of garbage. The sensor lights that the boy had triggered switch off one by one as the timer runs down. It's already past four in the morning.

When the doorbell rings he's in the middle of trying to put together the torn-up pieces of a bill that he had spread out on the floor. He found them in the garbage the night before. The bill, now held together by tape, is still missing some pieces. There are even times when he finds bills that haven't been crumpled. He's lucky if they aren't soaked with liquid from the garbage, but even if they are covered with food scraps, he doesn't mind. If he irons a bill after a quick rinse under the tap, there isn't a whole lot of trouble in making out the print. However, whenever they are ripped to shreds like this, he has to piece everything together like a child's jigsaw puzzle. The name starts to emerge with painful slowness. Kim, _____hoon. The doorbell rings as he's looking for the missing piece on the floor.

It seems that whoever rang the bell is leaning against the front door. When he tries to push the door open he can sense the heaviness of the person behind it. The door doesn't budge at all. Whoever it is—probably a man, guessing from the weight—must be propping himself up. Only after several attempts to shove open the door does the person on the other side seem to feel it shudder. Still, he takes a while to step away. It's a complete stranger, so drunk that he has no control over his own body. He's holding a large bouquet of flowers in one hand. His dress shirt, pulled out of his pants, hangs loosely over his thick legs like a tablecloth.

Don't worry.

The massive bear-like body falls on the man as if to pin him down. To prevent himself from being knocked over, he braces himself and fights the dead weight with all his strength. Even a wild guess tells him that this fellow is easily over a hundred kilograms. The man struggles like a monkey caught by a giant bear. The stranger looks down at him and mumbles again.

Don't worry. His foul breath hits the man directly in the face. The stranger keeps mumbling unintelligibly, continuing to crush him.

When the man plays the words over in his mind, it seems that the stranger is saying "I'm sorry." Barely managing to open his eyes that start to roll wildly in different directions, making him look cross-eyed, the fellow tries to gaze down at the man. Suddenly he sees that the man is wearing an undershirt instead of a proper shirt. His eyes flash with anger.

What? Who the hell are you? What are you doing here? With that, the fellow forces his way into the apartment.

The man pushes back, trying to resist him. *Hey, what do you think you're doing? Do you even know what time it is right now? You have the wrong house!* He doesn't stand a chance against this giant.

What did you say? I can find this place even with my eyes closed. Where is she? Hey! I know you're in there. Stop hiding and come out now! The fellow stops shouting and suddenly steps back. He starts to retch uncontrollably. Vomit hits the floor and splatters all over the man's dress shoes that are sitting in the entrance. *Isn't this 507? Sam Kwang Apartment, suite 507?*

As the fellow gradually sobers up, he becomes more coherent. The light in the stairwell has been broken for a long time. Whoever lived in suite 507 before probably hit it with his furniture when he was moving out. The man could see the filament inside the cracked bulb. The doorbells for 507 and 508 are right beside each other and in the dark it seems that the fellow meant to press 507, but pressed the bell for 508 instead.

Goddamn, I'm really sorry. Looking from the man to the mess he created, the fellow stumbles toward the stairs and flops down on the ground.

The vomit gives off a sour, acidic smell. While the man pours water on the ground and sweeps away the vomit, the fellow walks over to 507 and presses the doorbell. It's empty. For the last couple of days the man hasn't sensed any sign of life coming from the suite. If someone was inside, it would have been impossible to ignore all this commotion. The fellow continues to push the bell. Electronic cuckoo sounds chirp from inside the suite. When the door doesn't open, the fellow shouts and pounds on the door with a humongous fist like a boxing glove.

I said I was sorry! Please open the door!

Kim ____hoon. Even though he searches every corner of the floor, he can't find the missing piece. It probably got thrown out in another bag. He found these pieces of the bill in the bag with the kidney bean shells. He riffles through the pages of his notepad. Bean shells, seesaw, monkey bars, boy, puddles. Inside the garbage bag, there are plastic candy packages that crinkle and a fistful of chicken bones. This woman must be very diligent; someone who doesn't mind preparing foods that require a lot of time and effort. He also finds an old toothbrush with the bristles harshly flattened.

The doorbell rings again. It's the same fellow. He shoves the bouquet of flowers into the man's chest. It's a bouquet of roses. *Could you give these to the woman next door for me? It's her birthday today.* Bumping into the wall, he staggers down the stairs. The man counts the red roses. There are thirty in all.

For a few days now a pair of yellow socks has been hanging on the clothesline out on the balcony of 507. The heels and toes have dark stains that even soap couldn't remove. It's been three days since the incident with the drunkard, but the man still hasn't run into the woman. There's no sign of life next door. On his way home he circles the building on purpose, using the path out back. Standing by the wall, he looks up at 507. The balcony glass is shattered, all except for a few pieces that are still dangling. Their suites, 507 and 508, are the only ones with the lights off. People have been staying late at work. Once tax season passes they should be able to get off at the regular time.

The roses that he hung by the window have started to wither, the black spreading in from the edges as the petals curl. A single wall is all that separates 507 from 508. The man starts to move everything away from this wall to the opposite side. Half the morning goes by as he takes his wardrobe apart, moves it over to the other side, and then reassembles it. He drags his bed over to where his wardrobe used to be. The wall is twenty centimeters thick at most. He runs his palm over it. He lies down on his side facing the wall and puts his ear next to it. Whenever he hears the smallest sound, his senses sharpen. Besides himself, there are only two people who would come up to the fifth floor—the woman or that fellow. If he leaves his room door open, he can hear everything, even the sound of footsteps coming up the stairs. But to his disappointment, the footsteps always stop before coming up all the way. Just like dandelion spores suddenly blown in by the wind, curiosity had already started to sprout within him. He thinks he catches the sound of a key being inserted into a keyhole and the bolt sliding back into the door frame. That instant, the cover of the mail slot on his front door snaps open and a red rubber glove shoves in the morning paper.

From the bus stop he takes the long way and uses the back path again. He looks up at the balcony of 507. It's only after he sees the bare clothesline minus the yellow socks that he realizes the woman

184

is finally back. But when he rushes up, he doesn't hear a sound from her suite. Because of her, he has temporarily stopped his garbage work. Worried about the stench that might escape, he always worked with the bathroom door shut. But the sealed-up bathroom became an echo chamber, amplifying every drop of water that fell from the tap. It was impossible to hear any noises coming from outside.

So after an early dinner, he waits for the woman to come back for the day. On the bed, he stretches out on his side so he's facing the wall. He lies so close to the wall that his groin touches it. Afraid that the woman would slip past him again, he even resists nature's call. However, the pressure in his bladder forces him to get up from the bed. Coming out of the bathroom, he discovers a maggot squirming on the floor. Summer is coming, but it's still too early for maggots. He had mopped every corner of the suite with bleach several times. Writhing gently, the maggot moves toward something. He picks it up with a tissue and flushes it down the toilet.

He finds another maggot in a crack in the bedroom's threshold. The man crawls from the room to the kitchen, looking everywhere. He crawls toward the window where he hung the bouquet. He discovers a continuous stream of maggots crawling along the edge of the wall. Those that can't cling to the wall end up falling off; hitting the floor, they curl up into balls. A horde of maggots is writhing inside the cellophane that the roses are wrapped in. He opens the balcony door and hurls the bouquet out into the back lot overgrown with weeds.

In the morning while he's shaving, he senses that there is someone outside the front door. He runs into his bedroom, then dashes to the front door while trying to whip on his pants. He ends up taking longer to put on his pants since he's in too much of a hurry. He has to meet her. He needs to tell her about the fellow, he needs to tell her about the roses. He thrusts open the front door, but the corridor is already empty. The clicking of heels from the bottom of the stairs is fading. Urgently he leans over the railing and looks down the stairwell at the identical railings that zigzag all the way down to the first floor. Between the railings he sees something flash by and then vanish. It's as if a yellow butterfly suddenly took flight. Is the yellow he just glimpsed from the yellow socks that hung on her clothesline? He looks down at his own feet and realizes he forgot to put on his shoes. When did she come home? He stayed up waiting until 3 o'clock in the morning. During that time, he didn't hear any footsteps come up to the fifth floor. Maybe she never left the house in the first place, but was cooped up inside all this time.

Only a trace of her perfume lingers in the empty stairwell. It's not the perfume called Poison that was once so popular with the female staff at his workplace. It's a light, sharp scent. He inhales deeply, making his lungs expand like balloons. What kind of woman is she? It is then that he realizes he wants to get to know her.

When he lifts the stainless steel cover of the mail slot he discovers another flap inside. Shoving open the flap, he can see the front entrance of 507 through a rectangular opening the size of a postcard. His cheek, flattened on the cement floor, feels icy. He can see a pair of vinyl indoor slippers placed neatly in the entrance. They are mustard-colored with crudely embroidered flowers on the instep. Slipping his hand into the slot, he gropes around for the slippers. He can't reach them. Because he has to reach for them by feel, it's all the more difficult. He only has about ten minutes to spare before he has to leave for work. He works his arm further and further in until he realizes that he's in up to his armpit, causing the flap to pinch his skin. It's a slow process; he has to take his arm out repeatedly, look inside to estimate the distance, and then put it back in again. After some thought, he fashions a metal clothes hanger into a long hook like a fishing rod, and slips it into the mail slot. He hooks the slipper and pulls it toward him. Finally the slipper is in his hand.

The one-size-fits-all slipper is completely worn out. Judging by the flattened faux-fur insole where her heel rubbed, the woman has small feet. The vinyl on the instep is peeling off and its color has turned. Although it looks mustard yellow, it seems to have once been a bright yellow. He hides the slipper in the back of his closet. *Damn, late again*. He purses his lips and then heaves a sigh. To his surprise, he finds himself whistling a cheerful melody. *What? Me, whistling?* He skips down the stairs and runs all the way to the bus stop.

Half a month passes. Having resumed his work now that the woman had returned, he continues to lug garbage bags up to the fifth floor. The garbage truck empties the garbage bin every other day. If he skips even one day, he may never find her garbage. On the fifteenth day he finds the other slipper in one of the garbage bags. An indoor slipper embroidered with flowers. Her garbage bag is nearly empty. It's tied loosely so the knot comes undone easily. For half a month she probably turned her home upside down, trying to find the other slipper. Today she finally threw out the lone slipper, certain by now that its match won't ever turn up. There are purple fruit stains on the embroidery. He takes out the other slipper from his closet and places them side by side. The difference in their color is big enough to notice. Bits of cotton and sponge stick out through the worn parts of the vinyl sole. He opens up the bag and lifts up the contents. Used tea bags, thick orange peels, Diet Coke cans. All diet foods. He lifts up a plastic package that's tightly rolled up. It's an empty package of fabric softener, mimosa scent. Even though there are slippery grains of spoiled rice stuck to the package, he still catches a refreshing scent in the midst of the rotten stink. It's the same scent from the corridor. At the very bottom of the garbage bag is a three-tiered, fresh cream cake, untouched and gone bad. Grape stains cover the patches where the milky cream has rubbed off. A fluffy layer of mold is already blossoming on the top layer. There is a red outline on the cream where the cherry was. It looks like she picked out only the cherry, pineapple, and tangerine from the cake. He unfolds every little piece of paper, even an aspirin wrapper. One Mugunghwa (Rose of Sharon) train ticket to Gurye. In his mind he sees her from behind as she climbs Mount Jiri. The yellow socks that she's wearing get stained with dirt that won't come out. A seven-digit number scrawled on a slip of paper—maybe a phone number?

He also finds a past due notice for a pager. Once he has wiped off the cream, her name and pager number show up. Choi Jiae. 012-343-7890.

He stands in the middle of a large grocery store, holding a yellow plastic shopping basket. In it, he has placed a mimosa-scented fabric softener and jumbo container of bleach with a handle like a rum jug. A thick layer of dust covers the shelves that hold the products people don't tend to buy. In front of the cosmetics counter an employee is wearing thick makeup, her face painted on like a mannequin's. She latches onto passing customers to hand them questionnaires as she repeats the same thing over and over again.

We're promoting our new product. You will receive a free gift just by filling out this short survey.

Every year, a company launches dozens of new products. Even at his company, the staff working in new product development are anxious to come up with a hit product like Nongshim's Shrimp Crackers. In order to develop a new product that guarantees consumer satisfaction, thousands of surveys are distributed throughout the whole country. He has a thorough knowledge of his neighbors' different tastes and their patterns of consumption. Once he read in a book that there is a sociological discipline called "garbology," which examines the waste of residents in an area in order to learn about their actual behavior. Looking through a garbage dump is a more reliable way of getting sure answers than a vague survey. Garbage never lies. The real answer to a picture riddle? Garbage. This is what the man thinks about as he wanders down the aisles in the supermarket.

The fellow is sitting on a step on the fifth floor staircase. Because his huge body is blocking the way, the man has to wait on the landing for the fellow to move aside. Having felt someone approach, the fellow looks up, his eyes bloodshot, and recognizes the man at once. He sticks out his chunky hand in greeting. The man could feel the fellow's strength from his grip. There is a large cake box placed on the step where he was just sitting.

I'm sorry. I couldn't give her the flowers. I mean, I couldn't even meet her.

Yes, she went on a trip.

Then I guess you saw her?

Grimacing, the fellow rubs his face savagely as if washing it. *No, I heard through a friend.* He catches the man glancing at the box on the stair. *Oh, this here . . .* He lifts up the box and hands it to him. *I'm sorry to keep bothering you like this, but could you give this to her? Since she just came back from a trip, she shouldn't be going anywhere. At least, not for a while anyway.*

The man has no choice but to receive the box with just one hand because he is carrying his groceries in the other. The fellow's bloodshot eyes widen when the box slips a little.

Hey, you should be careful. If the box shakes, you'll squash the cake. At the words "you'll squash the cake," the fellow's broad face squishes up.

Is it a fresh cream cake? With fruit, like cherries or pineapple on top?

She's crazy about fresh cream cake. I'm a huge fan of fresh cream myself, the fellow snickers. *You think we'll ever be able to have some cake together?* He mumbles as if he's talking to himself.

After nodding goodbye to the man, the fellow starts to make his way down the stairs. The cake is heavy. While the man is opening the front door, he hears the fellow exclaim from the third floor. He must have tripped on that higher step.

Excuse me, the man calls down the stairwell.

The fellow's broad face looks up at him from a couple of levels below. The man is about to say, "You know, about her . . . ," but stops himself. The fellow has no clue that she doesn't like fresh cream cake. That could even be the cause of their breakup. But how could he let him know the truth without giving him the wrong idea? If he tells him that he looks through other people's garbage, the fellow will think that he's absolutely crazy. If he says that she told him herself, the fellow will become suspicious of their relationship.

What if something comes up? The fellow stares up blankly at his face. *Just in case. I mean, what if I don't get to see her like last time . . .* He lets his words trail off.

The fellow smiles brightly, revealing yellow teeth. *Then why don't you just go ahead and eat it?* His laughter grows distant.

The woman is on a diet right now. She doesn't hate the man; she just hates his body that weighs close to 100 kilograms. She's simply sick of having to eat the fresh cream cake that he's crazy about and she's sick of his mistaken belief that she shares his love for fresh cream cake—this is the cause of their breakup. If only the fellow had dug through her garbage, who knows? They might still be together.

Inside his fridge, the cake is slowly spoiling. He still hasn't run into her. They have just missed each other every time. Whenever he scrambles out after her, she is already gone, leaving behind only a trace of mimosa-scented fabric softener in the air. He opens up his address book. Choi Jiae. 012-343-7890.

Did somebody page me? The girl on the other end speaks in a dull voice while chewing gum.

Well, I'm supposed to give you a cake, but you're just impossible to run into.

She blows a bubble. The gum pops and sticks to her lips. *What are you talking about?* She uses her tongue to unstick the gum and starts to chew again.

I'm the man who lives next door to you, Miss Choi.

All of a sudden, the girl gets angry. *Oh my God, seriously, I've had enough. For a while there, a man kept calling, leaving weird messages and now this! You know what? I'm not, what's her name, Choi Jiae. I've had this number for over a month now.*

The front door of 507 is wide open. He takes the cake out of the fridge and rushes into 507. A middle-aged couple is repapering the walls. With all the furniture taken out, the suite looks bigger than he imagined. The smell of glue stings his nostrils. The man with pasted paper in hand climbs up a ladder and looks down toward the entrance.

Can I help you? Do you want your walls repapered? We offer very good prices. The missus smiles as she holds a brush dripping with paste.

The man steps out from the entrance as two workmen carrying a large sheet of glass come up the stairs. They go out to the balcony and remove the broken pane and start to put in the new glass.

The fellow is in the back lot searching for something. He raises his crimson face when the man gestures at him. He's out of breath. The man steps into the yard. Overgrown weeds come up to his knees.

I'm sorry. I ended up eating the cake. It took a whole week to finish it.

In the fellow's hand is a broken branch.

She moved out. But I guess you already knew that?

The fellow nods while he keeps beating the overgrown weeds with the branch.

Then what are you doing here?

Last summer, we went on a trip to Cheju Island. Jiae likes the ocean. The fellow's eyes look vacant, as if he's reminiscing.

It's not the ocean that Choi Jiae likes, it's the mountains.

Fixing his gaze off into the distance, the fellow keeps mumbling. *We bought a* tolharubang *there. You know the Cheju souvenir? The dwarf-like stone statue with holes punched in it like a pumice stone? That night when we got into a fight, Jiae went crazy and just chucked it out the window. It should have fallen somewhere over here. I've looked everywhere, but I can't find it.*

The man and the fellow are standing in the back lot. It's not easy to find a little statue in a thicket of weeds.

Then let's look again from opposite ends. The man looks around for a stick.

Are you sure you're not busy?

Picking up a branch, he answers as he walks over to the other end of the yard. *Time is the only thing I've got.*

He examines the ground as he beats at the grass with his stick.

When he glances up he sees the fellow using his sleeve to wipe the sweat pouring down his red face. It's a sweltering day. At noon the temperature hits about 28 degrees Celsius. *Tonight it's going to be the last time. I'm going to do it just once more and I'm calling it quits.* He takes off his tie and shoves it in his suit pocket. He unbuttons the top button of his dress shirt that's choking him. *There's really no other way of knowing. That's because the truth is rotting away somewhere in the garbage.* Savagely, the man starts to beat at the grass.

Raccoon World

by Park Min-gyu

Translated by Jenny Wang Medina

Respectable

" . . . that's respectable," B was saying sarcastically into the phone as I hung up on him. It wasn't because I didn't like him, or that I couldn't take any more of his belittling. It was because I could hear Team Leader Sohn's voice drifting toward me over three rows of desks and several clusters of office machinery. That guy shouting, "Yes, sir!" and running over to him is me—I'm an intern here at Moon Communications. I've been an intern here for four months. Even now, I still think

it's respectable. And I've been really good at doing this stuff for four months. There are eight interns total, all working to outdo each other. The pay isn't much to speak of, but I make enough to drive here and back. There's so much work to do that I have to stay up almost all night every night, but after the six-month training period, one intern will be chosen as a full-time employee. And the rest? Well, that's it for them. The personnel manager told us to "Think of this as good experience," but I definitely don't want to be one of the ones left behind.

The seven other interns are desperate too. It drives me crazy.

I can't let my guard down for a minute. And there are two girls in the group who have famously high scores on the TOEIC English test. Needless to say, it's intense, and the atmosphere is positively suffocating. Four of the interns are so-so and one's an idiot, but they're just as intense as the rest of us. You can never just say, "Oh well," and try to blame it on someone else if things go wrong. The fact is that that's just how life is, so

what can you do? Even I, I who made a name for myself as the singer of the rock group "Sam's Son" in college, can't do anything about it. All I can do is look things up, make copies, file, make phone calls, do research, and fetch coffee all day long. Yesterday I went and stood in for the department manager during his civilian defense training. Is that any sort of thing for a rock star to do? But it's respectable, respectable. Of course B, the drummer, was laughing so hard he cried.

Did you call me, sir?

Yeah, I thought you might be good at this sort of thing. Team Leader Sohn smiled at me. To make a long story short, I want to run this program, but it won't work. And . . . I want you to get it to work for me. Inwardly, I breathe a sigh of relief. Team Leader Sohn has such a bullish look about him that it always makes it hard to look him in the face. On top of that, the atmosphere was especially ominous that day because he was choosing his team for the big presentation competition.

This is

an old video game, from the looks of it. That's right, it *is* an old video game. Well, you need to download an emulator first, sir. An emulator? It would take a while to explain it to you, sir. I searched the Internet and simply found a MAME emulator, simply installed it, and ran Team Leader Sohn's simple program. It worked. Simple.

This is

what is it sir? It's Raccoon World, of course. Raccoon World, sir? Yup, Raccoon World. Sure enough, jangly, manic music started blaring from the computer, and a jangly, manic little raccoon appeared in the corner of the screen. Team Leader Sohn smiled with a look on his face that said, "See?" and immediately got into the game. The game consisted of moving the raccoon across platforms and up ladders, picking up fruit, and avoiding these bug-like things that chased you. You died if you fell on an upturned tack. It was completely pointless.

What do you think? Well, . . . I don't really know, sir. Is that right? Yes, sir. This is what I did for fun in middle school. Back then, some arcades even had to have ten Raccoon World machines in a row because it was so popular. I'm telling you, kids would line up to play it. You, me, it didn't matter what you had to do; everyone was completely obsessed with that Raccoon.

Those were good times.

How could they have been? I thought. But, if it was a time when middle schoolers were that tight with a raccoon, it couldn't have been that bad. I thought about that as I replied to Team Leader Sohn's question, "So, do you wanna try it too?" with, "No, I'm okay, sir. I don't know how it was in the past, but I've never heard of an intern being pals with a raccoon in this day and age. That's all I'm saying. Really."

I'm disappointed in you.

Excuse me? His response caught me off-guard and I nearly

jumped. Disappointed? What do you mean, sir? Well, I thought for sure that you'd like Raccoon World. You've always got your face glued to your monitor and you have the hands of a compulsive gamer, but I guess I had you pegged wrong. I'm sorry, sir, I said apologetically as I got up to leave. The walk back to my seat past those three rows of desks felt like an epic journey across three mountain ranges. How was I supposed to know that the Team Leader would like Raccoon World so much? Office life is such a bitch!

The afternoon was hectic as usual, but this time I was summoned by the personnel manager. I responded with a forceful, "Yes, sir!" as usual, and went running. Jealous glares came flying at me like arrows striking my back. It was those two girls with the high TOEIC scores. Hmph, they don't even know why he wants me.

Look here, just what do you think you're doing?

The manager asked the question as though he already knew the answer, but there was absolutely no way of knowing what I had done wrong. What do you mean? Team Leader Sohn, that's what I mean. I looked over at Team Leader Sohn and, oh crap, he was still obsessed with that raccoon game. Were you the one who opened that program for him? But I didn't . . . it's not that, it's . . . emulator, MAME . . . several words came to mind, but how, was I supposed, to explain, something like that, to someone over fifty? And the manager already had a look on his face that told me he wouldn't believe anything I said. It's been three hours already. In that time, he's scarfed down two bags of vegetable crackers and three bags of potato chips. He's showing all the symptoms. What symptoms?

Of Raccoon Rabies.

Excuse me? He's already been bitten. In America, they dump

anywhere from two hundred million to a billion dollars a year into trying to wipe out the disease. They even had to crop-dust the entire state of Ohio with an oral vaccine. Anyway, this is going to be a huge pain in the neck. The Raccoon in *my* department! Even if you didn't know what it was, you should have at least consulted me before you unleashed the Great Raccoon. Don't you think?

I'm in big trouble if it's going to be like this. Because it wasn't even my fault. And Raccoon World Rabies? What in the world is that? Listen closely. A long time ago, raccoons were just animals that stole from farmer's storehouses. Now, they steal things here and there from corporations. The only thing more dangerous than a spy is a raccoon. What the hell do they teach you kids in college? Raccoons are the biggest threat to all industry, the biggest threat to all mankind. Got it?

Yes.

Be careful from now on, because I'm telling you, they are deceptively cute. He chucked me under the chin condescendingly as if to say, "Strike three, you're out," and I was really pissed off. What the hell kind of company was this anyway? But all I could manage was a reflexive sigh. Rustle rustle. Team Leader Sohn was in the middle of tossing back his third bag of vegetable crackers.

What a Shame

It's just such a shame. He was such a good worker. The manager kept up a steady stream of laments as I formatted Team Leader Sohn's computer. We had to do this, the same way they sprayed all of Ohio with that vaccine. This was already the third time I'd formatted it. He wasn't kidding around about this.

Team Leader Sohn left the company yesterday. It had only been two weeks since it happened. The official word was that it was because of his failed presentation; only the manager and I knew that the real reason was Raccoon Rabies. Have you ever heard of a more pitiful reason for getting fired?

If you think this all sounds strange, well, obviously, it was. Very strange. That game swallowed Team Leader Sohn's life whole, and he suddenly gained a lot of weight too. Of course, gaining weight when you never stop eating is to be expected, but if you asked me what about the stripe around his eyes? I'd be at a complete loss. And there was no doubt that the area around Team Leader Sohn's eyes was covered with dark marks that looked like liver spots. If you saw him from far away, it looked like a perfectly symmetrical stripe. Wait, it's just like

a raccoon, can't you see?

people whispered. Of course, the marks could have come from playing video games too much—how could that possibly happen? After a while, people started avoiding Team Leader Sohn. The liver spots got darker as the days passed, and he became more and more like a raccoon with each passing day. Isn't there a cure? Nope. It's just such a shame. The manager's replies were always overly simplistic, and for that simple reason the Team Leader became a complete pariah.

I was Team Leader Sohn's only companion. Without fail, he would call for me immediately after our team meetings, which he was no longer invited to. I would shout, "Yes, sir," and scurry off, but doing so only meant that I would have to listen to a story so ridiculous it would make you go blind. And of course, the only thing he ever talked about anymore was Raccoon World.

Watch closely, this is Stage Twenty-three. Look, a big gap opens up here when this ladder comes down, and there's one long platform at the end there, see? I can jump across to there, but I don't know what to do after that. If I jump from there to the next platform, I'll fall onto that tack for sure. I completely forgot how to get across this part. But I'm telling you I definitely did it back then. It's just . . .

Why did you call me, sir?

Ah, yes, because I thought that you, at least, would know how to do this.

What makes you think that I would know how to do that, sir?

You're a good friend of the Great Raccoon, aren't you?

No sir, we're not close. We're not close at all.

That's disappointing.

Again, why are you disappointed, sir? There isn't anyone who would possibly know that.

Really? That's such a shame.

It was always such a shame, or something like that. Finally, I started avoiding him too. But then again, if I still wanted to have the kind of conversation I used to have with Team Leader Sohn, there were always the manager's summons. Everyone likes to say, "Yes, sir," and hurry away importantly, but when it's "What did Team Leader Sohn just say?" as he sits too close to you with his hand caressing your thigh—that's the kind of thing that would drive anyone crazy. At the time I didn't know what everyone else already suspected—that the personnel manager is gay.

Even though they cover it up

the whole world is in ruins. If there are people who turn into raccoons, then there are also homos who oversee corporate personnel departments, and there are rock singers who are so afraid of personnel's rules that they sit still to get their thighs stroked. There can't be anything worse than that.

The stress ultimately led to my downfall. I blacked out last night at Team Leader Sohn's going-away party and when I came to, I was lying on the cold, foul-smelling floor of a subway station. That was the first time I ever blacked out and had memory lapses, and it was also the first time I'd ever slept in a subway station. There were a few groups of homeless people lying near me, and the shutters at both ends of the passageway were locked tight.

I leaned up against a chilly wall and tried to collect my thoughts. I remembered everything up to the second bar we went to, and I remember being put in charge of making sure that Team Leader Sohn got home safely as everyone parted ways. The Team Leader lives in Inchon, which is why I came all the way out here, and I think I remember going to a sidewalk bar nearby to have another round of *soju*. Then my memory cuts off. I don't remember a thing. I looked around, but Team Leader Sohn was nowhere to be seen.

Hey you, are you alright?

Startled, I turned to see an unfamiliar older man staring at me. He was a homeless man in his mid-forties who looked like he was just trying to stick his nose in my business. Oh, um, yes. I lowered my head and blushed. Youth is really grand, for sure. I mean, to look that healthy after drinkin' so much? You know, I'll bet you your wallet's safe. Go 'head, check it. Startled again, I quickly shoved my hand into the inner pocket of my suit jacket. Just like he said, my wallet was there, safe and sound.

Don't you worry. We'd never lay a hand on anyone who came in with the Great Raccoon.
Did you say raccoon?
Didn't ya know? That's who brought you here yesterday.
Oh, I see . . . Would you happen to know where he went?
Well, since he's a raccoon and all, he probably went underground.

200

Did you say underground?

Yeah, underground. You know, down there in those tunnels where the trains go back and forth?

Wait. But he's really a human being . . .

I know. But seems he's nearly all raccoon now. When you get that far, you gotta live underground, see?

I'm not sure I understand you.

Our friend wouldn't happen to be stuck on Stage Twenty-three, would he now?

How did you know that?

I'm right, aren't I? That's when they all become raccoons.

I was under the impression that it was a disease.

Raccoon Rabies? That's just a story *they* made up.

Why would they do that?

Look here, the world's a much different place than you think it is.

Then what kind of place is it?

Stage Twenty-three. That's what this world is really called.

Don't Say a Word

Not a word. Listen, I slept in the subway station yesterday. Ha ha, what were you doing there? It was a peaceful night at the fishing hole. Luckily, I didn't have anyone else with me that day, so B and I were free to talk about almost anything. It had been a long time since we'd seen each other, and an even longer time since we'd been fishing. The sinker didn't budge for a long time.

So that's what happened.

So *that's* what happened. B nodded. Now that I think about it, it does seem awfully strange. That's why I'm so worried about it. Well, this is something we'll really have to think about. B pulled out a cigarette and puffed on it with the air of someone who was getting ready to do some deep thinking. I tossed the cigarette I'd been smoking away and started to roll more paste bait. The sinker still hadn't moved at all; it looked exactly like a giant nail that had been pounded into the water's surface.

It'll probably rust like that,

rust right up. B and I had been friends for so long that if we were made of metal, we'd have rusted. He was two years older than me, but we became friends somehow anyway. We met during my first year in college. We were at orientation, and some professor or staff person got up and was going on and on about something or other. I don't know why, but everything irritated me back then. So naturally, and since he wasn't saying anything important, well, anyway, I stood up and shouted

Shut up, you son of a bitch!

The entire assembly dissolved into a sea of laughter, and the disastrous event ended. At the end of the day, someone came looking for me. Who's the "son of a bitch"? Who said that? When several kids singled me out with their eyes, he approached me. Wanna start a band with me?

That was B.

After that, we became a fairly well-known band around campus. We were called "Sam's Son," but to the students, of course, we were better known as that "Shut up, you son of a bitch!" band, Sam's Son. Wow, they swear a lot so they must be worth watching. B always burst out laughing as he watched the kids going crazy and cursing at our shows. Those were good times. Back then, all you had to do was use foul language and you were a rocker. You didn't even really have to know how to play an instrument. If you just wailed on the drums or the guitar, people would go nuts. Looking back, it all seems like a dream.

Maybe it was because he was a philosophy major, but B was the kind of guy who always had something profound to say about everything. He knew a hell of a lot more than I did, to say the least, and he had had more diverse life experiences. I was the only male student in the school majoring in home economics, and as far as I was concerned, everything about B was completely admirable. I found out in the fall of our second year that B had taken the college entrance exam three years in a row before he got in and was two years older than me, which meant that the foundation of our friendship was different because, as he was older, I would have to be more deferential to him. But by then we were already too close.

Like a hook and sinker,

we went everywhere together. We drank together, met girls together, performed together, and went fishing together. Naturally, we graduated together, and only our plans to keep playing music together differed—I had to finish my tour of duty in the army. Strangely, I had a much more positive outlook on things after I got out of the army. My irritability melted away like snow, and I was transforming into a model student getting ready to join the professional ranks. Hey, this isn't the time to sit around playing music, you know. I jumped to attention.

And so, that's how it happened.

I see. B nodded again. And that was the end of it. The reality of the situation was that we broke up the band, and I became an intern at this company. I was sorry then, but nothing more, and I'm sorry now, and nothing more. Since then, it's always B who calls to see how I'm doing, not me, and going fishing today was B's idea, not mine. As for me—all I can do now is babble on and on about a raccoon.

Here's what I think.

B finally pulled himself out of his thoughts long enough to speak
The long nail stuck into the water's surface suddenly turned back
into an overturned sinker, but I didn't put any effort into it or try
to pull in the line. After all, this is a world where human beings
become raccoons. Who cares if a sinker turns into a nail, or a nail
turns back into a sinker again?

I want to say it's probably the "problem of pleasure."
The problem of pleasure?
You know, the raccoon.
That sounds complicated.

It's just that, well, I think you've reached that stage in your life.
You're standing on the threshold of Stage One right now and you're
realizing for the first time just how much the world hates raccoons.
The way I see it, you have two options. You can run away like a
raccoon, or you can simply renounce the Great Raccoon. It sounds
like your Team Leader was probably hiding the Great Raccoon for
his whole life. It must have been really hard for him.

Hiding it?

Naturally, at first. But as he passed through the stages, he started
to miss it subconsciously. And that's when it suddenly turned
up. He probably thought he'd cleared the trap of the upturned
thumbtack but now, no matter what anyone says, he's become an
honored raccoon.

My head is spinning. I don't even know which way is up
anymore. Then how did the raccoons become mankind's enemy?
Let me give it to you simply. Think about an agrarian society, for
example. Everyone is out working hard in the fields, but one little

raccoon shows up. Oh my god, it's a raccoon! someone shouts, and all the work is interrupted. Aw, c'mere you cute, cute, happy lil' guy!

Wait, they spoke English in agrarian times?

No, listen, that's just how it would have sounded. Because initially, raccoons gave people that kind of pleasure. After an hour or two, the raccoon would have completely drained those people of their souls. How do you think the team leader of that first field team felt? He must have wanted to kill that raccoon. That first team leader's hatred has been cultivated over a long, long period of time. And voilà, now we're in a late capitalist industrial society. Now the world has a firm grip on guys like that old field's team leader.

I had no idea something like that ever happened.

Those guys started exterminating the raccoons. I mean, it's the same as when they wiped out all the Indians. That vaccine that they sprayed over the entire state of Ohio wasn't really a vaccine, it was a poison used to kill all the raccoons. Why? Because there was never any Raccoon Rabies to begin with. That was an ingenious strategy, too, because on the other side, there were the people who were trying to protect the raccoons. As an endangered species, that is.

And why was that?

Well, at first, people thought raccoons were very rare and unusual. A raccoon was something you could only see at the zoo, and a nocturnal raccoon was something you might only see once in a lifetime. Then, of course, it was thought that if you managed to meet a raccoon somehow, you most certainly wouldn't be allowed to touch it.
Human beings are pretty scary, huh?
You're going to have to make a decision soon too. I mean, about this "problem of pleasure" thing.

Sorry for dumping all this on you.

Don't worry about it. The truth is, it's something I've thought about a lot. I was going to talk to you about it even if you hadn't brought it up.

Talk to me about what?

Well, actually, I want to become a raccoon.

That won't be too hard for you?

I guess I'll have to be on the run at first, but I've thought about it, and executing my plan will be surprisingly simple. All I'll need is an emulator to execute Raccoon World. Anyway, I think that the raccoon is the only thing God sent down to earth for the sake of mankind. That's the only thing I know for sure.

I guess we'll be living pretty different lives from now on then.

You lonely?

Yeah, I'm lonely.

Well, don't forget that there are raccoons out there.

Okay, thanks.

The sinker started bobbing. I grabbed the fishing pole and leaned into it. At the end of the line was a small young carp. After I took the hook out of its mouth, I silently dropped the little bugger into the net. Splat. The little guy flopped around violently, just like a person at the beginning of Stage One.

That's when we saw that strange body of light

floating gently above the acacia grove across from the fishing hole. It was definitely some sort of flying object, and was held aloft like it was filled with a giant balloon. The whole thing was enveloped in a flashing, semi-circle of blue vapor. It was stunning.

What the . . . is that . . . it looks like a UFO, just like in the movies!

As soon as the thought crossed my mind, the thing crossed over the reservoir and stopped directly above us. It was huge. The enormous machine was breathing slowly and heavily, just like a living being. Aaaah! we screamed, just like in the movies.

We watched as the UFO seemed to heave, and a small hole opened up in its center. A bright beam of light, different from the flashing lights in the surrounding vapor, shot straight down through the hole, and the instant we felt the pillar of light reach the ground the ship shifted with a giant roar. When we came to, the UFO had already disappeared.

And then we saw it. No more than five, six meters in front of us. Something was standing right where that pillar of light had touched the ground. It stood in a daze for a moment, and then it waddled over to stand in front of our lit lantern.

It was a raccoon.

Congratulations!

Congratulations! Click here! One hundred and fifty lucky winners! For one day only, we'll read your animal horoscope for free. Right here at EnjoyMall.com. Enter your date of birth now. Thank you very much! The patron animal for your birthday, April 27th, is, yes, it's the Raccoon! Your mascot is just like you—the cute and mischievous Raccoon. Why don't we read your fortune, you little Raccoon? Click here!

You are a very social person with a wide circle of acquaintances. You have lots of friends of all ages, don't you? Like you, your friends are very talented, and you get along well with the pleasure-seeking Monkey. The Pegasus, who doesn't get caught up in trivial matters, is also a good counterpart for you, Raccoon. Steer clear of the Ram and the baby Deer, however. The Ram, who holds his morality very dear, will always scold you, and of course the innocent, guileless Fawn will have a difficult time getting along with the likes of you.

You value experience and accomplishments, Raccoon. So it's no surprise that you're the type that's big on antiques and objects with some history. You also possess the special ability to take other people's stories and tell them as though they were your own. And that person who can discuss a movie they've never seen in more detail and with more animation than someone who's actually seen it? That's you, Raccoon.

You cope with change very well. Of course, that's one of the Raccoon's distinguishing traits. You can adapt easily to any situation, you're up for anything, and you tend to be rewarded more than other people. But when forced to make a choice between two harmful situations, you won't budge, not for anything. You always have specific places you're partial to, and when you order, it's always, "I'll have the usual." You like good food, which goes hand in hand with the Raccoon's tendency to place great importance on experience and accomplishments.

You are skilled at role-playing. You take on any role with ease, and you fully grasp each character's strong points. One of the Raccoon's greatest skills is its ability to take the tasks of each role it takes on and do them more efficiently. On the other hand, it's also easy for Raccoons to be seen as irresponsible. That's because of the Raccoon's signature absentmindedness. Absentmindedness is the Raccoon's tragic shortcoming. Of course, you yourself probably pay it no mind.

You also possess an unfounded self-confidence. You'd probably even say that your self-confidence comes from the fact that you're clearly the best of the twelve character signs. Overflowing with confidence, always cheerful and positive, you never fail to put a smile on everyone's face. People think you're trustworthy since you're always the first to pipe up with, "I've got it!" "Yes, sir!" and "You can count on me!" but the truth is, a lot of times your offers don't go any further than that exclamation point.

Raccoons get plenty of compliments from their superiors. This is because you have an upbeat, can-do attitude and more than your fair share of charm. With your propensity for placing great value on "experience and accomplishments," it's no wonder that your superiors and older people take to you so quickly. And even when people see how irresponsible or obviously obsequious you are, you have such a rare charm that no one can ever stay angry with you for very long. It's because everyone knows that you don't do those things on purpose. The Raccoon's charm, which makes it impossible not to forgive them no matter what they do . . . it's the envy of all the other characters.

You've got mail.

It was from the personnel manager. The subject line read, "Congratulations!" and it went something like this.

I know it's a little late, but it looks like we're going to make the final decision on the permanent employee sometime tomorrow morning. How would you feel about getting together to talk this over? Around nine o'clock tonight. Meet me at Climax in the Mukyo district. Oh, and don't get too excited about the subject line. I just wrote it as a joke. Well, hope to see you then.

The manager's e-mail came with a virus. My computer froze as soon as I finished reading it and closed the window. I guess I'll have to re-format my hard drive. I lit a cigarette. I felt lonely.

No matter how well they cover it up
people will always find out that our whole world lies in ruins.

And no matter how well it's covered up
you'll know that the raccoon is there in the end.

I'm so grateful

Thanks. For coming to meet me like this, I mean. The manager had arrived before me and was having a beer. It was a nondescript bar, not very bright and not very dark. What do you think of office life now that you've gotten a taste of it? the manager asked as he poured me a beer. It's great, I replied quickly.

Drink up.

I heard that you majored in home economics, of all things. Yes. Ahem, well, I started thinking that that's a very . . . fastidious major, don't you think? Yes, it is a fastidious major. Right, that's what I meant, I thought so too. Here,

drink up.

So, do you have any desire to work for us as a regular employee? To be honest, it would be great if they picked me. Good, good. A man's gotta have ambition, you know. Based on your performance, I'll try my hardest to help you out. What do you think about that? I'd be very grateful for anything you'd be willing to do for me. Good.

Drink up.

I'm not asking for anything that should be too difficult for you. It'd probably be easier if you just think about it as something that every young professional has to go through. You have to give something to get something—that's the way of the world, you know. I'm just trying to make sure you know that this isn't that big a deal. Here,

drink up.

Is life really that special? That's how everyone lives their lives. The way I see it, you have a quick mind and a bright future ahead of you. And you're so young and healthy. If you just had someone behind you, supporting you, you'd have nothing to worry about. Here,

drink up. The manager kept offering me more to drink, and he tossed back quite a bit himself. I could feel the effects of the alcohol. As time passed, I could hear the manager's breath gradually growing thicker, like the yeast swelling in beer as it ferments. That, and the beating of his heart as the alcohol spread through his veins.

It was well after midnight when we left the bar. The manager hailed a taxi and told the driver where to go. Inside the cab, he grabbed my hand and caressed my thigh, and when the taxi dropped us off, we were on some highway I would never have been able to find, in a neighborhood that I would never know how to get to again. There was a big building on the side of the road with a bathhouse in the basement and a big sign at the entrance advertising that it was open twenty-four hours a day.

The bathhouse was completely empty. Actually, it looked like the kind of place where the customers end up sleeping in the lounge next to the dressing room. No, actually, it looked like it might be one of those bathhouses that certain people go to for a certain purpose. My mind stuck on that thought for a minute before it gave up on thought altogether.

Just hang on a minute.

The manager wrapped me in a tight embrace from behind as I showered. It was odd, but I didn't feel a thing, and I decided to hang on for a minute, just like he said. The manager pawed my body for a while, then he carefully sat me down on a bath stool. His slick, clammy hands went to work on my penis, trying to make it erect. It was truly bizarre. Why did my penis, which I didn't think would get hard at all, suddenly get stiff? And why did "Stage Twenty-three" suddenly appear before my eyes right at that moment? Why didn't the world go step by step from Stage One?

It's lovely, the manager sighed as he stared at my erect penis. Then, after peeking his head around the partition to make sure no one was there, he got down on his knees between my legs. Just stay still. With that, the manager's mouth turned commanding, and started to suck. His right hand slowly reached down to stroke his own dick.

It was just a minute. I have no regrets. Looking back on my youth, I have nothing to be embarrassed about. I had a lot of competitors and it's hard to find a job. This is a crazy, mixed-up world. It was just a minute. Just a minute. It was just a minute. In just a minute, I'm going to jump over that gap—I'll jump across, and I'll land on that six-foot-long platform.

For a brief moment, I thought I saw white liquid spilling out of the manager's penis, then I thought I saw him rinse off his semen with the showerhead. I thought I felt him sigh again and press his hand into my shoulder, and I thought I heard him say, "Good work," with great feeling. Then, I thought I saw his tired-looking back as he left the bathhouse.

I sank down quietly onto the vast expanse of the bathhouse floor, and started to pour the hottest water my skin could endure over my head. Inside that steaming stream of water, I suddenly felt that I was all alone, that I was lonely, and that I was starting to sob.

It was right then.

I felt a presence behind me. I turned in the steam that was thick as fog, and there stood the biggest raccoon I'd ever seen, holding a loofah in his hand. He was huge. The loofah was nice, too. It was olive-colored, and created a nice contrast to the raccoon's brown fur. The raccoon took care of everything for me inside that thick white cloud of steam, nodding at me with a sympathetic look in his eyes. I nodded too. The raccoon slowly pushed the bath chair towards me and said,

Sit.

The bathhouse at dawn was silent, and in that silence, I entrusted the scrubbing of my back to a giant raccoon with a calm heart, the way I would with a good friend. I hadn't had my back scrubbed in years, and the raccoon was very handy with the loofah. It was strange, but I started to feel better as my back was scrubbed clean. By the time the raccoon finished his final scrub, I felt relatively happy. I started to stand up, but the raccoon pressed a heavy hand to my shoulder.

Not yet.

What did he mean, not yet? I was suspicious, but I found out the reason soon enough. He wanted to soap me down. The raccoon lathered refreshing soap all over my squeaky clean, freshly scrubbed body. I had no idea I could feel this good. Let me tell you, it was such a fantastic performance that I felt like I was flying through the air in an airplane over the state of Ohio. Aah, I was overcome with such deep gratitude that I nearly cried. Finally, a person like me is . . . I turned back to face him suddenly, but all I could do was say these trite words.

Thank you, oh Great Raccoon.

Five Poems by Kim Seung-Hui

Translated by Brother Anthony of Taizé
& Kim Hyong-Jin

A Parcel of Eggs

Someone is walking along.
That person must be extremely poor
with no proper clothes to keep out the winter cold,
just some old paper bags covering rags.

What did those bags once contain, I wonder.
On the paper covering part of the person's back some letters are
    printed:
"Fragile goods.
Handle with care."

There you are, placed before me.
Like a row of straw-packed eggs delivered as a parcel,
rib collides with rib and
one person makes another shudder as never before.

SANTA CELLO

Early in the morning in the back alleys of Sinch'on
a lot of last night remains, scattered along the roadsides.
Sitting huddled in the roadway, not realizing it's a roadway,
a white balloon is sleeping
slender-shouldered.

Someone blew that white balloon up, huff-puff, tied it loosely with a
      white thread,
then because a niece of mine ran away from home,
I got out of the car and started shaking the white balloon's body.
Look, it's daybreak, dear, the cars on their way to work are lined up,
      time you got up,
you must get out of here.
The white balloon remains huddled there, sitting on the roadway,
with, bluntly set down beside it, last night's empty soju bottles
and a small traveling bag like a letter of resignation.

Dear little girl, this shitty world, biscuit-like, where you're unwilling
      to lift your face,
have not the slightest thought
of lifting your face and looking up,
dear little girl, my runaway niece, Myŏng-ju, hmm? Myŏng-ju?

Still incapable of escaping from yesterday,
blocking today's roadway, that white balloon,
uncertain when it will leap out into the roadway
dressed only in its underwear, that white balloon
while dreamlike sunlight falls absently
into her hair like yesterday's boiled noodles,
the white balloon claims it's dead tired,

216

and I've been unable to meet her since she ran away to a dream of
    sunlight
several years ago, and now at last in a proper house composed of
    sunlight
sound asleep, that white balloon, unaware that today has come . . . .

I awoke one morning
to find my head was in a lion's jaws.
How did that happen?
My room had vanished, the floor had vanished,
while the bone-structures of the lion's scarlet mouth,
like a wilderness where wild beasts roar,
were approaching and closing right before my eyes.

There I was, my head stuck trembling in a lion's mouth—
is it too late?
I can hear the lion's teeth, like sharp swords, crunching
as they gnaw at my skull.
"I'm a dog."
"I'm a bird caught in a cage."
"I'm an unwilling good-for-nothing."
I can hear van Gogh roaring too,
blood is already trickling down and pooling under the lion's tongue
but I am quite unable to move my body.
Faint voices ring out.
"Pray withdraw this head from the jaws of the lion."
The voice of a research assistant from distant Pittsburgh rings out.
"Is this the end of my life, then?"

Inside the lion's jaws
will birdsong ever be heard again?
Will the babbling of a brook ever be heard again?

There's someone who lived for thirteen years unaware he had a
    bullet in his head.
That was possible because he did not know.

One old man lived fifty-six years with a bullet in his head.

As I stuff my head into the lion's jaws

I can't tell if I'll live another thirteen years or fifty-six years even.

It's me who gave up hope,

not hope that gave me up.

Days are coming when a spider will catch and eat a snake,

a snake swallow a crocodile.

Days are coming when not one bone of my head will be broken in
　　the lion's jaws,

not a hair of my head will be bruised,

and I shall survive to sing "Amazing Grace."

THE RAINBOW'S PROMISE

Did you see the rainbow?

It was a lofty clothesline

where Korea's laboring women,

arms knotted with bulging blue veins,

had hung lovely textiles to dry after laboriously plunging them in
  dark blue dye

and there I saw colored bandages flapping, a multi-colored arc

of several thousand tons of bandages

that had been stuffed silently into those women's hearts to staunch
  their bleeding

hanging flimsy layer upon layer of hues with the blue sky as
  background,

reminding me of a rainbow.

How could those bandages inside their breasts find their way up
  there?

How many thousand tons

how many billion light-years of bloodied bandages were dragged
  from so many thousand tons of women's breasts?

So very far

so very high

and even if they could have gone further

stopping there in a ring in midair like that

delicate foreheads bowed, gazing down at the world

dark eyebrows like lovely hearts

Because the washing flapped its wings, it went flying up to hang in
  the sky.

Perhaps one day the wind might bring the washing down again;

by telling it to flap its bloody, roughly bruised wings.

Because of the rainbow's promise

to lift it up again and plant it in all its lovely hues in the sky.

220

POTS BANGING

From the television,
a sound of pots being beaten in Argentina. Ah, Argentina!
A sound echoing from the midsummer night streets of Buenos Aires
as young and old, men and women, all take to the streets
carrying pots, frying-pans, ladles, saucepan lids,
and, once outside, bang on them
while they all utter a single, united cry.
Ah, Argentina!
Debts, the unemployed, destitute people, fortune-tellers, psychiatrists,
the dead, the wounded, all sighing together—
I feel like rushing out to join them
at the sight of people lined up, tight-lipped, for hours on end
in front of banks and employment agencies—
the silence reigning over such a scene.

As we gaze at the fuzzy television screen
we eat in silence.
Around the rickety table with its broken leg
no one says anything about it.
They just stare blankly at the bottom of the pot.
In the pot, radish-leaf soup, green paddyfields, ridges—
"Do you know what rice is? They say it's God's tooth.
Once, when people were wandering about, starving, God pulled out a
    tooth
and threw it into an empty field where it grew."
The spasms of the jerking meal-table are slowly stilled by mother's
    words,
the quiet meal-table moment
evening rain falling
pots banging.

AZALEA

Four Poems by Lee Moon-jae

Translated by
David R. McCann

BETWEEN HEAVEN AND EARTH

At the basement café
a late lunch alone,
stuffing down lumps of lettuce-wrapped rice,
solitary photosynthesis.

29th floor bathroom,
sluggish Han River's distant downstream
startles me back from the toilet bowl,
the sea's Han River mouth
opening so far upriver.

Outside the window,
a puff of cigarette smoke
gets sucked away into the stratosphere.

It's all a direct connection.

JOKE

All of a sudden feeling something beautiful,
thinking how great if someone were by my side
and how if a face came up, yours
would be the one I love.

Profound landscape.
Before a properly flavorful meal
a person who never thought of anyone
truly, that is a strong one,
or perhaps a truly lonely one.

To send the bell sound even farther
so must the bell be made to hurt even more.

HEART

www
cabbage patch drizzle

roots all grab the heel
cabbage insides open
wet soil from soil breaking apart
cabbage flowers letting the wet butterfly go
low atmospheric pressure going lower yet
gone on and looking back
those things my eyes long ago opened to

www
cabbage patch rain, falling,
clear, online

POET AND FARMER

Between the mouth and the food,
that space is most immense

In the space between mouth and food
the entire universe

no one, no
enlightenment
can close the space between mouth and food

circle of the universe
circle of the body
are cut from
the space between the mouth and the food
while between arse and the earth
no connection

that between
the food and the turd,
between turd and the food
is blocked

Run, Dad!

by Kim Aeran

Translated by Kevin O'Rourke

I cried a lot when I was a fetus. I cried because I was scared of the tiny darkness within my seed-small womb. I was diminutive; I had miniscule wrinkles, a small, rapidly beating heart and a body that didn't know what language was. I'm talking about a time without yesterdays or tomorrows.

I came like something in the mail, my arrival announced by mom, a parcel of flesh without language. Mom gave birth to me in a semi-basement room where summer sunlight rough as sandpaper shone relentlessly. She flailed around with only a shirt to cover her. And with no hand to hold onto, she simply grabbed a scissors. Outside the window she could see the feet of people walking by. Every time she felt she wanted to die, she stabbed the floor with the scissors. This went on for hours. In the end, she didn't kill herself; instead she cut my umbilical cord. Here I was, newly arrived in the world, and I couldn't hear mom's heart beating. The silence made me think I was deaf!

The first light I saw as a newborn was window-sized. I knew it existed outside of me.

I don't remember where my dad was. He was always someplace else, or he was late, or he didn't come at all. Mom and I held onto each other, heart against rapidly beating heart. Mom, naked, looked down at my solemn face and wiped it several times with her big hand. I liked my mom, but I didn't know how to tell her; I just frowned all the time. I discovered that mom laughed a lot when my face puckered with wrinkles. I think I concluded that love was not so much two people laughing together as one looking funny to the other.

Mom fell asleep and I was left on my own. The world was quiet; the sunlight lay over there on the floor like a polite "Dear John" letter, the first unpleasant note I received in this world. I had no pockets. So I clenched my fists.

∽

When I picture dad, it's always against the same background: he's running resolutely somewhere. He's wearing luminous pink shorts and has thin, hairy legs, and he's running straight-backed with a high knee action. He looks like a referee who's enforcing rules no one cares about. So he cuts a comical figure. I guess he's been running for twenty years, his posture and face always the same: a laughing red countenance sporting a row of yellow teeth like a bad painting someone stuck on him.

It's not just dad, though. Everyone playing the exercise game looks funny. It embarrasses me when I see middle-aged men in the park bouncing their bellies off the trunks of pine trees, or middle-aged women clapping their hands as they walk. They're always so serious about what they're doing and so enthusiastic. As if getting healthy entails looking more and more ridiculous.

I've never really seen dad running, but as far as I'm concerned he's been running all his life. I may have gotten this idea from something mom told me long ago. When she first told me this story, she had a washboard stuck in the V between her legs. She was scrubbing laundry in a welter of soapy suds and breathing so hard she looked very angry.

Mom says dad never ran to her. He wasn't the kind of man to come running: not when she said they should break up, not when she said she missed him, not even when I was born. People called him a gentleman; mom thought he was a fool. If mom made up her mind to wait for him on a certain day, he'd show up the next. And when he arrived late, he looked haggard. She always had a joke to greet her diffident lover—with his inevitable late-schoolboy look. He made no excuses, used no big words to explain himself. He just "came" with his thin lips and his dark face. I imagine he was afraid of rejection. He was the kind of man whose sense of guilt just wouldn't let him come. And guilt generated more guilt. In the end he felt so bad he decided that being bad was better than being a fool. This decision to be bad, I believe, removed him from the ranks of the gentle. When he behaved badly he made others feel bad, which probably means he was a bad man. I think of him as the worst man in the world, and at the same time as the most pitiable. But I don't really know what sort of man he was. A few facts are all he left behind. And if facts give us the reality of a man, dad was bad. If they don't, well, I don't really know him.

Anyway, the important thing is that my always-late dad ONCE mustered all his energy for a race. It happened a few months after he moved to Seoul to make some money.

Dad got a job in a furniture factory. Leaving home to make money in Seoul was a strange thing for him to do. That's how I see it. But he was just following the crowd. Dad and mom exchanged letters from time to time. His letter was always longer. Because mom was angry with him for going to Seoul in the first place.

One day mom came to dad's rented room in Seoul. She'd had a huge fight with her father—their relationship had always been bad—and made up her mind to leave home. With dad's address written on an envelope, she combed through a maze of twisty alleys until she found him. She had nowhere to go and planned to stay for a few days. Dad, of course, had different ideas. The day she arrived he launched a whirlwind courtship. A young man living with a girl he liked and sleeping separately? It was all so predictable. Dad's pleading, his cries of frustration, his blustering went on for several days. Mom was touched. Maybe she thought she wanted to carry him on her belly for the rest of her life. Eventually she said OK, but on one condition: she would share his bed if he bought her birth control pills.

That's when he started to run. He ran full speed from the top of Moon Village to the pharmacy downtown, red in the face as if bursting to pee and laughing enough to crack his lips. A dog began to bark at the sight of him and soon every dog in the neighborhood was barking. Dad ran and ran. Red-faced, hair flying, he jumped over stairwells as he sliced his way through the dark. He ran faster than the wind and in his haste tripped and fell into a heap of coal briquette ash. Covered head to foot with white ash, he shot back up on his feet and ran on as if his life depended on it, as if bound for places unknown.

Did he ever run as fast again? The image of dad running through Moon Village for a love tryst with mom made me want to shout, "Dad, you run a lot better than I thought," though I knew he couldn't see me or hear me.

Anyway, he ran so fast he forgot to get the instructions for the pills. Mom asked her ash-covered lover how many she should take. He scratched his head. "I think they said two," he replied.

For two months mom says she took two pills religiously every day. And for two months the sky was yellow and she felt nauseous all the time. Strange, she thought. So she asked the pharmacist and he told her to reduce the dose to one.

One day, she had to break the ice in the bucket in the moonlit yard to wash her private parts, and she was so numb with cold that she forgot to take the pill. That was the night she got pregnant. Dad's face got paler and paler as he watched her tummy swell. He left the day before he became a dad and never came back.

Jogging is the most popular sport there is; it doesn't matter where you are or how old you are. A blend of walking and running, jogging provides appropriate stimulation for heart and lungs. It's a complete body exercise that enhances your stamina. It doesn't require any special skills or high speeds and has the added advantage of not being restricted by place or weather. They say running demands stamina. What else does it demand? I don't know. Nor do I know

230

how to interpret the mind—and the energy—of someone who left me but keeps on running in the space he left behind.

Dad left home so that he could run. That's what I want to believe. He didn't leave to go to war, or to get a new wife, or to sink an oil pipeline in the desert of a foreign country. And when he left home, he didn't take a watch.

I don't have a father. That's not to say he doesn't exist. I see him in his luminous pink shorts. He's in Fukuoka, he's traveling through Borneo, he's running toward the observatory in Greenwich. I see him turning by the left foot of the Sphinx, slipping into bathroom 110 in the Empire State Building, crossing the Guadarramas in Spain. I can make out his figure clearly in the dark. His luminous shorts glow. He's running. But no one's applauding.

~

Mom raised me with a joke on her lips. When I'd get depressed, she'd lift me up with her wicked wit, which was often very vulgar, especially when I asked about dad. Not that he was a forbidden subject. He just wasn't that important to us, so we didn't talk about him much. And when we did, mom often indicated she was bored with the topic.

"Have you any idea how often I've told you about your father? Any idea?" she asked.

"*Alji*—I know," I said diffidently.

"*Alji*," she said gruffly, "is a bare bollix." And she laughed wildly.

From then on I associated *alji* (knowing) with something vaguely obscene.

The biggest thing I inherited from mom was the ability not to feel sorry for myself. She didn't treat me as if she owed me anything, or as if I was to be pitied. I was always grateful to her for this. When folks ask me how I am, I know they're just interested in how they are themselves. Mom and I had a sturdy no frills relationship that demanded neither sympathy nor understanding.

Whenever I asked mom about sex, she always answered with style. Not having a dad I was curious about many things. Once after an accident that left a man lame I asked, "How does he manage with his wife?"

"Does he do it with his foot?" she said curtly.

And when my young nipples began to develop, mom reacted not with alarm but with a sense of fun. She'd pretend to link her arm in mine and then jab her elbow into my breast. I'd run away from her with a shriek, but I liked the tingling sensation that spread across my chest.

There was only one other person in the world who was aware of mom's charm, and that was her father, and their relationship was bad until the day he died. I don't remember much about him except that he never spoke to me—I was a fatherless child after all—and that he invariably tore mom apart with his foul curses. I liked my handsome grandfather, but he neither made me his pet, nor gave me a hard time. Maybe I was so small that he didn't even see me.

Once, however, he *did* speak to me. He'd been drinking poppy tea and was in good spirits. He looked intently at me and asked, "Whose child are you?"

"Cho Chaok's" I answered loudly.

He asked again as if he hadn't heard. "Whose girl are you?" This time I answered in an even louder voice, "Cho Chaok's!"

And as if he were deaf, he asked again, slyly, "What? Whose girl?"

I jumped up and down with frustration and cried as loudly as I could, "Cho Chaok's, Cho Chaok's."

I could shout as much as I wanted in the concrete yard of my childhood. Granddad said, "Ah, ah, you're Chaok's girl." His face darkened. "Have you any idea what a terrible bitch she is?" he said suddenly.

He sat me down in front of him and regaled me with a litany of mom's childhood misdeeds. With big blinking eyes I listened to everything he said. He kept disparaging her, describing how she always counterattacked when he bad-mouthed her, not like my docile older aunt who was a wonderful daughter.

There was another side to the story. One of the things mom said to me most often was, "A good family is very important." If she hadn't left home after the fight with her father, she said, things would have been very different. I'd sit there, eyes blinking, listening quietly to her complaints just as I listened to granddad. Forget how much they hated each other; forget how granddad ridiculed her for having a fatherless child; forget how much she resented him for making granny wash his concubine's drawers. Forget all that. I still had a reason to respect him: something he said a few days before he died.

For someone who had dropped in casually, he sat there for an awfully long time until suddenly he grew awkward in the face of the inference of mom's silence, which was that surely now he had exhausted all areas for trivial complaint and interference. He thought for a moment about what to say and then began another harangue on the virtues of my docile aunt in comparison with mom. Having exhausted all the resources of foul language, again he found himself at a loss in the face of mom's silence. He fidgeted with his cup of juice, reached for his hat and stood up. Mom and I saw him off politely. He hesitated in front of the gate before throwing a strange parting shot over his shoulder.

"You know if it was love I was after, I'd pick the younger bitch over the older one."

Granddad died a few days later. I think he knew the little secret of mom's charm. With granddad gone, I'm the only one left that knows it.

~

Mom's a taxi driver. At first I figured she took the job so she could keep an eye on me as she threaded her way through the streets of Seoul. Then one day I surmised that maybe she drove a taxi because she wanted to run faster than dad. I imagined the two of them running side by side, now one in the lead, now the other. Racketing through my mind were images of mom's face, twenty years of resentment stamped on it as she hit the accelerator, and dad's face when his whereabouts were discovered. Maybe mom thought that the best revenge wasn't catching him, but running faster.

Mom found the taxi job tough. The distrust directed at an underpaid woman driver and the ridicule of drunken passengers were hard to take. It didn't stop me though from asking her regularly for money. Had I plastered politeness on top of my inscrutability, I think mom would have felt even worse. Of course, she never gave me more money because she felt she owed it to me. She gave me what I asked for, but I didn't forget what she said: "Everything I earn goes up the kid's hole while I fuck myself trying to make a living."

It had been a normal run-of-the-mill day for me. I got lectured by mom for eating with the TV on. I had to listen silently to her long-winded account of a fight with a passenger the night before. She got so worked up telling the story that she threw down her spoon and cried, "Fuck it, was I so wrong?" She was looking for solidarity from me, so I had to give a good answer. And as I slipped into my runners, I had to explain to her how I proposed to use the 10,000 won I had asked her for. Half-slumped over my desk at school, I watched the trainee teacher struggling to swallow his nonexistent saliva. For a fatherless child, there was nothing particularly bad or different about this very ordinary day. At least not until I got home.

Mom was sitting glum-faced in the middle of the room. She had a one-page letter in her hand. The envelope, torn open roughly, lay on the floor, the same floor she had once stabbed with the scissors. I knew from the address that it had been sent airmail. Mom couldn't read the letter, but she sat there looking at it, filled with a strange feeling of foreboding. Her face betrayed her unease; she was like a woman from the country who didn't know what to do.

"How long has she been like this?" I muttered to myself, snatching the letter.

"What does it say?" she asked, looking at me intently.

The letter was in English. I began a groping explanation of its contents, aware that it involved some loss of face for me. At first I didn't understand, but after reading it two or three times, I realized that it held very important news for us.

"What does it say?" she asked again.

I swallowed. "It says dad's dead."

She looked at me with the darkest of dark faces.

Mom always reacted with a witty remark when I wore that kind of expression. I wanted to say something witty too, but I couldn't think of anything appropriate.

In a way, dad had come home—gossamer like—in the mail, twenty years late. Dad had come home—like a statement of good will, motivation unknown—like thunderous applause at the end of an interminable play. A death notice with a strange intonation. In the end, maybe dad's reason for running to the four corners of the earth was to tell us that he was dead. He had traveled to distant places and had come back now to tell us he was dead. But dad hadn't really been racing around the world; he'd been living in America.

Dad's son sent the letter, which I deciphered in bed with the help of a dictionary. This is what it said. Dad married in America. I was a bit surprised by this. I couldn't understand why he had abandoned mom unless he didn't want a family. Either he loved the second woman a lot, or it wasn't as easy to run away in America. A few years later he got divorced. The exact reason for the divorce wasn't specified, but I guessed it had to do with his basic incompetence. His wife demanded alimony. Dad hadn't a penny so he offered to cut her grass every weekend. I remember hearing that in America you could get reported to the authorities by your neighbors for not cutting your grass. She promptly married a man with a lawn the size of a football field.

Every week dad pressed the doorbell as promised, stuck his face in front of the security camera, said "Hello," and trudged in to cut the grass. Imagine it. While she sat cozily in the living room drinking beer with her new husband, he crouched down outside tinkering with the lawnmower. In the beginning they might have been a bit put off by him, but I'm sure she said to her husband, "Don't pass any remarks, John." Dad soon became irrelevant. When he looked through the thick glass wall of the living room and saw them making out, he revved the engine and strode up and down outside. The boy who sent the letter insisted that this is what dad did—maybe he wanted to give his dad's bereaved foreign family some words of comfort. What kind of kid, I wondered, would write so pryingly and in such detail? Obviously he didn't think he was anything like his dad. I imagined the pair's lovemaking in the living room. Nipple and breath stuck fast to the glass; the blinds hurriedly pulled down. I look at them from a great distance, my eyes slit in a frown. Brrrng! Dad charges with his lawnmower. But his attack peters out, and he goes back to striding impatiently up and down outside. When the woman couldn't take it anymore, she gave him the latest automatic gasoline model as a present. But dad insisted on using the old model in the shed. He went around the garden making the same awful din.

One day dad and the new husband had a fight. It began when the new husband started criticizing the way dad was cutting the grass. Dad held his tongue though it was killing him; he just kept cutting the grass. The new husband's griping went on and on; eventually he began to curse. All this time dad had been silently cutting the grass. Suddenly he lifted the old lawnmower with its furiously whirring blade and charged. The new husband slumped to the ground in a blue paroxysm of fear. I don't think dad had any intention of hurting him, but unfortunately, he did get hurt. Now it was dad's turn to react with shocked dismay. At the sight of his own blood the injured man lost all control. Every curse in the language poured from his lips and he ended up reporting dad to the police. Dad took fright. He hesitated for a moment, then ran to the shed, saw the new lawnmower in the corner, hopped on it like a gunman jumping on his horse in a western, and with his heart pounding, switched on the ignition, spurred the mower out of the shed and dashed out onto the road. Dad fled at the top speed the mower could muster, scattering the smell of fresh grass cuttings behind him. Where was he heading?

The letter ended by saying that dad was killed in a traffic accident. The son said the family had been truly saddened by his death. They held a simple service at the cemetery. Regrettably, the son said, he never liked dad very much. When he was a kid, he said, dad left him in front of the TV to go to work and he used to wait there all day. That's how he grew up. He was hoping now he would be able to forget dad. Though he had never met his foreign half-sister, he wanted me to know that he also grew up waiting for dad, so he knew the pain. "I found your address in my dad's belongings," he continued. "My mom doesn't know I'm writing this letter."

It all seemed like lies.

Actually I was the real liar. I told mom that dad had been killed in a traffic accident, but I didn't tell her what kind of accident.

"Why is the letter so long?" she asked.

"English is always longer than Korean," I said.

Then she asked if there was anything else in it. How he lived, who he lived with? Was there really nothing else? No one knew the answers to these questions. She probably wanted to ask why he'd left home that night. But then again maybe that was the one thing she really didn't want to ask. "Dad . . ." I began. She looked at me with the expression of a whipped puppy. "Dad always felt bad," I said. "He felt guilty all his life. That's what it says here." Her eyes danced. I chanced a further comment. "And mom, this bit was really lovely." "Which bit?" she asked with trembling voice. I showed her the bit that said he came to his wife's house every week to cut the grass. "This bit here," I said. Mom looked like she would burst into tears as she looked at the part of the letter I indicated and rubbed it fondly. It was the first time I ever saw my witty mom who never cried with a lump in her throat.

That night mom didn't come home until dawn. I lay in bed with the covers pulled up under my chin and thought about dad, about his life and death, and about cutting the grass, that sort of thing. But still he keeps running around inside my head. Images that have been in there for so long aren't going to disappear that quickly. It occurred to me that I kept imagining him because I could not forgive him. Maybe the reason I kept him running in my mind was that I was afraid I would charge at him and kill him the moment he stopped. I felt sad. I better go to sleep, I thought, before this sadness dupes me.

~

Mom came home after the peak-fare time ended. I thought she'd try not to wake me, that she wouldn't put on the light, that she'd take off her clothes very carefully. Instead she poked me in the ribs.

"Ya!" she cried. "Are you asleep?"

I stuck my head out from under the covers. "Are you crazy? My God! The taxi driver's drunk!"

Mom said nothing. She just laughed and tumbled down on the covers. She curled up small like a clenched fist. I thought of tossing the bedcovers over her but didn't. In a little while, she slid in under them, maybe because she was cold.

In the dark mom's breathing gradually got gentler. She smelt of cigarettes. I was angry with her. You're bad, I thought, folding my arms. Mom had her back to me, sleeping like a shrimp. I was staring up at the ceiling. The long stillness caressed her breathing. I thought she was asleep, but suddenly she spoke, curling up even more tightly into a ball. There was no trace of malice toward the dead man in what she said.

"So, what do you think, is he rotting OK?"

I didn't close my eyes all night long. I kept looking at the ceiling, reviewing the various images of dad in my imagination. I saw him in Fukuoka, crossing Borneo, approaching the Greenwich

Observatory, turning by the foot of the Sphinx, going through the Empire State Building, climbing the Guaddaramas. My laughing, racing dad. Suddenly I realized that all this time he had been running in the blazing sun. I thought I'd imagined everything he needed for running. I dressed him in those luminous pink shorts, put on his cushion-soled runners and his airy running vest. But isn't it strange that I'd never thought of giving him sunglasses? I'd forgotten that even the most rubbishy man in the world gets sick like everyone else, likes the things everyone else likes. All those years I was picturing dad in my mind, he was always running, his eyes sore and swollen from the blazing sun. So I decided tonight to put sunglasses on him. I imagined his face. He wore a little smile; he was filled with anticipation but trying hard to conceal it. He closed his eyes, like a boy waiting for a kiss. With my two big hands I put the sunglasses on him. They suited him really well. He'll run better now, I thought.

242

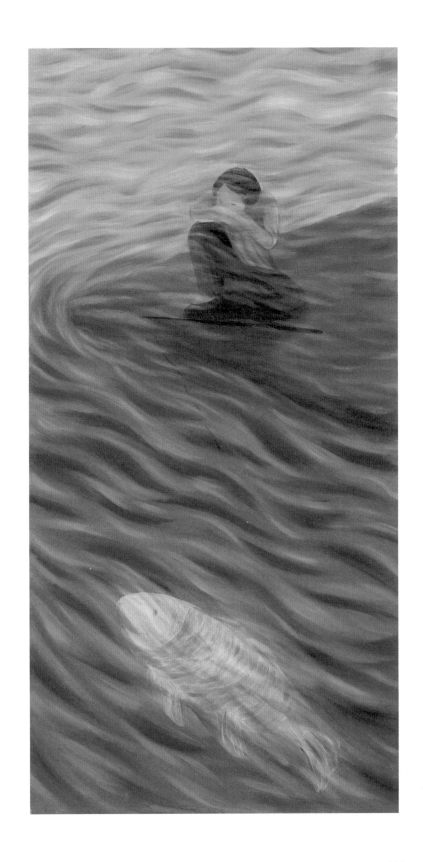

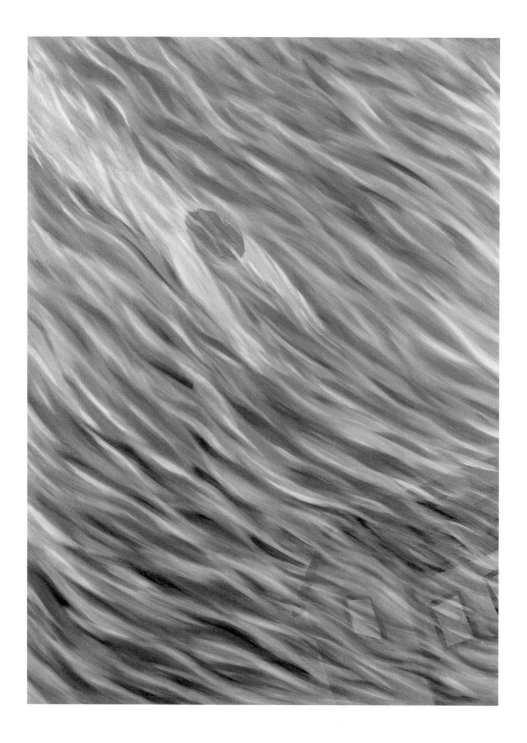

"1953"
Photographs by
Joe Savitzky

Between Us and the Rest

by Lee Hye-kyung

Translated by Jessica Lee and Young-Jun Lee

"But . . . isn't it better than suffering?"

Kyŏng-ŭn's husband breaks the silence as he accelerates on the highway. Perhaps her husband is right. The doctor did warn that her father only had a few days left to live. "At least he can die with dignity," Kyŏng-ŭn thought. The air is crisp and moist from all the rain over the last few days. As she stares out the car window into the sunny sky, Kyŏng-ŭn recalls how sunny it was the day she marched in her mother's funeral. Deep in her heart, she knows that she has already given up on her father. And yet her husband's words still pierce her heart like a sword. "Would you say the same thing if it were your father?" she wants to ask. Kyŏng-ŭn tightens her mouth before those words can escape. "Why am I so tense?" she wonders.

Three months earlier, Kyŏng-ŭn's eighty-year-old father had surgery for a cerebral hemorrhage. One day, when she was folding cotton diapers, she got a phone call from her sister. Her sister lived two and a half hours from the town hospital and got to see their father regularly, unlike Kyŏng-ŭn, who stayed home all the time. The smell of boiled laundry filled the air. According to the weather forecast a typhoon was passing by to the south and the rainy season was beginning.

"His kidneys almost stopped functioning and now he's having trouble breathing. They say he only has one or two weeks left. . . .

AZALEA

*Between
Us and
the Rest:
Lee Hye-
kyung*

Kyŏng-hae and I are going to visit him as much as possible in the time remaining. I have to talk to her later again tonight, but I'm thinking about going there tomorrow."

Before she had time to think, Kyŏng-ŭn blurted out, "I want to go too."

"Do you think you can make it? I know it's hard for you to travel right now, but it would be good for you to see him at least once before he passes away. . . . You want us to pick you up?"

Kyŏng-ŭn quickly retracted her offer. "Actually, I'm not sure if I can go. Even if I do, it'd be better for me to take a train than a car."

With her ballooned-out belly, Kyŏng-ŭn barely managed to waddle down the stairs of the train station. Once on board, she took out a book. She read about childrearing, using her belly as a desk to prop up the book. "No parents are perfect. A child is not simply a possession but a gift from God." These words comforted Kyŏng-ŭn, who at thirty years of age was becoming a mother for the first time. Did my father suffer alone from anxiety his whole life? She closed the book and looked out the window.

When Kyŏng-ŭn left her house it was drizzling, but now the raindrops were much bigger. They splashed on the window and crawled downward, leaving thin tails of water in their wake. They looked like living organisms. Kyŏng-ŭn's parents had her thirty years before. Among the infinite numbers of sperm her father released that day, one reached her mother's egg, fertilized it, and created Kyŏng-ŭn. Maybe she would be different if some other sperm had swum faster. She tried to calm herself, as her mind raced like the fleeting raindrops on the windowpane. At her age, it was possible to be widowed or even outlive your children. Anyone can lose their parents. My father is just going back to where he came from. She felt a little calmer.

Interpreting her silence as anxiety, Kyŏng-ŭn's husband presses the gas pedal even harder. The thought of her mother-in-law on the phone crosses her mind as the speedometer inches toward 70, then 75, then 80 mph.

"I heard about your father. You want to go see him, right? I know you're expected to go, but . . . I still think you should stay at home. You haven't visited in a long time anyway. Why not be patient a little longer?"

When Kyŏng-ŭn didn't reply, her mother-in-law backed down. "Be careful and have a safe drive. I hope everything goes well. Let us know right away if anything happens." Was it those last words that were making her so tense?

"I know how you must feel, but do you really have to do that? We already have a big family. . . ."

The town hospital's intensive care unit is narrow and long. Seven beds side by side with an aisle between them. The beds are very close together; there is hardly enough room for a folding chair.

"What if something happens . . ."

Those ominous words hang over Kyŏng-ŭn's head as she recalls an incident from a few months ago. Her eldest sister was visiting, perhaps to check up on Kyŏng-ŭn since she had been homebound for so long, as the doctor ordered. Her sister used to crave watermelons when she was pregnant with her first child, but she never got to eat any since it wasn't watermelon season and they were expensive. She handed Kyŏng-ŭn a slice of watermelon, but snatched it away before she could take it. "This must be some kind of a special baby, forcing his mom to stay at home like this. Come here and say hi to your auntie." She reached out to touch Kyŏng-ŭn's belly, but Kyŏng-ŭn flinched and drew back. Her sister's hands looked awkward, frozen in mid-air.

"I'm sorry. I'm pretty sensitive right now," Kyŏng-ŭn apologized, but she still didn't let her sister touch her stomach.

"Maybe you've really been spending a lot of money on this baby. You must be under a lot of stress from the in-laws. I guess there's nothing wrong with being extra careful." Kyŏng-ŭn's sister pulled back.

"Even if something went wrong, where would you be safer than

AZALEA

Between
Us and
the Rest:
Lee Hye-
kyung

right here at the hospital? Don't worry about me. Just go and get some rest. Also, tell my husband to get some sleep."

Other than the sound of visitors passing through, the hospital, located in the middle of a forest in a small suburb, is dreadfully quiet at night. In the stultifying silence, the patients have to struggle harder to stay alive.

"Father, go. Shed the lifelong burden inside your heart, and go on. Fly away, father," Kyŏng-ŭn whispers as she puts her hand underneath his hospital garment and caresses his chest. Until last week, her father would open his eyes whenever she'd say the word "father." But now, he seemed irretrievable. His face used to be cleaner than the faces of the other patients, but now it was swollen and his cheeks sagged like a pair of water bags. He had a tube inside his neck to collect phlegm, a tube for urine, and other medical equipment clustered around his body. The backs of his hands were bruised and his back was covered in ribbon-shaped bedsores. Even if he regained consciousness, he would feel humiliated for the rest of his life living in this state. What she hopes for her father is a peaceful end, not a recovery.

Two years before, sitting at her father's sickbed, she had prayed for him to recover. That was when her father had been taken to the hospital near where she lived and had surgery for a hip fracture. The surgery was successful, but because of the sudden failure of his lungs the next day, he became deathly ill again. Kyŏng-ŭn's husband was going on a four-day business trip. She visited the hospital after seeing her husband off at the airport on a night flight. When she opened the door to her father's room, she noticed a strong smell of *soju*. It was her eldest brother's turn to take the night shift, and he was drinking. "Everyone else went home a few minutes ago," he said. "I need some alcohol in my system if I'm going to pull an all-nighter in here." He sunk into the cot and began to snore loudly. The sound of snoring woke her father. He looked sad and empty as he gazed at his son. Kyŏng-ŭn felt sorry for her father. She had never seen him like that before. There was no trace of vigor in his eyes. He looked as if he'd given up everything and was ready to die. Afraid, she stayed awake by his side for three days. After three days, her father's eyes seemed to regain some clarity.

Kyŏng-ŭn no longer hopes for a full recovery. After his hip surgery, her father had his eightieth birthday party. Watching his father walk back to his room after the birthday dinner, the eldest son said, "I think it's best to live until seventy—no more than that." For his sons, who made thoughtless comments by what they assumed was his deathbed, and for his daughters, who were mere onlookers, having no rights when it came to making family decisions, the news of his recovery had the same effect as an announcement in a theater to a tired audience. They had watched the show out of courtesy and were now rising from their uncomfortable seats to leave. The theater announcer reminded them that the play was not a one-act play, but a two-act one, and that they needed to return their seats for the second act, which was going to start shortly. Kyŏng-ŭn was afraid of how the audience— including herself—would react to such an announcement.

"Old man, you did it again! Stop doing that," the nurse scolds an old patient as she walks over to the bed next to Kyŏng-ŭn's father. The oxygen mask that was covering the man's nose and mouth is clinging by his ear and the contours of his jawbones make his face appear skeletal. After she places the mask back on his face, she goes to the man in the next bed who has chocolate-colored skin and is suffering from liver failure. She pulls the blanket over him but he kicks it away. He is naked from the torso down and his saggy genitals lay exposed, the scrotum that was once full of sexual desire.

"Father, forget everything and leave. You've suffered enough in this lifetime. Maybe you'll be born into a better household next time and live more comfortably."

All seven of his children grew up educated and got married. Years of hard work earned him a fair amount of wealth, and neighbors regarded Kyŏng-ŭn's family as a reputable one. But all this did not

AZALEA

*Between
Us and
the Rest:
Lee Hye-
kyung*

satisfy her father; he was never happy. Whenever Kyŏng-ŭn visited him, he would always complain about his anxieties. "Father, you are being greedy. How many families have what we have? Raising seven children is not easy. I don't have a child, but all your other children gave you grandchildren. You don't have a single physically or mentally ill grandchild. None of us went through a divorce. No child of yours even came close to going to prison, and everyone is living a good life. Believe me, this is all because the ancestors are watching over us. So if you wish for more, you are asking for too much."

As if there is nothing more immoral in this world than getting a divorce, as if not going to prison guarantees a person's goodness, as if not having a disorder is something to be proud of. Kyŏng-ŭn felt like a clown reciting things she didn't believe. A clown trying to reason with a king who has unfair expectations.

"Who are you?" asks the patient next to her father. His clear, lucid eyes do not betray that he is on the brink of death. His family visited him briefly during the day but didn't come back. Kyŏng-ŭn walks over to the old man's bed and places the loose oxygen mask back on his face. It's something she can do without calling the overworked night nurse. Kyŏng-ŭn nods and looks at his face. Suddenly, she hears a voice saying, "What are you doing? You are in no condition to take care of someone other than your father. Why worry about a stranger?" She glances over at her father but his eyes are shut. Suddenly, she can sense her father's life permeating the room like dust. She sinks into her chair.

The walls of the funeral home are covered with many stainless steel doors. One door is decorated with a wreath made of artificial flowers. Kyŏng-ŭn stares at her father's name on the wreath. A man once full of life and blood, now lying there, a cold, bloodless corpse . . . what did he want from life? She feels a poison burning inside her.

The problem started with a hundred dollars. Her father died on July 7th at 2:25 P.M. As soon as the doctor announced his death, her family began to rush out of the room like an audience trying to escape from the theater all at once after a spell had been broken. There were arguments over whether to rent a VIP suite or a small room for the funeral ceremony, arguments over the cost of food at the reception. What kind of food is reasonably priced and won't damage our reputation? The aroma of the chef's spicy beef soup filled the air and close acquaintances began arriving one by one. Then the incident occurred. One of Kyŏng-ŭn's brothers' friends, who came to help, had a favor to ask Kyŏng-ŭn's eldest sister. "We need more change for our card game. Could you give us a hundred in smaller bills?" He was a familiar face to Kyŏng-ŭn's family, always coming over to play ever since he was little. Kyŏng-ŭn's eldest sister told the eldest brother—the chief mourner and the funeral director— about the request. It was common for the house in mourning to lend some change to those who played cards and stayed at the ceremony overnight.

Her brother shot back, "Do you think I have that kind of money? And even if I did, why should I lend them money when I don't even know when they will pay me back?"

The eldest daughter could not believe her ears. She knew that her brother had used their father's money to pay the hospital bill. "For crying out loud, what kind of family doesn't have a hundred dollars on hand?" she cried.

"That's none of your business," her brother replied.

Some families are so poor that they don't have a hundred dollars to spare. She knew that some people didn't even have enough money for a proper funeral and donated the body of their loved one to the hospital for medical research. Kyŏng-ŭn's eldest brother inherited all of his father's money just because he was the eldest male of the family, yet he never had to live with his father. How could he say what he said, when he obviously spent an outrageous sum renting an entire floor of the funeral home as a VIP suite? Ordinarily Kyŏng-ŭn would ask her husband to get some change and settle the matter quietly, but not this time. "If you don't have any money, at least try to make some," said Kyŏng-ŭn.

AZALEA

*Between
Us and
the Rest:
Lee Hye-
kyung*

Her brother turned around and responded, "I don't know *how* to make money." She shouted back, "You rotten son of a bitch!" The sting from Kyŏng-ŭn's words was more bitter than bile and stronger than stomach acid. Her poisonous words spread through the air and made her own skin prickle.

"Look, father. That is your son." At that moment, she realized she was condemning their dead father, not his son. If the eldest son is that way, what does that make his father?

But the problem was bigger than this one incident. Her eldest brother obviously thought he had the right to talk to his sister that way, his sister who shared all the family responsibilities without having any rights.

"Father, I am sorry I cursed at you. But there is nothing I can do about it. You know I always speak my mind."

"I should ask about the recording now that the youngest child is here," said the stepmother as casually as possible, as she took out a cassette player.

Whenever Kyŏng-ŭn called their home to see how her father was doing, her stepmother would always say, "We don't need anything, just focus on your health and on giving birth to a healthy child." But one day, the stepmother called her and asked her if she could borrow a tape recorder. Kyŏng-ŭn thought that the old couple was going to use it to record some songs.

Kyŏng-ŭn slid an unused tape into the deck and pressed the record button. "Ah. Ah. Testing. Let's make sure it's working," she said. After rewinding the tape, she heard it replay the first few words, and then the tape got stuck. She took it out and tried again, but the cassette player had not been used in a long time and decided to stop working at this particular moment. "It's not working. We'll try to fix it later," she told her stepmother.

"Damn it! I wanted to record when the youngest was here," said the stepmother, looking distraught. Kyŏng-ŭn was surprised by her reaction and by the desperation she detected in her stepmother's voice. She was particularly fond of Kyŏng-ŭn, perhaps because she was the youngest of the family, or maybe because she always mailed her stepmother allowances to help treat her bad leg.

"What did you want to record anyway?" Kyŏng-ŭn asked.

"Your father mentioned transferring the ownership of the house to me, but he never set it in stone, and since I have nowhere to go after he dies, I wanted to record that promise while you were here. . . ."

Her words sent chills down Kyŏng-ŭn's spine. Basically, she was forcing her father's will to meet her needs. "Do you really have to do that? Everyone in the family knows about the deal," Kyŏng-ŭn said, with no small amount of contempt in her voice.

"Still . . . the eldest son doesn't even greet me when he comes over . . . Everything's useless once your father dies," the stepmother sulked. When she moved in, she had agreed to take care of Kyŏng-ŭn's father under the condition that she would gain ownership of his apartment after he died. Out of courtesy, Kyŏng-ŭn called her "stepmother," while the rest of her siblings called her "grandmother."

Maybe her own children were pressuring her to be more aggressive about securing the apartment before the old man dies.

"If only she had waited quietly, everything would have taken care of itself," Kyŏng-ŭn thought.

"I asked your brothers to go and change the deed so it's in the stepmother's name, but they refuse to do it. I would do it myself, but ever since my hip surgery I haven't been able to walk much," her father used to say, as he paced around the house with a cane. "Might as well . . . Look what has happened to the principal, Mr. Han . . ." he continued.

"Oh, father!" Kyŏng-ŭn shouted. He was referring to the rumor going around about the retired principal at the local middle school, who'd transferred the ownership of his house to his second wife. She sold it off immediately and ran away with the money. How inappropriate to mention that in front of the stepmother.

Rather than peace and harmony, in her first visit home in a long while Kyŏng-ŭn found naked self-interest, people ready to attack each other with their canine teeth. The stepmother, who

AZALEA

*Between
Us and
the Rest:
Lee Hye-
kyung*

wanted to make the house hers as quickly as possible. . . . The
father, who shamelessly accused her of having ulterior motives
to her face. . . . She felt a surge of anger—born out of a mix of
her father's discontent and the stepmother's frustration. "You
still want to change the ownership, father?" Kyŏng-ŭn had asked.
"Yes, of course," he'd say. She wanted to believe him. After all,
the stepmother was the one who fed him and kept him company
throughout these lonely years. She even massaged his weak
legs. Considering the fortune each of his sons received, Kyŏng-
ŭn wondered if the apartment was even enough for all that the
stepmother had done for her father.

Kyŏng-ŭn wrote down the word "Contract," her father and
stepmother's names, and their social security numbers. "I hereby
agree to transfer my own apartment to _____ when I
die." She wasn't very good at filling out documents; she sometimes
had to write something three or four times before she got it right,
even if it was as simple as filling out an automatic transfer request
form at a bank. Yet that day, she was writing as though she had been
preparing for this moment all her life. Both Kyŏng-ŭn's and her
father's signatures were on the contract, and she made two copies,
one for her and one for the stepmother.

Suddenly, the stillness in the room sheltered from any
commotion shatters, as if a membrane protecting inside from
outside had burst. "Oh, Lord! Nooo . . ." There is wailing in the
air. Kyŏng-ŭn's stomach tightens. Everyone is chatting about the
cost of funeral garb and the size of the coffin, but when they see
real mourners, they all get up and wail loudly again. It's a different
type of wailing from what people usually hear when someone is ill.
It sounds like someone is heaving up all his internal organs. The
heart-wrenching cries continue. A middle-aged woman kneels over
a dead body under a white sheet and weeps. "My son . . . Young-sik
. . ." "How would it feel to part forever from one's children?" Kyŏng-
ŭn wonders as she wipes the tears streaming down her face. "Father,
don't be scared. You are not alone anymore." As soon as this thought

escapes her, she feels ashamed. "How selfish am I to worry about my father being lonely when I stand in a sea of parents mourning their losses?"

When Kyŏng-ŭn wrote the contract for her stepmother, her anger toward her father intensified. He cared more about his sons, who rarely ever visited him, than the stepmother, who took care of everything for him for more than ten years. At the same time, it also occurred to her that her father may have intended for things to work out this way. Since her long-held desire for the house wasn't a secret, no one expected the stepmother to wait around until she got what she wanted. Her father was more cunning than the stepmother. She was satisfied with a piece of paper, which may not be legally sufficient even with his signature. And she was so naïve that she even apologized for being so demanding. Her father never said a word about the house after that. If there were any problems with the contract, he knew that the stepmother would fight for the house, no matter what it took.

"But what if . . . what if her father didn't know things would turn out like this?" The thought unleashes a cloud of bats from the depths of her mind, their wings fluttering in the air.

A bat hangs upside down, wiggling its body. The camera zooms in to reveal that the bat is in labor. The head of a baby bat slowly emerges from its womb.

Kyŏng-ŭn cringes at the sight. How lonely the mother bat must be, giving birth to a baby all alone. Seeing this makes her dizzy. She reaches for the snacks next to her but stops short, her hand suspended in midair, as she thinks of her baby's autopsy. Instead, she gets up and grabs some oranges from the refrigerator, her eyes still glued to the television screen.

According to the documentary, bats usually go hunting after giving birth. Once the mother bats return, the baby bats suckle all day.

The producers of the documentary did an experiment to see if

AZALEA

*Between
Us and
the Rest:
Lee Hye-
kyung*

bats that live together can distinguish their babies from others. They did an experiment with a Guano bat and found that mother bats easily found their own and protected them from other bats.

"That's right. Even animals can recognize their own from the rest. So that's what life is—separating my own offspring from everyone else's, my blood from everyone else's blood. But is that really all there is to life?" Kyŏng-ŭn wondered.

Seven years of marriage. If Kyŏng-ŭn added up all the pressures she faced since her marriage, they would be enough to propel a small train. Every New Year's Day, her father-in-law always told her, "Take care of yourself. And make me a grandchild this year." "How many siblings did you say you have?" her mother-in-law would ask in the middle of a television show. "I like that you have many siblings, especially since our family is so small." Some accused Kyŏng-ŭn of using contraceptives in order to maintain her career. Eventually, she was forced to go to an oriental medicine clinic and infertility clinics. Doctor confirmed the size of an egg with an ultrasound and called her husband to have intercourse at that particular time. "Today at about four o'clock." Filming their every move . . . having intercourse during the so-called "right time" to make egg and sperm meet . . . had the human body been reduced to a reproductive machine? There was a lady Kyŏng-ŭn saw frequently at the infertility clinic. She underwent artificial insemination to have a baby. "If I collected all the money that I spent in this hospital, I could probably build another hospital," she said. Maybe Kyŏng-ŭn didn't spend as much as that woman, but she still spent quite a bit—enough to build at least a couple of rooms in the hospital.

Kyŏng-ŭn quit her job after she became pregnant. She was even excused from attending obligatory family events. "Don't even think about visiting just because it's my birthday. I'm just going to the hot springs," the mother in-law assured her a week before her birthday. Her sisters would check up on her all the time. "How is your morning sickness?" "Do you feel any movement?" "Is there anything that you want to eat?" One day, the husband decided to ban all visitors. "I'm sorry, it's just that she's so sensitive these days." Television helped her pass the time. Soap operas, documentaries, movies . . . The Sea of Galilee gets fresh water from the upper reaches of the Jordan River and returns it downstream to the river. Hundreds and thousands of fish and vegetables grow because of the Sea of Galilee. Some of the water from the Jordan River also travels to the Dead Sea, but water cannot flow there so nothing can live in it. Kyŏng-ŭn tried to remember the names of all these places so that she could teach them to her child.

Locked inside the house, she felt like she was drowning in a bottomless sea. She had trouble breathing, as though something heavy lay on her chest. She jumped whenever the phone rang. Her fear of going outside was nauseating, as though she were trapped inside a submarine on the bottom of the ocean. The thought of her baby did not comfort her. The seed-like eyes and tiny little feet of her unborn child reminded her of an anti-abortion campaign poster, and tears ran down her face. It must have been mild depression.

"Come on, Mrs. Kim, you're worrying too much. You may not be a perfect wife, but I'm sure you'll be a great mother," Kyŏng-ŭn's husband said half-jokingly, as if all her fears and anxieties were irrational. She guessed that his confidence in her child-rearing abilities came from what he had seen at their outing a few weeks before their marriage.

One Saturday, Kyŏng-ŭn took him to a disabled children's shelter that she had been visiting every other week. She played with the kids, folded diapers after they had been washed and dried in the sun . . . such were the responsibilities of the volunteers. A greedy and wild child named Chi-hae always fought for Kyŏng-ŭn's attention. One child sat on her husband's lap and patted his face with small hands. These were children who had been disowned by their parents because of their disabilities. They were too hungry for affection to be shy around strangers. Her husband seemed to be at a loss but still embraced the child in his arms. A boy named

AZALEA

*Between
Us and
the Rest:
Lee Hye-
kyung*

Chae-min leaned his weight on Kyŏng-ŭn's back, and Theresa, who usually stayed in the background, reached out to touch Kyŏng-ŭn's thigh with her foot while looking away. These little bits of contact and warmth meant a lot to the children.

It was a fine spring day and white bridal wreaths were in full bloom. The couple barely managed to extricate themselves from the children dangling from their necks like monkeys. Kyŏng-ŭn suddenly stopped and said, "It's here. This is where the scent is the strongest." This was the place where the smell of flowers seemed to bless the passersby.

"After our child grows up, it would be nice to visit these disabled children in our free time," her husband said as he breathed in the sweet air. Kyŏng-ŭn knew that this was just a fleeting impulse, the kind that made people who avoided their poor relatives for fear they would ask for money suddenly pick up the phone one day and donate after watching an ad for charity. But at that very moment, she wanted to believe in the sincerity of his words. Perhaps watching him play with the children made her feel more optimistic. She hadn't expected him to get a lot from the visit, but only wanted to show him why she visits these children. Her hope was that he would realize that love must extend beyond the family, beyond simple blood relations. She thanked her husband for coming with her. She offered him the scent of the bridal wreaths as a gift and finally accepted the reality of her marriage.

"Cuckoo, cuckoo." The cry of the cuckoo echoing across the fields at night sounded like a sudden sob after long weeping. The motel was a seven-story building surrounded by tall trees. Kyŏng-ŭn's white funeral clothes glowed under the blue motel lights. The front of her funeral skirt, too short for Kyŏng-ŭn to begin with, was hiked up even higher because of her swollen stomach.

"I'm sure none of you have been to a 'love hotel' since nobody here has had an affair. Let's take a quick look inside," Kyŏng-ŭn said at the entrance. To everyone's surprise, the motel looked very clean.

Even though it had been built for lovers rather than sleepers, the rooms and the bathrooms weren't flashy and the beds seemed clean. Fresh forest air from outside swept through the opened window, filling the room.

All the nephews of Kyŏng-ŭn's mother arrived at the funeral home at once. They sat on the couch in the hallway, far away from those who were drinking after paying their condolences. "You guys should come sit out here with us. The funeral is over and the mourners are sad to death, but you can't all die and follow him," one of the nephews told Kyŏng-ŭn's sisters, whose eyes were red from crying. He told some funny stories about the relatives and made some of the sisters laugh, but when they did, he suddenly changed his tone and scolded them. "I know how y'all are happy that uncle died in peace, but mourners aren't supposed to laugh. You should suppress your laughter and let it out only when you're alone in the bathroom." As if contradicting his words, his eyes had a kindly crinkle.

The majority of mother's nephews, or Kyŏng-ŭn's cousins, were nearing sixty. All of them, at some point in their lives, had lived in Kyŏng-ŭn's home. Their family was so poor that having one less person at the table helped substantially, and Kyŏng-ŭn's family always had plenty of work for them. The boys helped at the store and the girls took care of housework and chores. After one stayed with Kyŏng-ŭn's family for a few months, another would come to take his or her place. Compared to Kyŏng-ŭn's father's side of the family, her mother's side was far more generous in helping those in need.

After Kyŏng-ŭn was grown up, she often thought of her cousins. Her father never pressed anyone for money, but he was not very generous either—not even to his own family. Her second aunt would always come to help her mother during family events. Kyŏng-ŭn's father would be especially harsh toward his wife whenever the second aunt was over. Kyŏng-ŭn's heart sank every time she thought of her aunt and her cousins and what memories they must have of her father's place. They insisted on staying up all night and waiting until the funeral cortege left the funeral home the next day, but Kyŏng-ŭn urged them to stay at the motel overnight because she felt somehow indebted to them.

AZALEA

Between
Us and
the Rest:
Lee Hye-
kyung

Several years before Kyŏng-ŭn got married, her mother passed away. A few days after her mother's funeral, she got a phone call from her aunt, who had just returned from the funeral. "You've disobeyed your parents all your life. Find someone to marry soon and don't disappoint your father before he passes away." Then she asked to talk to her father. "Why does she want to talk to my father?" Kyŏng-ŭn wondered. Her father and her aunt were not that close. Kyŏng-ŭn's father looked uneasy as he took the receiver. "All right . . . all right." He repeated short responses. "What did she say?" Kyŏng-ŭn asked after he hung up. Her father wiped his face with his hand and said, "She thanked me for taking care of your mother when she was ill. She is such a noble person, your aunt . . ."

They say my father found fault with everything my mother did and would hit her, especially when my aunt was over. My aunt had to watch her sister going through all of that. How did she deal with all those memories?

The man is the sun, the woman is the moon. The man's grave is always placed on the left and the woman's on the right, aligned with the Chinese characters Sun and Moon (日月). When they dug the left side of Kyŏng-ŭn's mother's grave, they discovered that the color of the soil was bad. So they decided to move the father's to the right.

"Auntie, what happens when son and moon are switched?" Kyŏng-ŭn's young school-age nephew asks after hearing the geomancer's explanation.

This nephew closely resembled his grandfather. Indeed, people used to tease her sister-in-law, saying that she must have really hated her father-in-law during her pregnancy for her son to be his spitting image. Ever since Kyŏng-ŭn was little, Kyŏng-ŭn's father traveled across the country with a geomancer to find a propitious site for a grave. Incidentally, the site he chose was only a half an hour's drive from Kyŏng-ŭn's place.

"What do you think happened? Maybe the woman became stronger since she switched places with the man," Kyŏng-ŭn suggests to her nephew. He gives her a look, as if to say, "Oh, come on. That's silly." She tries to stifle her laughter at the sight of her nephew's reaction. She drops the cell phone. Kyŏng-ŭn bends over to pick it up, but she immediately regrets doing so as her stomach knots in pain. Fortunately, her family is busy looking at the workers digging the grave. She walks toward the forest away from the noise.

"Hello?"

"Mrs. Kim? It's Mary's Adoption Center. Congratulations. Your baby is here."

Kyŏng-ŭn suddenly turned around and looked back. The workers were busy ramming their shovels into the soil next to Kyŏng-ŭn's mother's mound. Mourners in their funeral garments were disappearing into the distance.

"Are you there? The baby is healthy and adorable."

Kyŏng-ŭn's husband agreed to adopt after they learned that her weak womb wasn't the only reason for her miscarriages. Her husband was sexually deficient. Several years earlier, he had reacted completely differently when she brought up the issue of adoption while watching a television program about adopted children overseas searching for their biological mothers. "You don't even know who the father is . . . What if the biological mother shows up later on?" He strongly objected. "Go ahead and do what you want but don't think of coming back." Her father was even more vehemently opposed; he threatened to disown her. Her sisters were no different. "Once you do it, there's going to be trouble. We can't let you go through that."

After Kyŏng-ŭn and her husband decided to adopt, he said, "I hope it's a girl. I heard that mothers naturally favor girls over boys." He said it as if there was no one in the world more considerate of his wife. Only when she reminded him of the in-laws' expectations did he reveal his innermost thought: "If it is a girl . . . she'll be lost to us when she marries into another family." Kyŏng-ŭn couldn't

AZALEA

*Between
Us and
the Rest:
Lee Hye-
kyung*

refute that. "It would be nice if the parents are healthy, and even better if they are highly educated and grew up in a decent family." Her husband sounded like a stranger talking at an adoption agency interview. "I hope the baby was made in love." She wondered if he'd memorized some kind of script. His words resonated with her, because she grew up believing in the purity and decency of love. He was saying what Kyŏng-ŭn believed, but did not dare say.

"We are currently out of town. My father passed away . . . We'll be back in a few days."

"I see. I'm sure you're occupied with a lot of things. Don't worry about it and give me a call when you get back. By the way, the baby is adorable."

"It's amazing how babies slowly come to resemble their foster parents," said the social worker during the home visit. She added, "We recommend an open adoption. Of course, many parents do not reveal the adoption because they worry that it might scar the child. But the child has a legal right to know where he or she came from."

A wave of sadness swept over Kyŏng-ŭn as she thought of the baby whose soul had wandered the universe to reach her after nine months of her fake pregnancy. She would have to make up a story about her conception dream and be congratulated by everyone. "My baby, I am so sorry," she murmured, as she wrapped the stomach band around her belly. She felt sorry for not being able to receive the baby as a gift from heaven but instead through the back door as if it were something shameful. Words were locked up inside her and began to fester. Witnessing this necrosis within, Kyŏng-ŭn cried often. She cried over the baby's biological mother, who had to send her baby away. She cried over her stomach, which would turn flabby because of the failed pregnancy. She cried over the baby, who would be thrown into a world that divides people according to blood. She cried over herself, because she had lived by deceptions. Finally, she cried over her father's death. On the day she switched to a stomach band designed for nine months instead of six, she cried at the thought of her belly being a grave mound rather than a cradle of life. As she went shopping for baby supplies during off-peak hours, to avoid encountering gossiping housewives, she cried. Her family thought she was going through a pregnancy-related depression. Those were dark days, dark as a grave.

It was a secret she would carry with her to her deathbed. Someday, the child would ask where he came from. "Mommy, mommy what happened back then?" Each time, Kyŏng-ŭn would feel another brick being piled on her heart. She felt lost, as if deep in a bamboo forest. The people she occasionally saw seemed like bamboo trees. She wanted to scream the truth to everyone: that what she had conceived was not a child, but a lie.

After returning from her father's three-day funeral, Kyŏng-ŭn will feel a sudden pain in her stomach, three weeks ahead of schedule. Her water will break and she'll go to a nearby obstetrician. Because the clinic is too unsanitary and crowded, she'll come home a day after her delivery. The week-old baby will look like a newborn. It's a well-known fact that traumatic events, for example a single mother's unwanted pregnancy, can cause premature birth. Her father's death could serve as justification for the early arrival of the baby.

Kyŏng-ŭn waddles towards her husband—the only person who shares the burden of her secret with her—to inform him about the birth of their child. The grave mound is almost complete. Pine branches in the middle of the mound look like a crown on a person's head. They distinguish her father's mound from the rest. As she's about to call her husband, someone shouts, "Where are the sons-in-law? It's time to finish the mound."

AZALEA

Five Poems by Hwang In-sook

Translated by David McCann
& Kim Jean Young

I WISH TO BE BORN AS A CAT

Let me in my next life be
reborn as a cat.
A black tabby with glossy fur.
Tiny cat hopping lightly
as a big magpie,
curling my whole body into a ball.
I won't be dozing on the porch,
won't lick milk from a porcelain bowl,
but instead I'll go out to the open field,
threading through thorny thickets
to play with the meadow mouse.

Hungry, I'll attack a flock of sparrows.
Scared of me, they'll dash off in a rush.
Ha! Ha-ha!
I'll run, hopping after.
Baby sparrow
I will not catch but pretend,
dabbing at its fluttering heart with a paw.

Off at a ramshackle run
I'll swipe at the biggest magpie.

The sun will go slowly down,
the wind rise.
Meadow mice and sparrows all gone,
I'll be left alone in the dark field.
I won't go back.
Tasting the darkness, I'll look for a stack of stalks,
warm and cozy with the smell of straw.
I'll jump on top and settle in,
my bed shining bright in the moonlight.

Or I might wander the empty fields
in cold rain and gusting wind,
but not a single bit of my fur will get wet.
I'll dream
the dream of running in a sunlit field
after the magpie I missed that day.

PINK BIRD

Stretching, hands raised, I saw
the mysterious bird on the chimney.
Really a pink bird,
or the sun waking to play?
As I was rubbing my eyes,
it disappeared somewhere over the roof.
Are you listening or not?
I say I saw a pink bird.
Are you listening or not?
Do not be wondering
was it a metaphor, a symbol?
I saw a pink bird,
and I am saying that I saw it.
That is all.

DROWSINESS

The snail is crossing the brook.
The snail is crossing the brook.
The snail is crossing the brook.

The snail is crossing the brook the whole day long.

The snail on the windowpane
is crossing the brook the whole day long.

REGRET

So thoughtful,
my thought after the act.
More honest,
my tongue than my mind.

Look, here is the sky.
No one can peer into it,
and no one does.
Only the birds, soaring up, holding their breath,
raise cries of joy,
trailing the awful trap of freedom along;
only birds can pluck
the strong blue string:
Tin-Tin-Tin.

Five Poems by Kim Chiha

Translated by Young-Jun Lee

THERE WILL BE NO RETURN

There will be no return
once I step, once I sleep here
sleep will fall deep down in my body
there, the white room of sleep, there, the bottomless dizziness

There will be no return
Stand up,
like blood on the wall, like old screaming,
surprised to stand up to surprise once
I sleep then never ever
ah to the barren road,
as a traveler never again

Sound of heeled shoes all night
walking on the ceiling
in the room beyond scenes faces hands traits
laughing loud
there the white room there bottomless dizziness

Eyes gaping wide at the pain of a nail being torn out
shouting as a lump of flesh is broken
perhaps I
can survive as a soul alone and
standing on the road

In vain
in vain, fallen friends,
fallen asleep under the blanket of shame in vain
under the beatings under the kicking foot under the contempt in vain
fallen friends who once
smiled once
wept once
had something good

Ah, there will be no return
Once I fall into sleep,
unless struggling and writhing
with mad burning eyes never
to the wind-raging road
with my brothers
as a traveler, never again.

FIG

Leaning against the stone wall supported by my friend,
I threw up and wiped tears and blew my nose and
tried to look up at the gray sky but
a fig tree blocked my sight.

Hey, I say to my friend,
I have had no season of flowering.
But getting fruit without blooming,
it's a fig,
no?
My friend raising his hand and rubbing my back said,
Hey,
blooming inside the fruit
is the fig,
no?

As we staggered along the blackened streak of sewage
a black alley cat quickly
crossed the dark trickle.

At Haech'ang

Two men barely standing
in the abandoned port town of Haech'ang,
once prosperous but now
closed for the opening of Kochŏnam.

They are dimly standing,
one drunk one sober,
not even a dog barking.
Only the wind blows where the diner used to be.

On a day when clouds were drooping low, to that very place
I came
half drunk half sober,
split into halves barely standing
in the waning sunset.

Quivering faintly, the sound of a cargo truck
leaving town,
and after the truck disappeared over the hill,
so did the two men.

FIFTY

Is it age?

Everything appears dim to my eyes.

The eyes are the soul's net.

Everything seems dark to my soul.

Even dawn comes as sunset

in the dark room where I am always hungry

and I wait for the sound of scissors that comes so late

and a cockroach comes to my side and

I keep silent.

I wonder, outside

is it falling, the frost?

I feel a chill at my tooth breaking, a thread,

my jacket lost a button a year ago

and outside,

sharp-sighted, my wife

returns,

treading on lingering warmth.

Is that the sound of scissors?

SIMULTANEOUS PECKING FROM INSIDE AND OUT

Deep blue stars are rising
in evening's body,
rising at the groin,
in the middle of the chest, at the belly button,
even in the brain.

The tree that burned me grows within me.
I died and
on the tree
rise as the crescent moon.

Love,
tell me of
the subtle time of birth.

I will emerge from the shell
kick loose and emerge
to become the cosmos,
to be resurrected.

Book Review

The Guest, by Hwang Sok-yong, translated by Kyung-
ja Chun and Maya West, Seven Stories Press, 2005,
$27.95, hardcover, ISBN 1-58322-693-1.

Perhaps more than most Asian peoples, Koreans live
with ghosts. Most often these are the spirits of someone
they knew in life, someone who died an untimely or cruel death,
someone whose soul cannot find peaceful repose. Ghosts may
startle when they appear, but they do not frighten because, after all,
they are a part of one's past.

So it is for the protagonist of this novel, Ryu Yosop, a Korean
Presbyterian minister living in Brooklyn in the 1990s, who decides
to visit his hometown in North Korea, a place from which he had
been separated for forty years. The ghosts he meets there are those
from his boyhood, people he had known since birth. They perished
horribly, in the midst of recrimination and torture, in October 1950
at the beginning of the Korean War. In North Korea, Reverend
Kim sees the museum near his hometown filled with photos of
slaughtered victims, posted as a testament, the guides proclaim, to
the atrocities committed by American troops upon innocent Korean
civilians. The museum actually exists in the North Korean district
of Sinchon in Hwanghae Province, and is full of photographs of
long-dead victims slaughtered, according to the commentary, by
American soldiers.

In October 1950, Yosop was a boy of fourteen and he remembers
the story differently. He remembers that when the Korean

Communist cadre arrived in the village, many of its poorest
members quickly joined the Communist Party. Their status
was elevated by party membership and they helped to direct the
arrests of those who had once held land and power. The Korean
Presbyterians in the village, a well-organized group of small
landowners, denounced the Communists as followers of Satan
who would never allow the countryside to become Christian. The
American troops, having landed at Inchŏn and then advancing
northward toward the village, were said to be crusaders whom the
Korean Presbyterians would aid by eliminating the Communist
sympathizers in their village. The Christians began to arrest and
execute the Communists, expecting the American reinforcements
to arrive soon. The Communists, of course, were most often fellow
villagers.

So began the brutalities, torture, and executions that the villagers
on both sides, once neighbors and childhood friends, carried out
against each other. By the time the American army arrived, the
fratricidal killing had mostly ended. In the novel, Yosop's elder
brother had been one of those Christians who killed whole families
in the name of anti-Communism. He had recently died in the
United States and his spirit is one of the ghosts accompanying
Yosop on the journey back home. Once in the village, the ghosts
of two boyhood friends appear to greet Yosop. The ghosts are
murderer and victim, together as when they were children, their
spirits having passed beyond the cruelties their human bodies did
not survive.

The facts behind the novel's account are true. Witnesses to the
slaughters, living in the United States in the early 1990s, recounted
the story for the author. The museum in North Korea demonstrates
how photographs can stand as mute documentation for different
narratives. It is the ghosts and their presence who populate this
novel, who shadow the main characters, and who, ultimately, force
the reader to ponder the events of the story.

Hwang Sok-yong, the author of this thoughtful work of fiction, is a household name in South Korea and in the North as well. He is respected as a fiercely independent voice determined to speak about human beings as complex, selfish, and forgiving people. In 1989, he defied laws of the South Korean government by traveling to North Korea to speak with Korean writers living in the North, at a time when contact between both sides was proscribed. After voluntary exile in New York and Germany to avoid being imprisoned by the government in the South, he returned to Seoul in 1993 because, as he strongly felt at the time, a writer needs to live in the country of his mother tongue. He was, as expected, jailed by the conservative government that preached its fear of the North. Following the persistent intervention of Amnesty International and PEN, he was pardoned in 1998 by a more liberal South Korean government under Kim Dae Jung, then seeking to improve ties with its counterpart across the 38th parallel. Hwang's novels and short stories have been widely published in Europe and Asia. He has won many prestigious literary prizes in South Korea, and his name has been on the Nobel Prize shortlist. When *The Guest* appeared in Korea, critics in both the South and the North, unnerved by the harsh realities exposed in the novel, fired off criticisms against Hwang. He currently lives in London under the sponsorship of London University. This novel is his first major North American release.

Many times in modern Korean history, the guests who came to reside in the peninsula were not welcome, but stayed anyway. One of the early guests was smallpox, a Western disease that many Koreans called *sonnim*, meaning the guest. In this novel, two other Western guests are present and, like smallpox about a century earlier, they impose themselves upon the Korean people. The two guests Hwang writes about are Marxism and Christianity. Both were imports from the West and both were highly deterministic ideologies whose followers claimed that absolute truth lay with them.

As a way of ridding themselves of unwelcome guests, of cleansing the events of an undesired past, Koreans often turn to Shamanism, asking the shaman to perform an exorcism. Given the bloody events in Sinchon district in 1950 and the slaughter between brothers that took place, Hwang felt that the healing and restorative power of the shaman could help to assuage the lingering remorse. *The Guest* is structured in the form of a Shamanistic exorcist ritual, where the spirits come into the everyday world so they can communicate with their kin still on earth before receding back into the realm of those no longer among the living. In the Shaman ritual called *Chinogwi*, an exorcism practiced in Hwanghae Province, twelve separate rounds take place where the dead and the living simultaneously cross and recross the boundaries between the past and the present. Following this pattern, Hwang's novel has twelve chapters. The rich traditions that influence the structure of the novel set its pace of surging and hesitation as ghosts appear and then withdraw before the story unfolds another step. This pace, marvelously maintained by Hwang, mirrors the rhythm and dance steps of a Korean Shaman ceremony.

In spite of its welcoming attitude toward the spirits, this is not a story about the supernatural, and it is not a ghost story. Hwang uses the ghosts to reveal the shared humanity of all living beings, because the spirits of the departed seek emotional closure and mutual forgiveness. They harbor regret for the mistakes they made while alive. When the ghosts speak of their actions in the past, and when they come out together for their final expressions of remorse before bidding farewell to Yosop on his final night in the village, the novel exhibits the universality it holds for all human beings of moving beyond hotly held youthful passions to the thoughtful mellowness of maturity. It is the universality of wishing one could undo some actions in the past.

The message imparted by the deceased spirits is that living on this earth can seem to be a tedious chain of mundane actions and thoughts, and at the same time, humans can be unspeakably cruel toward each other. But in its totality and in its simple pleasures, human life is also overwhelmingly precious. Hwang's highly acclaimed and richly thoughtful novel is for all humanity and for all time. Through the ghosts who populate the story, Hwang shows us how the past and the present are very often one and the same.

Ronald Suleski
Harvard University

Five Poems from
Maninbo (Ten thousand lives)

by Ko Un
Translated by Brother Anthony of Taizé & Lee Sang-Wha

ŎNNYŎN IN SIBERIA

In the 1920s
some Koreans
made their way beyond Mongolia
into Russia,
journeyed all the way to near Lake Baikal
and settled in a ruined hut that had to be propped up.

Such a long way to go to live.

Despite blizzards
and days so cold their urine froze,
they managed
not to freeze to death.

Such a harsh way to live.

On a freezing morning, a girl in Korean dress, long skirt and blouse,
a water pot on her head
went on her way

to fetch water
carrying a club to smash the ice.

Not yet called Anna or Tatiana,
just Ŏnnyŏn, Pretty Girl.

Her father had not come home for several days.
Boarding a sledge,
he went off to a hunting lodge
in Bear Forest.

Ŏnnyŏn had
two younger brothers
and two younger sisters.

The family had grown as they journeyed on.

They're not yet called Sergei or Josip or Boris but
First Twin
Second Twin
Tong-sŏp
Kŭt-sŏp
Below Ŏnnyŏn
Little Girl
Last Girl.

Once she turned eight, Ŏnnyŏn became an adult.
She had been living the days
she was destined to live.

HALLELUJAH

Outside Kanghwa town on Kanghwa Island
there's Kapkot, a place where breezes blow.
In the fields of Kapkot,
once the special February wind subsides,
the March wind comes along.
Skylarks venturing upward are injured by the gusts.

Across the whirlwind-stirred sea,
in the haze of the Kimp'o plains
the April wind makes the seedbeds sprout with young rice.

The seedlings are planted in May.
As people are planting the rice they shout:
Hallelujah
Hallelujah

Once Christianity arrived at isolated villages,
believers
and non-believers
became deadly foes.

In a single village Baptists
and Episcopalians,
each other's enemies,
could not intermarry,
could not attend each other's wedding parties.

A member of the Holiness Church, Kwak Il-kyu,
who shouts Hallelujah one hundred times a day,
is getting married to Hong Sun-ja of the same church,
who shouts Hallelujah two hundred times a day.

Episcopalians dare not attend
the wedding,
even though they're cousins
or distant relatives.

Former co-workers,
former close friends and kin
vanished,
became one another's foes.

The moment the North Korean armies arrived
those on the left arose, killed those on the right.
Once the North withdrew
the right was left
having slaughtered all those on the left.

The churches prospered.
The churches distributed
American relief food and goods.
People came flocking
to collect wheat flour.
They even received a secondhand suit of clothes.

All were forced to shout Hallelujah!
Out in the fields at harvest time too:
Hallelujah!
Hallelujah!

YI JŎNG-YI'S FAMILY

They walked all the way from Chinnampʼo in North Korea
to Hongsŏng in South Koreaʼs Chʼungchŏng Province.
They walked and walked,
for twenty days they fled.

Yi Jŏn-hae
and her sister Yi Jŏng-yi
with their parents following them.

All day long walking with nothing to eat.
When they found a well
they drank then walked on in the flesh-biting cold.

They dreaded the American troops
so they smeared their clothes
with their own shit.

They spread soot from kitchen chimneys
over their faces.
The mother became
a beggar-mom,
her daughters beggar kids.

Their bodies stank of shit.
Instead of American troops, dogs came running.

Their robust father
likewise
blackened his face. The teeth inside his lips looked stronger still.

When snow fell
they ventured into a village
and were saved by a shed
or an empty cowstall.

Three hundred miles they walked,
arrived at Hongsŏng, settled there.

When China attacked in January '51,
they never reached there,
being held back near the 38th parallel.
They began a new life amidst the hills and fields of Hongsŏng,
purchased a big hospital.

One daughter, Yi Jŏng-yi got married,
became the poet Kim Young-Moo's wife. Never late for Mass.

DDT

Soon after Liberation,

Seoul

began to teem with 370 different political parties and civic groups.

Every morning when you woke up

several more had hung out their signboards.

Parties with just five members appeared, lacking even a signboard.

The commander of the occupying forces, General Hodge,

detested the Koreans, calling them cats or worse.

All the Koreans working in Hodge's headquarters

and the Koreans in the streets

outside his headquarters

were liberally doused with DDT.

Smothered in that poisonous powder

the Koreans would giggle helplessly

while they boiled with seething shame.

Thanks to the Americans who came for the war

in 1950 Korea again became a land of DDT,

fleas, bugs, and the plentiful lice and nits about their bodies,

even invisible microbes,

were uncivilized Koreans

so the Americans drenched the Koreans

in plentiful quantities of DDT.

All the orphans likewise

were baptized in Hallelujahs and DDT.

Offspring with neither dad nor mom became the offspring of DDT.

Ch'oe Johan, a war orphan,

his family name was that of the director of his orphanage, Zion

Home,
his given name
the John of St. John's gospel.
His original name, Pak Sun-Sik, was completely forgotten.

Since his room happened to be next to a stinking cesspool,
Ch'oe Johan's blanket
always smelt of a mixture of DDT and sewage.

Ah, home, sweet home.

Kwŏn Jin-gyu

His Japanese wife died.
Love lost.

Alone he molded clay,
chiseled stone.

The sculptor Kwŏn Jin-gyu
had a room in Seoul's Tonam-dong district.

The sculptures were quite at home.
The sculptor
was a guest squatting on the edge of a camp bed in a corner.

One clay figure breathing.
One sculptor gasping.

It seems there are cliffs in art.
He failed to avoid the cliff,
walked over the edge,
and after that there was nothing.

He ended his life.
Not because he hated the world
Not because he hated himself. Art driven out.

Another
Perspective

Cranes

by Hwang Sunwŏn (1915-2000)
Translated by David R. McCann

(Story originally published in 1953)

Beneath the high, clear autumn sky just north of the 38th boundary the village was quiet and alone.

In the empty houses, there might be just a white gourd on the dirt floor between rooms, leaning against another white gourd.

Old people met by chance would turn aside, pipes held behind their backs. And children, being children, turned away at some distance. Everyone's face was marked by fear.

The area showed no signs of what might be called the broken remnants of the present conflict. But it somehow did not seem like the old village where he had grown up as a youngster.

In the chestnut grove on the back hill, Sŏngsam halted his steps. There he climbed one of the trees. It seemed as if he could hear from a distance the shouts of the old grandfather with the wen: "You little son-of-a-guns, climbing someone else's tree again!"

The old grandfather with the wen had probably passed away in the time since. He hadn't been among the old people encountered in the area so far.

Holding on to the chestnut tree, for a moment Sŏngsam looked up at the blue autumn sky. Even without the branch being shaken, one of the remaining chestnuts opened, and the nut slipped out, and fell.

As he reached the front of a house, the temporary headquarters for the Public Peace Corps, he saw there was some young fellow tied up in handcuff rope.

It didn't seem to be anyone he had seen before in the village, so he went up close for a look at his face. He was stunned. Wasn't it his closest childhood friend, Tŏkchae?

What was going on, he asked the Public Peace Corpsman who had come over from Chŏnt'ae with him. *Vice chairman of the Farmers Collective Committee, this one was, caught hiding out in his own house.*

Sŏngsam squatted down there on the dirt floor, a lighted cigarette in his mouth.

Tŏkchae was going to be sent off to Chŏngdan. One of the Public Peace Corps members was going to take him.

Lighting a new cigarette from the one he had just finished, Sŏngsam stood up again.

"I'll take this sunnavabitch."

Tŏkchae all this time kept his face turned away and did not even try to look in Sŏngsam's direction.

The two came out of the village.

Sŏngsam smoked one cigarette after another. The cigarettes seemed to have no flavor. He just kept drawing the smoke in deep, and letting it out. After a while, the thought came to him that this Tŏkchae fellow, he might want a cigarette too. He remembered when they were young, how they would make cigarettes out of pumpkin leaves and smoke them behind the wall, so the grown-ups wouldn't know. But how could he offer a cigarette to a guy like this one, today?

Once, when they were young, he had gone with Tŏkchae to swipe chestnuts from the old grandfather with the wen. It had been Sŏngsam's turn to climb the tree. Next instant, the old grandfather was shouting at them. He slipped and fell out of the tree. The chestnut burs pierced his backside, but they just ran. Only when they had gone far enough so the old grandfather with the wen couldn't follow, did he turn his backside to Tŏkchae. It hurt like anything, pulling out the chestnut burs. He couldn't help the tears that trickled down. Tŏkchae suddenly reached out with a fistful of his own chestnuts and stuck them in Sŏngsam's pocket. . . .

Sŏngsam threw away the cigarette he had just lit. He makes up his mind not to light another while escorting this fellow Tŏkchae.

They reached the hill road. The hill is where he and Tŏkchae had gone all the time to cut fodder, until two years before Liberation when Sŏngsam moved to a place near Chŏnt'ae, south of the 38th.

Sŏngsam, overwhelmed by sudden anger, gave a shout.

"You son of a . . . ! How many people have you killed so far?"

Only then does Tŏkchae look over, then lower his head again.

"Sunnavabitch . . . ! How many people have you killed?"

Tŏkchae raises his head and turns his way. He shoots a look at Sŏngsam. His expression turns darker, and the edges of his mouth, surrounded by his dangling beard, quiver and shake.

"So, that's how you killed people?"

Sunnavabitch! Somehow Sŏngsam's heart feels relieved at its core. As if something blocking it has eased and fallen loose. But,

"Some guy gets to be vice chairman of the Farmers Collective Committee, why didn't you run off? Hiding out with some secret mission?"

Tŏkchae says nothing.

"Go ahead, tell the truth! What sort of mission was it you were hiding out to do?"

But Tŏkchae just keeps walking silently along. Clear enough, this one is feeling caught. It's good to see their faces at a moment like this, but he keeps his face turned away, and doesn't look over.

Grasping the pistol that he carried at his waist, Sŏngsam says, "It's no use trying to defend yourself. You're going to be shot, no doubt about it. So you might as well tell the truth right here and now."

Without turning his head, Tŏkchae replies,

"There's nothing to defend myself about. I'm just the son of a dirt-poor farmer. I'm known as a guy who can handle the hard work, and that's why I was made vice chairman of the Farmers Cooperative Committee. If that's a crime to get killed for, there's nothing to be done about it. All I'm good at, all I ever was good at to stay alive, is digging in the dirt."

He pauses for a moment.

"My father is laid up now. It's half a year already."

Tŏkchae's father was a widower, a poor farmer getting old, caring just for his son Tŏkchae. Seven years ago his back had already given out and his face was covered with age spots.

"You married?"

A moment, and

"Yeah, married."

"Who with?"

"Short Stuff."

No. Short Stuff? This is great. Short Stuff. Kind of fat, and too short to know the skies were high, just how wide the earth is. Sort of a loner. They hadn't liked that, so he and Tŏkchae, together they used to tease her all the time and make her cry. And now Tŏkchae had gone and married Short Stuff.

"So, any kids?"

"The first is coming this fall."

At this, Sŏngsam could hardly keep himself from laughing. He was the one who had asked with his own mouth if there were any kids, but when he heard that the first was coming this fall it was almost more than he could bear. Even not pregnant, Short Stuff's little body had a tummy almost too big to reach around. But realizing this was not the time to laugh or make jokes about such a thing, he says,

"But don't you think it's suspicious, you hanging around, not trying to get away?"

"I thought of trying to get away. They said when they came up from the south this time, all the men, all of them would be caught and killed, so all the males between seventeen and forty, they were made to go north. I thought of getting away too, even if I had to carry my father on my back. But he said no, he couldn't. Where would a farmer go, and leave the farming? And besides, my father, he grew old doing the farming, trusting in me; I wanted to be the one to close his eyes with my own hands. People like us, all we know is working the earth to stay alive. What good would it do us to run away?

Last June, it was Sŏngsam who had fled. He had told his father secretly at night that he was going to flee. Sŏngsam's father had said the same thing then. If farm workers left the farming, where would they go? So Sŏngsam had fled alone. As he wandered the strange streets and hamlets of the south, always in his head was the farm work he had left to his old parents and young family. But

fortunately, they were all as healthy now as they had been then.

They crossed the ridge of the hill. Now it was Sŏngsam who walked along with his face turned away. The autumn sun was hot on his forehead. He thought, a day like this, the weather was perfect for threshing.

As they came down from the hill, Sŏngsam gradually slowed down and halted his steps.

Over in the center of the fields, looking like some people wearing their white clothes, backs bent, surely that was a flock of cranes. The place that had become the demilitarized zone along the 38th parallel. Even though people had stopped living there, it was still a place where the cranes continued to live as before.

Once when Tŏkchae and Sŏngsam were about twelve, without the grown-ups knowing, the two of them had set a trap and caught a crane. It was a Tanjŏng crane. They had tied it up, even its wings, and every day the two of them would come and stroke its neck, ride on its back, making a fuss over it. Then one day, they heard the grown-ups in the area whispering about something. Someone had come from Seoul to shoot a crane. He even had some permit from the government-general for collecting specimens. The two had run off down the road. It did not matter that the grown-ups might find out and give them a scolding. All they could think was that their crane must not die. Without stopping to catch their breath, they crawled through the weeds to untie the lasso around the crane's legs and loose the rope from its wings. But the crane could hardly walk. Probably from being tied up for so long. Holding it together, the two of them heaved the crane up into the sky. Suddenly there was a shot. The crane flapped its wings two, three, four times, then sank down again. Had it been shot? But at the next instant, as another Tanjŏng crane spread its wings wide in the bushes right beside them, their own crane, the one that had come down to earth, stretched out its long neck, gave a cry, and flying up into the sky, sweeping in a circle over the heads of the two boys, vanished into the distance. For a long time the two boys could not take their eyes away from the blue sky into which their crane had vanished . . .

"Hey, time for us to go crane hunting," Sŏngsam suddenly announced.

Tŏkchae was stunned, not knowing what was going on.

"I'll make a snare with the rope here. You chase a crane over."

Sŏngsam had untied the rope and was crawling away into the weeds.

The color drained from Tŏkchae's face. The words flashed through his mind from just before, "You're going to be shot." Soon a bullet would come from where Sŏngsam had gone crawling off.

Sŏngsam turned his head back toward him.

"Hey, what are you waiting for? Chase a crane or something over here!"

At last Tŏkchae understood, and began crawling through the weeds.

Just then, two or three cranes, their huge wings spread, went soaring through the clear autumn sky.

Another
Perspective

David R. McCann

H wang Sunwŏn (1915-2000) was seen as a fine writer, though critical judgment seemed to weigh against him for his purported avoidance of the themes of his day: the Japanese colonial occupation (1910-1945), the division of Korea in 1945, and the Korean War (1950-1953) and its aftermath, notably including the repressive political regimes running from Syngman Rhee through Park Chung Hee, Chun Doo Hwan, to Roh Tae Woo. Originally published in 1953, "Cranes" in particular seems to elicit a reaction against what is viewed as too romantic an ending—the cranes flying off into the blue sky—for its subject, the brutal Korean War. Yet the story is far more complex than its scant number of pages would suggest, its shifting point of view having a resonance with the events of the war and the years preceding that stands as a bold challenge to the tragic political uncertainties of that time in Korean history. It demands a second reading, and stands as its own demonstration that the structure and movement within a narrative are as significant as the contents.

While they may be considered elementary by some, the notes that follow are meant as soundings, to record the depths of a story that many readers view as simple and romantic. This is an anti-reading, and if some or most of it seems obvious to our readers, then let that stand as a measure of the superficial nature of the usual construals of Hwang Sunwŏn's work. It is not the case that he was a simple and romantic writer as the typical reading suggests.

The story opens with a swooping movement down from the autumn sky to the ground, from the "high, clear" overarching sweep of the sky to a place on a map, "north of the 38th boundary." The reader arrives on the ground in a quiet village filled with empty houses, yet occupied by old people and children, all their faces "marked by fear." A character appears, someone who had "grown up as a youngster" in the village, who immediately climbs a chestnut tree into recollections about his childhood. The character, now named Sŏngsam, looks back up at the autumn sky which framed the story's beginning; then within the more local and restricted purview of his gaze, the same descending movement that started the story repeats itself, as a chestnut falls to the ground. The narrative is full of movement, up and down, back and forth between present and memory, while it sets in juxtaposition the figures of the young boys stealing chestnuts and the old grandfather who owned the trees. We have noted the fear in everyone's face, and may have ascribed it to the general atmosphere related to the war, the "broken remnants of the present conflict." Quickly and deftly, the story opens with what seems a simple entry of a person into a place, but sets up a situation marked by edges, borders, accusations, and characters who share both residence in a place but also tensions in their interrelationships.

The next sequence of the story moves in a somewhat similar way, though on the ground rather than down from the sky. As he makes his way into the village, Sŏngsam comes to a particular house that has been turned into the headquarters of the Public Peace Corps, where he sees someone tied up in the handcuff rope used historically as well as into the present time both to restrain and also to mark a prisoner as guilty: "*chairman of the Farmers Collective Committee, this one was, caught hiding out in his own house.*" But the narrative then turns to deconstruct that label of the prisoner as it brings the two friends back together through their recollections of childhood events. Tŏkchae, first presented to the reader tied up in prisoner rope and labeled by the highest rank that local village leaders were given as North Korean troops moved into local territories, turns out to have been the truly filial son, while Sŏngsam, the character through whose eyes the reader first encounters the scene of the story, is revealed to have been the unreliable opportunist who left his own father and young family as he snuck off one night to seek a better fortune in the south.

As the two characters talk, they begin to reconnect through their memories of Short Stuff, the woman Tŏkchae has married. Sŏngsam asks, empathetically, "But don't you think it is suspicious, you hanging around, not trying to get away?" Tŏkchae's answer not only reverses who was the good and loyal son, which he turns out to have been; it also reparses the opening of the story, shifting its entire framework. As Tŏkchae explains why he had stayed in the village despite the warning that those from the south would kill all the men between the ages of seventeen and forty, the reader realizes that the fear in the faces of the villagers at the beginning of the story is not some generalized anxiety related to the conflict, but fear at the sight of Sŏngsam as he walks into his old village, a member of the much feared southern forces, with the reader following closely behind.

For a story published in 1953, this reframing of the meaning of *southern* might have been a hazardous political statement indeed—that the forces of the south could be as murderous as the communists were reported to be. It is also a deft narrative move, forcing the story to double back reiteratively upon itself. Readers may also note that the passage at the very center of the story, the shift in the presentation of Tŏkchae, through Sŏngsam's altering vision of him, from murderous commie to dedicated son and farmer to husband of Short Stuff, is marked by a shift from simple past tense to the present tense. Not nearly as visible in the English translation, there is another shift as well in the resonance of the phrase "sunnuva!" The old grandfather's shout at the boys is "*Yŏnom ŭi chasikdŭl!*" *Chasik* means *offspring*; *nom* means *fellow* in a

Dickensian sense, as in *The Pickwick Papers*. That is, it often means a bad fellow, a verbal prelude to a physical fight. *I noma!* means "This fellow hey!" but more like the English "All right you!" But with different intonation, when said to a well-known pal, it simply means "Hi, it's you." The old grandfather's shout, then, means "You little brats," but also "You children of a guy from here!" The narrative's frequent repetition of the term as Sŏngsam expresses his intention to punish, perhaps kill, Tŏkchae has the effect of invoking the other sense of the term as well, the bond between the two.

The story sweeps to its close with the image of the great white cranes soaring through the clear autumn sky where the story first began. Some find the image too simple, too romantic, not true to the brutal reality of war. I read the cranes as invested with their white-clothed human counterparts, the farmers "in the center of the fields . . . wearing their white clothes, backs bent," and the soaring movement as a deliberate reinvocation of the story's opening, a move that requires the reader to imagine what will happen next, what story will follow. After the two men replay their childhood game of chasing the cranes, where can they go? Can Tŏkchae, having escaped, go back to his village now occupied by the troops from the south? Having lost the prisoner, where can Sŏngsam go? Hwang Sunwŏn's subsequent stories can be read as a continued engagement with the ground-level implications of the questions raised and joined by his 1953 short story "Cranes."

Another
Perspective

by Lee Chang-dong
Translated by Heinz Insu Fenkl

T he mule is gone, thought Taegi. I'll never see him again. His fingers shook as he unbuttoned his pants, and he leaked a few drops before he was quite ready. Facing the tall smokestack of the Slurpy Bar factory across the open sewer, he spewed his piss, his body trembling all the while.

Twilight stretched itself across the sky above the factory. Taegi closed his eyes. That scarlet light—the same glossy sheen of the mule's back when it was brushed, scrubbed, and combed—would vanish without a trace if he opened his eyes to look.

Slowly the scarlet changed into a deep purple, the color of the dried and clotted blood trailing from the mule's dead body. The city was swallowing everything up into its dark abyss once again—the smoke shooting out of the factory smokestack was spreading like ink in water, blotting out the sunset.

Taegi didn't even think of buttoning his pants. He stared vacantly up at the smokestack that rose high into the sky. It stood tall and firm whenever he happened to see it. Taegi looked down at his penis, as if to compare, but it must have been insecure from the start, buried there in his pubic hair, so small and stubby it was nearly invisible. It just lay there inert, shriveled like the remnants of a plucked pepper.

317

But the smokestack—if not for the building that stretched out
beneath it—would have been hard to imagine as a mere factory
chimney. It loomed too high, like a giant tower, a monument, or the
pillar of the world holding up the sky.

Taegi spat, still holding his wilted penis in his hand. He
straightened and tucked it back into his pants, lifted up his bag, and
looked back for a moment at the levy road he had walked along.
He could hear the whirring of the factory and see the mule-colored
twilight descending. Along the open sewer a low, flat housing
project lay wrapped in a silent funk.

The open sewer was thick with the factory's wastewater. It got
the runoff from the dye factory at Sangryo and sometimes it flowed
a brilliant yellow, or as red as a virgin's period. The water was black
and murky now. Last summer a six-year-old kid had drowned in it.
The people in the projects spent all night searching, but the child
was never found.

The projects—that was what they called the houses that
stretched along the bank of the sewer. After a major manufacturing
plant moved in on the other side of town, the civic authorities had
relocated the people who lived there and put them here in houses
made of cement brick. Low and flat, following the sewer—at first
glance they looked like a species of long beetle, and if you looked
closer, they looked like dead, crumbling shells; and the people—
every possible species of them—lived in the projects in hordes,
like ants marching in and out to consume the beetles' dessicated
remains, and Taegi, a part-timer in the city sanitation department,
was one of them.

Across the open sewer, an enormous industrial site was being
constructed. Each day, garbage trucks would speed down the
roadway along the sewer bank, relay after relay, dumping their
loads in the vacant lot not yet occupied by the factory. The garbage
covered the fields and paddies with shocking speed. The city was
like an obese animal that shed its fur each day, or an old man with
intestinal problems puking up everything he had eaten. Taegi

318

worked for the city, loading and hauling that garbage. Twice a day, he led the mule from one side of the city to the other, sweeping and collecting. From where he happened to be—at the garbage dump, or in one of the many partitioned units in the projects—Taegi watched the tall buildings raise their shining heads high above the pale dust at dawn. He saw the fantastic explosions of dust at midday, and at night he heard the breathtaking throbbing sounds of the factory machines.

Now he was about to take his leave of all those things. He slowly shuffled in the direction of the levy road, which was gradually growing dark.

A drunk staggered toward him down the path, mumbling something unintelligible. As he got closer, Taegi realized it was the words of a song.

Yesterday, when we made love,
We become one for the very first time—

"What's this?" The man stopped and brought his face up close under Taegi's chin, stinging his nostrils with the reek of liquor. "Brother Kim, right? Where are you headed?"

Taegi recognized his laugh. It was very familiar, but much to his regret, he couldn't immediately place who this person was.

"Come on, it's me. Me! Don't you recognize me?" He unfastened a few shirt buttons, half exposing his chest, which was flushed from the liquor. His hair was cut short like a draftee's.

It was probably the close-cropped hair that made him hard for Taegi to recognize. But now that he tilted his head back, just the slightest bit, and raised a hand toward his hair as if to brush a long strand away from his face—that habitual gesture made Taegi take a closer look at his face.

"Hey, it's Kidong!"

"Damn! You're sharp! As you can see, I've been drinking."

As far as Taegi knew, Kidong never drank. Everyone who lived

AZALEA

The
Dreaming
Beast:
Lee Chang-
dong

in the projects knew what a miser he was, though he went around wearing garish Hawaiian shirts and pants that hugged his ass. He worked at the Slurpy Bar factory, and all he did from the beginning of the work day was flirt with the female employees. Whenever a girl his age happened to walk by, he wasn't happy until he had stuck his fingers in his mouth and whistled to his heart's content. Taegi was more than familiar with the sound of Kidong's pop songs carrying across the sewer embankment at night.

Kidong wore his hair long. It was his great pride—glossy and stylishly flipped back. Whenever he had a spare moment, the first thing he did was take out his hand mirror so he could admire his hair.

"So, brother, what's your business out here? It's nearly dark." Kidong swayed back and forth, grinning and laughing as if to prove he was drunk. He had an unusual grin, one side of his lip curled up in a sneer, subtly exposing his teeth, one eye squinted shut. It was something he had designed especially to use on the female workers at the Slurpy Bar factory but—perhaps to keep in practice—he used it on everybody.

"You look like an entirely different person," said Taegi.

"Oh," Kidong replied glumly, his energy suddenly gone. "You mean this hair? These things happen." Once again, he tilted his head back and made the sweeping gesture with his hand, as if his hair were still long.

"Let me buy you a drink," he said, pulling Taegi by the arm. "I'll buy you a drink to celebrate getting my hair cut today."

Taegi did not decline. He walked in whichever direction Kidong was leading him. He hadn't intended to tell anyone in the projects that he was leaving, but now that he'd run into Kidong, he didn't see any particular reason to shake him off.

The street converging with others at the entrance to the bridge was already brightly illuminated—the streetlights had come on. With the windfall of industry, the place was suddenly booming: a theater, a tailor shop, a clothing store, a butcher, a beauty salon, a café, a real estate office, and even an employment office, all clustered there. Occasionally the headlights of a car flashed quickly by; light flowed out of the stores lining the street; people staggered out of the drinking establishments, arms flapping in the air—and sometimes they were all lit up, rushing toward your eyes, or spinning in circles. The whole street, now that alcohol had begun to flow, was properly intoxicated, humming, feeling good.

"After tonight, I'm leaving on the first train. . . ."

Kidong stumbled again and clutched Taegi's arm. "So where are you planning to go?"

Perhaps it was because he'd been thinking of leaving, but as he looked at the frenetic energy of the street, it felt to Taegi as if his chest had been hollowed out, as if he'd been the victim of a cold-hearted whore. Even after he was gone, the people who came reeling out of the bars would go back in, the lights in the display windows would still shine, and the street would go on thriving with the energy of a boom town.

"I think I'll leave on the night train."

"Where to? Are you going back home? You got news that your old man's sick?"

"I'm not going back for a visit. It's permanent."

Kidong stopped and whistled sharply. A large group of women was walking by on the other side of the street, as if they were just leaving the factory after work. "What will you do with *him*?" Kidong jabbed his hands into his pockets and strutted with some style now, as if his drunkenness had just evaporated. "I mean the one with four legs."

"He's dead," said Taegi.

Kidong stopped. "Are you kidding?"

≈

As he lay dead in the street, the mule's unfathomably deep eyes were looking upward, as if he were dreaming about something.

AZALEA

The
Dreaming
Beast:
Lee Chang-
dong

The warm steam of his breath still leaked from his nostrils, and the flow of blood from his cracked skull lay sticky on the asphalt. It was the end of him. The cop from the neighborhood police box asked Taegi his name and address and filled out a simple accident report. "I swear it's not my fault. That crazy pony suddenly ran out in front of my truck. No one could have avoided him!" The truck driver laid out his explanation, the nape of his neck gleaming with sweat, his veins bulging. All the while, Taegi just stared silently at the mule's eyes—which looked as if he were still alive, deep in thought about something—and the dark blood covering the surface of the street, beginning to clot. "Hey, why did your pony run out in front of the truck?" asked the cop, turning toward Taegi. "Is this man's explanation correct?" When Taegi did not answer, the driver shouted, incredulously, "Look at him! He knows his pony was crazy!" After listening to several more accounts from witnesses, the cop finished filling out the accident report. But when he wrote that the casualty was a pony, Taegi finally spoke up. "He's not a pony." "What?" The cop lifted his head, narrowing his eyes. "What do you mean it's not a pony?" "He's a mule. Not a pony and not a donkey. He may just be a dead animal, but he deserves to be identified properly. Please write that he was a mule."

~

"That's really sad," Kidong said with an appropriately sympathetic expression. "He was like part of the family in the projects. Why do you suppose he suddenly ran out in front of a truck? He didn't really go crazy, did he?"

"Hey, let's leave it alone now, all right?"

"It means your meal ticket is gone, doesn't it? But then you also get to leave this place. Well, in either case . . ." A food vendor was parked along the street; Kidong pulled Taegi toward the tent wagon. "I can't just send you off quietly, without even a drink, can I? If you're not gonna drink on a day like today, then when? Don't worry about it. There's a train first thing in the morning, and don't you worry about missing it." Kidong pulled the canvas flap aside and entered first.

"Welcome."

"Give us each a glass of *soju* and a skewer of fish cakes with soup," Kidong said.

They perched on the wooden stools.

"From what I've heard . . ." Kidong took a sip of the soup and turned his head toward Taegi. He put his little finger in his mouth, sucked on it loudly and then wiggled it back and forth under Taegi's eyes. "Is it true that the mule had an underdeveloped prick?"

Taegi grabbed Kidong's little finger with one hand and yanked it down. "He wasn't underdeveloped. He just couldn't reproduce."

"It's the same thing, isn't it? I once saw them castrate a pig when I was out in the country and it was so awful I couldn't bear to watch. But they say that after it's cut off, the pig gets fatter and the meat tastes better. So I guess you never know. You learn, but sometimes you don't understand."

The carbide flame flickered and danced in the wind. Kidong carefully picked up one of the *soju* glasses that was turned upside-down on the counter. He peered inside, and continued, "If you really think about it, we're no different from the mule."

The mule's penis was incredibly large. So large that it seemed not to be just a reproductive organ, but an organ designed especially for him. Taegi remembered how at times it would grow to an unbelievable length, as long as a warrior's sword you saw only in movies, so long its tip touched the ground; and he remembered the mule's eyes at those times, glowing like an oak tree in flames. His organ would grow abruptly, at the most unexpected times.

Taegi never understood the mule's strange sexual arousal or why it would start so suddenly in the middle of the city. In the deep shadows between looming apartment buildings, in the middle of the street with traffic rushing by, he would suddenly stop walking and stand there as if his hooves were stakes driven into the earth. At

AZALEA

The
Dreaming
Beast:
Lee Chang-
dong

those times Taegi had no choice but to stand there and wait for the mule's huge erection to calm down. For a long time, the mule would stand, frightening and motionless as he restrained his urges, his two eyes burning as if he were dreaming; and then he would slowly resheath that blade he had drawn, his whole body would tremble, and then he would begin walking again.

"I'll tell you a story. Will you listen?" said Kidong. The second glass of *soju* went into his throat. It was cold going down but hot when it reached his stomach. Kidong put down the glass with a loud *clack!* and began.

"This happened at the factory. As you know, we make hot buns in winter and in summertime we make an ice cream pop called a Slurpy Bar or Slorpy Bar, whatever. . . .Well, a strange rumor was going around this past summer. The heat—it wasn't normal. It was enough to kill perfectly healthy people."

Because of the heat wave, everyone ate Slurpy Bars. On the street, in their homes, at bus stops—people were sucking on them everywhere, and women especially liked them. Whenever Kidong saw some coltish girl sticking a Slurpy Bar in her mouth and shamelessly sucking on it, he couldn't help feeling naked. True, the Slurpy Bar was sweet and cool, but Kidong knew it was a cheap frozen product made of artificial ingredients that gave a passably sweet taste, mixed with plain water, and injected into a vinyl bag.

It was beyond belief, the huge number of Slurpy Bars that melted and disappeared into that huge number of mouths. But if you thought about the people of the city sucking away, it was as simple as this: they did it for the sweet taste and the coolness; it lingered momentarily inside the mouth before it was gone.

Whatever the reason, people wanted Slurpy Bars every summer, and sales were good for the factory. It ran 24 hours a day in two 12-hour shifts, and yet there were always complaints that the product was in short supply. Then a strange rumor started to circulate. It was said that each day, some of the Slurpy Bars in the factory disappeared and piles of empty Slurpy Bar wrappers were found in the women's restroom. The rumor spread like a contagious disease, and soon there was no male factory worker that didn't know about it.

"You know what was going on—according to the rumor?" Kidong stopped talking and emptied the last drop of *soju* from his glass into his mouth. "What does the Slurpy Bar look like, exactly? Something all the girls desire? Same size, same shape?"

As the *soju* went down his throat, Kidong's whole body trembled. He looked over at Taegi's expression. Just then, the owner of the tent wagon raised his face over the hissing flames of the charcoal briquettes and laughed.

"It's true. They look just like the real thing. They probably made them that way on purpose to sell more."

"That's exactly what I'm saying! So whenever they had the chance, the female workers would hide them one at a time and then go off to the bathroom. In that heat. . . it probably gave them chills all the way up to their tits."

"Sounds like a complete lie to me," Taegi said. He watched the fish burning over the charcoal flame, the smelly smoke occluding the interior of the tent like a pale smokescreen.

"True," Kidong nodded, his face red and hot, "but you can't know for sure if it's a lie. I didn't believe it either, at first. Maybe it's a story somebody made up to keep from falling asleep on the night shift. Your body gets heavy, you get drowsy, your eyes sting like they're full of sand. . . . Well, later, there was this other rumor. If the girls kept sneaking off and doing that, they got sick and ended up sterile. Sterile, you know? They couldn't have kids. Because the Slurpy Bars were so cold it wasn't good for women. Like they say, a rumor ends up biting its own tail. Damn it, you should be able to tell how much is a lie and how much is true." Kidong brooded awhile, watching the undulating shapes as the carbide flames grew longer and shorter.

The owner of the wagon tent replied, "Well, you can't know whether that last part was made up by the factory management. You know, to stop the loss of their product."

Azalea

The
Dreaming
Beast:
Lee Chang-
dong

"In any case," said Kidong, "the story about the female workers getting sterile is a serious mood killer. Give us another round here. No—give us a whole bottle."

"Don't overdo it. You're already drunk," said Taegi.

"What's the matter? Like I said, if you don't drink on a day like today, then when do you drink?" Kidong quickly lifted the bottle of *soju* that was in front of the owner and poured. His enormous shadow trembled where it was projected on the canvas inside the tent.

"Think about how many female workers are in the factory. Lots of those girls are pretty. I even poked a few of them myself. You see their faces going into the factory at the beginning of the morning shift, all gleaming in the sunlight, and it really makes your sap rise. Their work area is separated from the men's, but I see them coming out at lunch time and sitting on the grass in their green uniforms. I can't stand not whistling at them. But, Kim, to say they can't have children—how would that make *you* feel?"

It *was* a real mood killer. It had been a long time since Taegi had had an erection. The Slurpy Bar factory operated continuously, 24 hours a day in two shifts, day and night. The 6 A.M. siren that signaled the change in shifts was what chased Taegi from sleep each morning. As he awoke, the very first thing Taegi would do was to reach into his shorts, slowly sliding his hands down his belly to where his penis hung, until he felt it with his fingertips. He aspired to see his penis hard and erect, but that hope went unfulfilled, and each time he held in his hand a shriveled member—with no vitality and no pulse. It was soft and pliable like a fish cake limp from being dunked in hot soup.

From the time he had left home to come up to the city, Taegi had not been able to get it up, no matter what. At home, imbued with the fresh power of the ocean at dawn, his penis had stood as stiff as the base of a bush clover, poking his shorts up into a little tent. That was how it used to be. But here, from the time he had started dragging the mule from one corner of the city to the other with white dust coating the rims of his nostrils, it had just wilted without a pulse. Taegi thought of himself as a cripple. A prick that can't stand has no use, and since his tool was useless, he was the most pitiful of cripples.

"Hey, since we already brought it up, how about one more?" Kidong's face grew redder and redder and his speech was less inhibited. "I also heard this at the factory. The old man who's the president of the company—he's got tons of money, the factory is running smoothly, his kids all got their turn going to America to study and now they're managing director and executive VP. What worries could he have? But like they say, there's no end to human greed. These days he keeps fresh young girls around himself all the time to enhance his vitality. Quality-assured fresh virgins."

"Enhance his vitality by having girls around? He'd probably drain it," the owner pitched in as he put the fishcake skewers in front them.

"You don't know what you're talking about," said Kidong. "Girls gushing all over with their sexual energy—as long as he doesn't screw them, all that energy gets absorbed by him. There's no medicine as powerful as that for cultivating an old man's *yang*."

"Damn, it's a strange world these days. Not enough brains to imagine that stuff."

"Yeah, but it helps to have plenty of money. Hey, why are you getting up?"

"I've got to go now." As he stood up, Taegi realized that he had gotten quite drunk in that short time.

"Sit down. I'll pay," said Kidong. "Hey!"

Taegi settled the bill, hugged his bag to his side, and staggered out, pushing the tent flap aside.

"Are you really leaving today?" Kidong followed, close by his side, staggering to the same rhythm. "I'll walk you to the station. We can't just part like this, can we?"

They walked, scrawling nonsense on the ground with their footsteps. They crossed the intersection at the walk signal and

AZALEA

*The
Dreaming
Beast:
Lee Chang-
dong*

passed a bank with its shutters down, then a brightly lit display window, still open. In front of a dark building that was under construction, the two of them stopped simultaneously. They stood shoulder-to-shoulder, facing a wall, and started to piss. Taegi's stream was a mess—drunk, his penis was like a broken rubber water gun—and it scattered weakly at his feet.

Suddenly, Kidong doubled over. He belched and started puking on the ground. Taegi pounded his back.

Kidong stuck his fingers in his mouth and finished throwing up. "Just look at us!" He got up, tears welling in his eyes, and took his wallet out of his back pocket. He handed Taegi something—a promotional photo. "Look at who it is."

It was done in imitation of a pop singer or a movie star, a typical ad or a show poster. In the picture, Kidong's hair was beautifully long and he had that oddly crooked smile, one side of the lip curled up in his usual sneer.

"I may look like this now, but I used to have the most fashionable hair at the factory. And this is a secret, Kim. Do you know who did my hair? The top barber in the city. And it was for free."

Kidong's face shone pale in the darkness. Again he made that gesture with his hand—flipping back his long hair to show it off. But his hair was so short now even the strongest wind couldn't have mussed it, and when Taegi saw that odd gesture it felt as if he had an itch—in that certain spot in the middle of his back where his hand couldn't reach.

"I used to get my hair cut once a week. I'm a model. You know what I'm saying, right? 'Number One Beauty Academy.' Once a week I sat up there in front of the students and the instructor did my hair. In the current hottest style." Kidong made an effort to stand up straight and shook his head as if he had a headache. "I had my hair cut today. It's Sunday and the factory's closed, and as I was coming back after my haircut a cop called me from the local police box. And do you know what he said to me? After I'd just had my hair cut? He said it was too long! And he cited me right there.

But wouldn't you know it—he was a real master at diagnosing my crime." Kidong giggled, and flapping his arms around, he shouted, "Exhibits antisocial tendencies and clear potential for criminal behavior!"

Taegi looked at the vigorous energy of the booming city, the lights suspended along the street spinning round and round before his eyes. He realized there had never been a time when he was part of it. He was just a part-time employee of the City Sanitation Department. When he dragged the mule from one corner of the city to the other, sweeping up, he was just cleaning up the garbage spat out by the thriving city, a city that had nothing to do with him.

"You know, I realized maybe it was a mistake to bring that animal with me here in the first place."

"What's that?"

"A city is no place for a mule to live."

People would gather around the mule and watch, laughing and giggling. Once the mule was aroused it was as if all four of his hooves were staked into the ground—he was helpless and immovable, and his organ, growing to that incredible length, was something they liked to gawk at. When they saw his gun barrel protruding down, frightfully grand, they marveled, they laughed lewdly, they pointed; and the neighborhood brats would throw stones and laugh uproariously. But even then, the mule seemed unconcerned. He would look up at that certain spot in space, piercing it with his gaze, and he exuded a frightening aura, as if he were dreaming something. Why the mule had begun to get sexually aroused in the middle of the city, what he was visualizing behind his eyes, what he was dreaming—Taegi, for the life of him, could not understand.

"What do you plan to do when you go back home?" Kidong asked in a voice now low and gloomy.

For a long time, Taegi looked out at the city's vitality, the darkness growing brighter and brighter. "You know, I never thought about it. I'm just going back there because it's where I was born."

329

AZALEA

The
Dreaming
Beast:
Lee Chang-
dong

But when they reached the train station later, Taegi found his path blocked. The waiting room was so jammed with people that he and Kidong had to push a path between them to get inside. A crowd of campers, who looked to be about college age, had spread out so densely there was hardly room to place a foot between them. Taegi realized it was Sunday—they had probably been camping at a nearby sightseeing spot and were on their way home. And now, though they were squatting on the floor waiting for their train, they still exuded the fresh energy of the mountain as they played their guitars, kept time clapping, and sang along. The small half-moon aperture of the ticket window was firmly shut. A sheet of white paper taped above it read, "Today's tickets sold out."

"Damn, it's just like they say," Kidong complained as he watched the young girls clapping and laughing. "Every time you want to go somewhere, it's a market day."

"This isn't a market day, it's more like a celebration."

"If it's a party, then we're uninvited guests." They looked at each other and laughed.

When Taegi saw the closed ticket window, he had had the strange feeling he already knew it would be like this. There was nothing he could to do but take the train the next morning.

They walked out of the station plaza as the speaker behind them announced departure times.

"Where will you go now?" asked Kidong.

The light changed at the crossing and people walked out onto the street, but the two of them stood there. Shutters were coming down over the storefronts. The light had suddenly waned into darkness, and people hurried by.

"What wretched luck, huh? Are you going back to your place now?"

"I'll spend the night here somewhere and take the first train in the morning," said Taegi.

At the bus stop, people were running back and forth looking for their buses.

"Wait here—just a moment," Kidong said, suddenly running toward the darkness of the station plaza.

Taegi clicked his tongue. Kidong had a nose like a dog—even in the dark, he had spotted a couple of young women in the distance. He said something to them, and at first Taegi thought Kidong's charm must have worked, because he could see one of the girls walking back with him. But Kidong seemed oddly reluctant. The girl was clinging to his arm, pressing herself tightly to his side.

"Is this him?"

Up close, Taegi could see the sloppy makeup job on her face.

"Come on," she said. "We'll give you the best service." She tugged on his arm.

"What the hell is this?"

"Well, I thought they were two girls who came to go hiking and missed their train," Kidong said.

The girl burst out laughing. Busy passersby turned to look disapprovingly, and Kidong stood there not knowing what to do. The girl was clinging to him like a leech.

"I'll give you a discount. It's like fate, after all, isn't it?"

Taegi roughly removed the girl's hand, but then she grabbed hold of his belt and shouted, like she was making an announcement to everyone, "Look! This man has a tiny penis!"

Taegi cringed, as if he had pissed his pants, and turned around. The girl was still laughing—a properly coquettish laugh. She made as if to bury her face in his shoulder and said in a nasal voice, "Ho ho. . . . You should have cooperated in the first place."

The girl stood between Taegi and Kidong and walked with her elbows linked in theirs. They turned down an alley of squalid buildings that stretched out, shoulder-to-shoulder, with plexiglass signs reading, "Female Boarders" and "Student Lodging."

The girl stopped in front of one of the boarding houses. As they stepped inside, a fat middle-aged woman with disheveled hair slid open a frosted window and stuck her face out.

"How many?"

AZALEA

The

Dreaming

Beast:

Lee Chang-

dong

"Two," said the girl.

The middle-aged woman looked them up and down. A nauseating smell wafted in from somewhere. Taegi avoided her eyes and Kidong lowered his head and let out a quiet, fake cough.

"They have to pay in advance."

"All right."

The woman looked them up and down once again, then slid the frosted window shut with a bang.

"Take your shoes off and bring them with you," said the girl. "Come with me."

By the light of the mini bulb dangling from the boarding house ceiling, the girl's face, with its heavy makeup, looked different than it had on the dark street. The dim light brought out a pale carnality that made their hearts beat fast, and the two men were momentarily stunned; they obediently picked up their shoes and stepped up onto the raised wooden floor of the hall. The stairs creaked with each step, and in front of them, the girl's hips swayed back and forth in synch with the sound.

Kidong abruptly grabbed Taegi's arm. "Kim. . . . I – I'm losing my nerve. What do I do?"

"What are you talking about?"

With a shoe in each hand, Kidong looked at Taegi, and with great effort, he forced a laugh. "To tell you the truth, I've never done anything like this before. I'm starting to shake. . . ."

"What are you guys doing? Hurry up!" the girl called from the top of the stairs.

They glanced at each other's faces. "Damn it. . . ."

Kidong went up the stairs first. As his eyes came level with the floor, the first thing he saw was the girl's legs. Behind her there was a narrow hallway just wide enough to let a single person pass. More mini bulbs hung from the ceiling. There were three doors. The girl opened the one to the room at the end of the hall.

The same wallpaper pattern, old and discolored with dark blotches, covered the entire room. The ceiling was the same veneer as the hall with water stains here and there from rain leaking in. On the wall hung a single picture cut from a calendar. An actress smiling, in a suggestive swimsuit that covered her anatomy in such a way that after a first look you would immediately have to look again, more carefully. They stared up at it vacantly, as if by agreement, because it was the only familiar thing in the room. The actress—she was so familiar they felt as if they were in her room; and her naked smile—so gracious, telling them they could have anything they desired from her—quickly put them at ease with their private fantasies.

"Ho, ho. . . . You guys come into a girl's room and have such grave expressions. Like you're at someone's funeral," said the girl. When she entered the room, the atmosphere seemed less charged.

"There's two of us. Why only one of you?"

"You worry too much. A girl's got to get herself properly ready for her wedding night." She let down her hair, which had been split into two tails.

The second girl came in. She had permed hair, and with her skirt hiked up above her knees so they could have an eyeful, she plopped herself down and handed them the bill for the night.

When they had paid, the girl with the perm said, "It's time to pair up. The one who's sleeping with me go over to the room across the hall." She looked at the two of them one at a time. "Who's going?"

Her hand hesitated for a moment over Kidong's knee, but then she gripped and squeezed, making him blush. Kidong stood up, wavering, as helpless as if he were pulled by an irresistible force. The girl laughed and supported him with her arm around his back.

Before the door closed, Kidong turned to look back at Taegi, hesitating, as if he were about to say something. But the girl pushed him, and as he went, the only thing he could communicate was his twisted smile with the curled lip. It seemed to linger even after the veneered door slammed shut.

Taegi sat with his back against the wall, feeling absolutely lost. The tiny room was so stuffy he felt like he couldn't breathe in it, but

AZALEA

The
Dreaming
Beast:
Lee Chang-
dong

at the same time, he felt as if he had been cast out, all alone, onto a vast and empty plain.

The girl got up quietly. She spread out the blankets that were folded up on one side of the room and stood in front of Taegi. Facing him, with a voice full of modesty, she said, "Please receive my greeting."

She drew her hands together at eye level and slowly knelt, lowering her head. It was an old-fashioned traditional bride's bow. Taegi watched her, bewildered. "My name is Mija," she said, still on her knees. "I am at your service."

Taegi had no idea what to do.

The girl suddenly lifted her head and burst out laughing. "Ho, ho. . . . That expression on your face—you look just like a new groom."

She walked over toward the wall on her knees and flipped a switch down. Suddenly the room was filled with utter darkness.

Taegi knew exactly what he was supposed to do then, but he could not move his body. All those words, separated by thin partitions in his head, full of restless rustling sounds that came from some unknown place—suddenly they stopped and there was not a single sound.

"You want to hear about a dream I had?" the girl said as she lay there. "I had it last night. In the dream, you know, I wore really nice clothes. I was made up pretty and I was waiting for someone. People were all making a big fuss—brushing my hair and fixing my makeup. The person coming to see me must have been some really handsome big shot. But I didn't know who it was. My heart was pounding. I was looking at my beautifully made-up face in the mirror, and I just waited for that guy to come quickly. And then I woke up. Isn't it strange?"

To Taegi it sounded like the girl's voice came from a dim and distant place. Though he tried to drag his body up to the other side, he was sunk in the depths of the earth beyond the reach of hands. His entire body was paralyzed, stiff—he couldn't move a finger.

He saw the image of the mule hit by the truck, sprawled out in the middle of the street. Even after death the mule's eyes were still open, gazing upwards as if he were dreaming. What was he dreaming? When he returned after lunch, he knew the mule was aroused again. The neighborhood brats were sitting around him laughing and giggling. His huge penis was stretched out to its full awesome length, long enough to touch the ground. He saw the kids put a long thing up to his penis. It looked like a pole, but by the time he realized it was a metal rod they had heated in a fire, it was too late. The mule raised his head and let out a terrifying shriek. The kids scattered like mountain rain and the mule ran, mad with pain, into the middle of the street, into the flood of backed-up traffic. Though he lay with his head on the asphalt, his eyes were still gazing into space as if he were alive. Those steady eyes, deep in thought and steeped in dream.

"Would you like a Slurpy Bar?" the girl said into his ear, her voice sticky and surreptitious in the darkness. And before he could even be shocked, she pushed something soft and warm into his mouth.

"It's a *real* Slurpy Bar—you can suck it for free. I'm letting you have it as a special treat on the house."

A young woman's breast, unbelievably soft and pliable. Taegi touched her carefully, treasuring her as if she had endured so much wear and tear that she might fall to pieces at any moment. A vague sadness surged through him in waves, and behind it he felt the hot blood coming, filling him. His throat dry with an unbearable desire, he called out to the girl, "Hey!"

"Don't 'Hey' me. Call me by my name. I told you my name is Mija."

The girl stroked him gently. A few strands of her long hair caught between Taegi's lips, and the fishy smell, which made him want to spit and curse, wafted around inside his mouth.

"Mija?"

"Yes, sir?" The girl answered in hoarse whisper, her body pressed close to his.

Azalea

*The
Dreaming
Beast:
Lee Chang-
dong*

Taegi swallowed back a wad of hot saliva. "Can you have a baby?"

She made no sound for a long time, but then she let out a high, lilting laugh. Taegi looked into the inky darkness that filled the tiny room, stubbornly waiting for her answer.

"You know, that dream I told you about?" she said, restraining her laughter. "It's a lie. It's a story I made up. I tell that same dream to every one of my customers. I tell them I had that dream last night and I ask them to interpret it for me. Every one of their interpretations is different. And each of those times I think things will happen exactly like the interpretation. 'That's a big deal!' 'Be careful not to get carbon monoxide poisoning.' 'It's a dream that you're gonna win big in the lottery if you buy a ticket.' Do you know what one guy said? He said he was a genuine psychic and the dream meant I was going to have a baby. . . ."

The girl fondled Taegi's body, her hands methodically covering each and every corner, one side to the other. The inside of his mouth grew parched with desire, and from that certain corner of his body something stood up, squirming. Taegi knew what it was. It was his lifeless, wilted organ, and it was rising—unbelievably—like fresh bamboo shoots poking their heads up through the earth, still damp in the morning with fallen rain. As it grew, Taegi felt an unbearable joy overtake his whole body. It rose, grand and arrogant, towering, pointing up at the sky like the thing he saw across the sewer each morning—the smokestack of the Slurpy Bar factory.

In the darkness, Taegi felt around for her sheath, and into it he slipped his blade, so stiff it was on the verge of snapping.

~

Taegi opened his eyes at first light. The interior of the tiny room was dimly lit by the morning sun. He could see the dark blotches on the wallpaper. The girl was still sleeping.

Taegi listened for a moment to the quiet sounds of the street—cars, people talking loudly, things he couldn't quite make out.

Now a beam of light pierced the girl's hair, tangled like a wad of threads, and illuminated her upper lip. Her mouth was half open in a faint smile. Taegi put on his clothes carefully so as not to wake her from her sweet dream.

As he walked down the wooden stairs and came out into the alley, the main thoroughfare outside was already congested with traffic. With the morning sun reflecting from their glossy tops, the cars flashed quickly by like silver arrows. It was a fresh morning—for everything. Someone tapped Taegi on the shoulder.

"I thought you had left by yourself," said Kidong.

Taegi took his hand. They looked at each other like two people just meeting. But Taegi could see Kidong's hair growing, growing beautifully like the mule's mane gleaming blindingly in the morning sun.

"Are you really going?" asked Kidong.

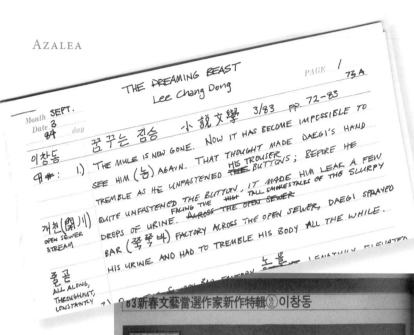

Another
Perspective

Heinz Insu Fenkl

first started translating Lee Chang-dong's "The Dreaming Beast" late in the summer of 1984, a few days after I arrived in Seoul to begin my Fulbright Fellowship. I had read it the previous year in a literary journal called *Sosŏlmunhak*, a publication that came free-of-charge with the Korean women's magazine my mother often bought at the local Korean market in Marina, California. I still have those first several pages of translation notes neatly printed in technical pen, dated September 3rd.

"The Dreaming Beast" was a timely story for me to read in 1984. I had studied psychoanalytic theory as a graduate student, so I was both fascinated and puzzled by Lee's overt depiction of sexuality and use of sexual symbolism. How to convey his simultaneously conventional and unusual use of that imagery in English translation was a problem I could not tackle at that time.

What struck me about the story—and I remember this very clearly—was how its imagery seemed to transcend the words that conveyed it. The language wasn't all that elegant—in fact, it was rather coarse in places and sometimes awkward—and yet there was a visceral quality to the images that outlasted the dispersal of words in memory. I held the images of that story in my head permanently—like the memory of a good film. The only words I recalled from it, for many years, were the characters' names, Taegi and Kidong, and

AZALEA

On Lee
Chang-
dong:

Heinz

Insu Fenkl

the odd Slurpy Bar; and I remember that I had initially misread *nosae* (mule) as *noŭl* (twilight). The image of Taegi looking out across the twilit sewer at the looming smokestack—that stayed with me as vividly as my own experiences. Perhaps it was because I had grown up outside ASCOM, the American army post near Inchon, which also had an open sewer along one of its boundaries with the local town of Pup'yŏng. You could see smokestacks from outside in the local camptown the GI's called "Sinchon."

When I saw the film *Oasis* last year, I felt an odd familiarity. It was as if the camera were my own consciousness playing memories back at me. In the opening scenes, when Jong-du, freezing in his Hawaiian shirt, does something as simple as eat the brick of tofu (a traditional ritual after release from prison), I felt tears well up in my eyes. He was just like a cousin of mine. The particulars of the world he lived in—oddly down to specific camera angles—were those I remembered from my own life, and the use of illumination—from the mundane scenes to the fantasy sequences—also felt oddly familiar to me. I did not realize that Lee Chang-dong was the director until I watched the DVD for the second time.

I went back to look for "The Dreaming Beast," digging up my old translation notes and the original text. The magazine itself was badly yellowed, the cheap newsprint having decomposed via its own acid in the intervening years. Something about the shadows of branches projected on the oasis tapestry in the film had also reminded me of "The Dreaming Beast"—its weird title page from back in the days before Photoshop. And there he was, Lee Chang-dong, looking oddly feral in his puffy coat, posed in front of a painting of tigers.

Even while it generated a great deal of controversy, *Oasis* won numerous international awards. In 2002, Lee won the Chief Dan George Humanitarian Award at the Vancouver International Film Festival and he won Best Director, the FIPRESCI Award, and the Cinema Verine Prize at the Venice International Film Festival. Moon So-ri, who played Kong-ju, won Best Actress in Venice in

340

2002 and at the Seattle Film Festival in 2003, where Sol Kyung-goo also won Best Actor for his characterization of Jong-du. Lee had established himself as a significant force in the world of film, a director whom many now consider Korea's best. And yet many of my Korean friends had found *Oasis* impossible to watch because of the visceral discomfort it aroused; nearly all of the Western critics tended to note this excruciating quality, though they understood it as an integral part of the film's themes.

I think that for Koreans, *Oasis* was, in an ironic way, too familiar, too close to home. It was a brutally realistic depiction of a part of Korean society that many found embarrassing and dissonant. Lee certainly understood precisely which buttons to push. But for those who could endure the discomfort, *Oasis* also offered a kind of transcendent release by its conclusion, and this was not only due to its power of characterizations and the underlying moral consciousness; a lot of the film's force had to do with the technique behind its cinematography, which I found to be already present back in the early '80s in Lee's first major short story.

~

"The Dreaming Beast" is a narrative about the underlying human cost of industrial development. At its outset we are presented with a deceptively simple set of symbolic contrasts as the main character, Taegi, gazes across an open sewer at the towering smokestack of the Slurpy Bar factory. Taegi's mule has just died, hit by a truck, and he is comparing his own shriveled member to the gigantic phallic symbol whose smoke is blotting out the twilight. It's a particularly vivid and cinematic moment in the story; it serves as an imagistic establishing shot, but in this case what Lee establishes are not only character and setting, but the central tropes that propel the story.

On the one hand "The Dreaming Beast" is, to the Korean reader, a simultaneous homage to and response to a spectrum of modern short fiction. There are major allusions, for example, to Sŏnu Hwi's "The Season When the Buckwheat Blooms," Kim Sŭng-ok's "Seoul, Winter, 1964," and Hwang Sunwŏn's "Twilight." The agrarian sentimentalism, urban existentialism, and nostalgic confessionalism of these three stories play throughout "The Dreaming Beast," paralleling it to its subtexts; but Lee pays homage to these works in a way characteristic of film and not literature. The allusions are not made into literary collage for the sake of irony or satire; they are here to create a palimpsest-like quality. Lee updates his subtexts, sometimes critically, while remaining respectful of their spirit. Those previous stories form the infrastructure of this one in the way the history of narrative film integrally weaves through any contemporary film as part of its technical and aesthetic infrastructure. The allusions are layered under the surface of the story, so "The Dreaming Beast" doesn't play like a Tarantino film, which relies on the viewer's conscious response to allusion; it is more like a Wim Wenders film, whose allusions are more organic.

342

Of course, what I am trying to show is that the story plays ultimately like an early example of a Lee Chang-dong film conveyed in text.

Here, for example, is the opening of Hwang Sunwŏn's "Twilight":

> It was an enchanting twilight, a brilliant twilight that seemed to spread its evening radiance like a giant fan across the horizon, and then, in an imperceptible instant, to fold it up again. The scarlet, so clear until now, was turning a deeper shade of red. Was it the season, now verging on autumn, that made the twilight as beautiful as this? Or was it because the sky had just cleared after a hard rain and the clouds were dispersed so lightly like cotton across the western sky?
>
> A twilight this beautiful was only visible once in a lifetime, and yet it could disappear at any moment.

Hwang's title is actually "*Chŏnyŏk Noŭl*" (literally "Evening Twilight"), and the passage sets us up for a confessional story full of nostalgia and sentimentalism. Lee begins "The Dreaming Beast" very bluntly, with "*Nosaenŭn chigŭm ŏpda*"—literally, "The mule is now gone." He plays on that odd association of *nosae* and *noŭl* (mule and twilight) before presenting his own description of a twilight, alluding to Hwang's, that turns it into the image of the dead mule, still figuratively present:

> Twilight stretched itself across the sky above the factory. Taegi closed his eyes. That scarlet light—the same glossy sheen as the mule's back when it was brushed, scrubbed, and combed—would vanish without a trace if he opened his eyes to look.
>
> Slowly the scarlet changed into a deep purple, the color of the dried and clotted blood trailing from the mule's dead body. The city was swallowing everything up into its dark abyss once again—the smoke shooting out of the factory smokestack was spreading like ink in water, blotting out the sunset.

AZALEA

On Lee
Chang-
dong:
Heinz
Insu Fenkl

Hwang's story includes an important moment in which the young boy gets up at night to pee; Lee's opening scene happens while Taegi is pissing. While Hwang's "Twilight" hinges its tragedy on a woman's pregnancy (i.e., her fertility), Lee's story hinges much of its thematic power on the issue of fertility (i.e., the possibility of a prostitute conceiving a child by the figuratively castrated Taegi). This sort of parallel interweaving of allusions also happens with Lee's numerous other subtexts, and I would not have noticed had I not translated Hwang's "Twilight" back in 1984, shortly after reading "The Dreaming Beast."

This syncretism of allusion was difficult for me to convey as the translator; it was one of those problems that makes for easy rationalization and avoidance. Perhaps for a Western reader, unfamiliar with modern Korean fiction, these qualities are not necessary to point out. But many of Lee's subtexts now exist in English translation. Is it the translator's job to re-create allusions in the target language to other previously translated texts? Perhaps, ideally.

≈

It was especially difficult for me to convey the sense of ironic earnestness in "The Dreaming Beast." On the surface, the imagery in the story is easy to read in English as Freudian hyperbole. It would be very difficult for a Western story to pull off the apparent symbolism without being self-consciously sarcastic, satirical, comic, or absurd. Yet in Korean (circa 1981), these symbolisms are not Freudian symbols. They are simultaneously more matter-of-fact and more profound. In conjunction with the action in the story, they produce an effect that closely approximates what Lee does two decades later in *Oasis*, which also succeeds in transcending a set of potential pitfalls and, despite its predominantly mundane surface, creates something both viscerally powerful and aesthetically elegant. What a Western reader might take as a use of universal

Freudian sexual symbology is integrated with culturally specific allusions. Let me begin by talking about a parallelism that occurs at the level of action and is thus most *visible* in both works.

There is a particularly touching moment in *Oasis* when the mentally retarded Hong Jong-du asks about Han Kong-ju's name. He tells her that he is the 18th-generation descendant of a great general named Hong Kyung-rae. He resolves to call her "Your Highness" and she calls him "General." He bows to her, as if she were receiving him in state. The scene is heartwarming, but as a depiction of a mentally retarded man playing general with a physically disabled woman playing national princess, it is also an uncomfortable mockery, a political statement. As Kong-ju explains to Jong-du, his ancestor was not so much a great general as a traitor to the state.

By the end of the film, the political allegory becomes clear. In a country in which the state and the family are analogous, in which Confucian familialism remains both a corporate and national ideology, Jong-du betrays his family as his ancestor betrayed the nation. Likewise, Kong-ju's family has exploited her handicap (abandoning her in a dark and dumpy apartment, leaving her vulnerable to rape) in the same way the nation has exploited its

AZALEA

On Lee
Chang-
dong:
Heinz
Insu Fenkl

young women. "Princess" is a Korean euphemism for prostitute, particularly in the term *yang kongju*, "Yankee Princess," meaning a prostitute who services American soldiers. Jong-du is also the *18th*-generation descendant of Hong Kyung-rae. In Korean, 18 (*ship p'al*) sounds like "to fuck" (*ship hal*). Indeed, Jong-du initially rapes Kong-ju, and though that incident goes undetected by Kong-ju's family, it is their discovery of consensual sex between the two characters that results in the ironic rape charge that precipitates the ending of the film.

"The Dreaming Beast," also features an important bowing scene in which Taegi and the prostitute act out the ritual of the wedding night, with the layers of irony similar to those in *Oasis*:

> The girl got up quietly. She spread out the blankets that were folded up on one side of the room and stood in front of Taegi. Facing him, with a voice full of modesty, she said, "Please receive my greeting."
>
> She drew her hands together at eye level and slowly knelt, lowering her head. It was an old-fashioned traditional bride's bow. Taegi watched her, bewildered. "My name is Mija," she said, still on her knees. "I am at your service."
>
> Taegi had no idea what to do.
>
> The girl suddenly lifted her head and burst out laughing. "Ho, ho. . . . That expression on your face—you look just like a new groom."

This is a parallel inversion of the scene in *Oasis*, in which the "general" bows to the "princess." Here the "bride" bows to the "groom," but instead of a real bride and groom, we have a charged set of stand-ins. Taegi is a part-time garbage man with a small penis, and his name ironically evokes "great flag" (implying the pole) or "great *qi*"; though without the *hanja* we may read it as "abomination," "abhorrence," "great talent," or even "atmosphere"— all in keeping with the interwoven themes in the story. Hardening the T sound in Taegi's name to TT turns it into the diminutive suffix *ttaegi*, which is similar to "-ling," in keeping with his small member. Bowing to him is a prostitute in thick make-up, who calls herself Mija, literally "beautiful child," which, in the context of the story, also invokes "beautiful letter" (or, for a glimpse of nationalist politics, "American master"; the sound of her name is as close to *mijae* as Kidong's is to *kidung*).

What Mija says to Taegi when she bows to him does not translate easily because of the underlying cultural context. In Korean, what she says is actually "*Chal put'ak hamnida,*" which translates, literally, as a petition for Taegi to treat her well. Even when the sentence has become a figure of speech in Korean, its irony tinges the scene with complex layers of resonance. It is a mockery of the wedding night; it reminds the reader that johns typically abuse prostitutes; it reveals Mija's irrational and pathetic hopes tempered by harsh sarcasm; and yet it also evokes sentimentality and nostalgia.

Like *Oasis*, "The Dreaming Beast" ends shortly after a sex scene in which the complex tropes (that play out the theme of growing industrial power and diminishing human *qi*, or life force) all converge in what would, on the surface, appear to be an obtrusive Freudian cliché:

> In the darkness, Taegi felt around for her sheath, and into it he slipped his blade, so stiff it was on the verge of snapping.

But once again, the story transcends its conventional symbolism through its orchestration of the imagery that follows—imagery, which I found, in retrospect, to be highly appropriate for a writer who was destined to become a major director. Since it involves the central trope of light and illumination, I will begin by discussing a couple of prominent examples of its use in *Oasis*, where it is actually visible to the viewer, before returning to the ending of "The Dreaming Beast."

AZALEA

On Lee
Chang-
dong:
Heinz
Insu Fenkl

In two of *Oasis*'s scenes—which some critics have called "magical realist"—Kong-ju plays with her hand mirror and, contorting her face with effort, her hand gnarled by cerebral palsy, she reflects sunlight onto the ceiling of her dim apartment. The bright patches of light transform into white doves that flutter about in her room. Later, after she smashes her mirror, the fragmented pieces reflect smaller patches of light that become white butterflies. The doves and butterflies exist only for her—when other characters enter the scene, they turn back into mere blobs of reflected light.

Through this technique, Lee visually represents Kong-ju's imagination for the viewer. We understand, intuitively, that we are seeing Kong-ju's fantasy made real for us. This idea carries over into the main fantasy episode in the film, in which Jong-du and Kong-ju are dancing, the images in the oasis tapestry coming alive in the room, and we see Kong-ju, for the first time, the way she would

appear if she were "normal." This technique makes its counterpoint use of shadow and darkness all the more poignant: when we see the image that frightens Kong-ju—the quivering black silhouettes of the bare tree branches, reminiscent of her contorted fingers, projected onto the oasis tapestry—Lee does not visualize her imagination for us. The *viewer's* imagination amplifies the terror in the same way a horror film engages the viewer's to represent the unimaginable monster.

At the very end of *Oasis*, in its denouement, Lee floods the interior of Kong-ju's apartment with new light, and though she is reading Jong-du's correspondence from prison, the tone is romantically optimistic. All the trauma and negativity of "the night before" has been transformed into a bright condition full of hope and potential. As Kong-ju sweeps her apartment with a hand

AZALEA

*On Lee
Chang-
dong:
Heinz
Insu Fenkl*

broom, the dust motes float in the air like luminescent snowflakes.

"The Dreaming Beast" ends similarly, with the trope of light transforming an earlier darkness, both literal and figurative. The story, if you recall, opens with an ominous image of darkness:

> The city was swallowing everything up into its dark abyss once again—the smoke shooting out of the factory smokestack was spreading like ink in water, blotting out the sunset.

At the end, just after the obtrusive knife-into-sheath scene, Lee reiterates the movement of the story as a whole by beginning once again with darkness. Then, he slowly brings up the light (I have italicized the relevant words for clarity):

> Taegi opened his eyes at *first light*. The interior of the tiny room was *dimly lit* by the *morning sun*. He could see the dark blotches on the wallpaper. The girl was still sleeping.

> Taegi listened for a moment to the quiet sounds of the street—cars, people talking loudly, things he couldn't quite make out.

Now *a beam of light* pierced the girl's hair, tangled like a wad of threads, and *illuminated* her upper lip. Her mouth was half open in a faint smile. Taegi put on his clothes carefully so as not to wake her from her sweet dream.

. . . .

With the *morning sun reflecting* from their *glossy* tops, the cars *flashed* quickly by like silver arrows. It was a fresh morning—for everything. Someone tapped Taegi on the shoulder.

"I thought you had left by yourself," said Kidong.

Taegi took his hand. They looked at each other like two people just meeting. But Taegi could see Kidong's hair growing, growing beautifully like the mule's mane *gleaming blindingly* in the *morning sun.*

"Are you really going?" asked Kidong.

The story ends with the same optimistic and post-cathartic affect as *Oasis*. The figuratively castrated Taegi and Kidong have proved their potency. Kidong, whose name could be read as "wonderful child," "prodigy," or "starter," had been sheared like the biblical

AZALEA

*On Lee
Chang-
dong:

Heinz
Insu Fenkl*

Samson, but now his hair is growing back as light. In fact, Lee seems to be playing with the resonance of Kidong with *kidung*, and the revitalized Samson pushing down the pillars of the Philistine temple (before Delilah cut off his hair, Samson killed 1,000 Philistines with the jawbone of an ass). *Kidung sŏbang* also happens to be a reference to a pimp, and Kidong was the one who procured the prostitute, albeit by accident. Together, with the combined physiognomy of their names, Taegi and Kidong symbolically knock down the polluting smokestack and replace the polluted darkness with a bright new atmosphere.

∼

My purpose, as a translator, is to convey qualities of the original work that go beyond the surface of the text, to weave together the effect of underlying connotations while trying, at the same time, to provide lexical equivalents of words. The process requires a kind of kabbalistic imagination, especially necessary for a language like Korean, in which multilayered wordplay is so prominent. It also requires—at least for me—a clear interpretation of the text I am translating. I need to believe I know what the story is *really* about on its various levels before I can re-create its effect in English. (To give an extreme example, I could not finish my translation of Jo Kyung-ran's "Looking for the Elephant" until I was able to re-create her Polaroid Spectra photo of the elephant.)

By the time I completed the first draft of my translation of "The Dreaming Beast," I was analyzing its prefiguring of *Oasis*. I had also realized that the inexplicably redemptive/transcendent ending of *Oasis* somehow works like confession and absolution. I have come to believe that *Oasis*'s true power is in demonstrating to viewers the universality of Jung-du and Kong-ju; suggesting that we, like them, have potential for goodness trapped within deceptive surfaces that may be willfully misunderstood, abused, and exploited by society. This element of universality may relate to many viewers'

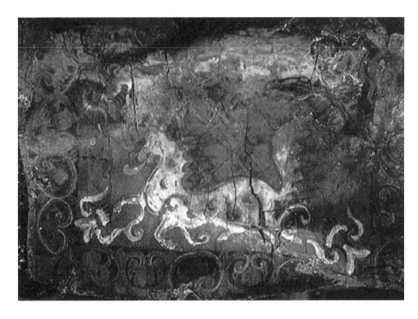

http://www.marymount.k12.ny.us/marynet/TeacherResources/SILK%20Road/html/sillatang
.htm (The image from the birch bark saddle in the Heavenly Horse Tomb in Kyongju.)

simultaneous revulsion at and identification with the film and its characters. With its redemptive ending, Lee suggests that, under our ugly surface qualities, there may be authentic love and light.

Given its prominent images of sterility, pollution, castration, and squalor—and its ironic focus on the dead mule, sterile despite its incredibly long penis—it might seem surprising that a similar redemptive trajectory emerges in "The Dreaming Beast." But a similar trajectory does begin to emerge, once one answers the question implied by the title. What is the mule gazing at? What is he dreaming? What would a mule like him idealize?

When I finished the translation, I knew the answer was a horse, the celestial white horse of Korean myth and legend, associated with divine favor, protection, salvation, and power. The iconography of the white horse is pervasive in Korean culture—one finds it in shamanic dreams, in pseudohistories, in Kyongju's Heavenly Horse Tomb of the Silla period, in legends of great savior generals. The

AZALEA

On Lee
Chang-
dong:
Heinz
Insu Fenkl

White Horse Brigade was legendary for its fierceness in Vietnam; the winged *Chollima*, associated with morning, is an important icon in North Korea.

In "The Dreaming Beast," the main characters are all initially associated with the dead and infertile mule, but by the end, I could see the horse associations throughout the text, some of them quite subtle. The girls at the factory, for example, are directly compared to horses. Kidong's Elvis-like sneer is horselike and his hair is associated with a mane. Mija's laugh could be taken as a horselike snicker, and when she acts out the wedding night with Taegi, there is an implicit allusion to the custom of a groom riding a white horse.

But there are two especially important horse allusions in the story. The first occurs when Taegi is anxious about what to do with the prostitute after she turns the lights out. In the darkness, the "words, separated by thin partitions in his head, full of restless rustling sounds" turn into silence. These words, in Korean, are *maldŭl*, homophonous with "horses," telling here because the image is reminiscent of a stable. The words in Taegi's mind are like restless horses in their stalls, compartmentalized in the same way he occupied his box-like home in the projects and the prostitute works in her tiny stall-like room in the boarding house. (By coincidence, a pimp's girls are called his "stable" in English.)

The allusion is even more telling because of what Mija says shortly after she breaks the silence to talk about her dream: "*Kkum sogesŏ nan marijyo.*" It is a simple sentence fragment, which I translated as the phrase "In the dream, you know . . ." because of its context. But Lee could easily have joined it to the next sentence as the introductory phrase, which it is. The fact that he left it as a fragment draws particular attention to its layered meanings, which all play thematically in the story. "*Kkum sogesŏ nan marijyo,*" read as its own sentence, taking the words literally and out of context, could be read as, "In the dream, I'm a horse."

By this point in the story, we realize that all the characters are "The

354

Dreaming Beast" of the title. In fact, one could say that all humans are "dreaming beasts." And with this realization, the relationship between the story and the film finally came together for me.

The "magical" sequences in *Oasis*, which rely on the reflection of light from a hand mirror, show that Kong-ju, too, is a "dreaming beast." A hand mirror, oddly enough, is also associated with Kidong's dream in the story:

> Kidong wore his hair long. It was his great pride— glossy and stylishly flipped back. Whenever he had a spare moment, the first thing he did was take out his hand mirror so he could admire his hair.

Kidong's characteristic sneer is parallel to Kong-ju's distorted facial expressions, which are highlighted for the viewer when she looks upward, like the dreaming mule in the story.

I realized that Lee's short story had not only prefigured much of the film, but that it was also aware of its own medium—it was a subtle piece of metafiction. The fragment, "*Kkum sogesŏ nan marijyo,*" literally, with the words out of context, could also be read as:

> "In dream, I am words."
> "They are words born in a dream."
> "It is a horse born in a dream."

This is a kind of literary synesthesia, ultimately linking the darkness-to-light imagery of the story; it is parallel to the twilight/mule becoming the morning/horse and illuminates the power of the word. The fact that the mule (*nosae*) is associated with sterility, castration, and disempowerment is consistent with its association, at the beginning, with the twilight (*noul*). Likewise, the mule's enormous penis (*pal-ki*), its symbol of phallic power, is nearly homophonous with illumination (*palg-ki*), and the hopeful ending is heralded by horse imagery, sexual intercourse, fertility, and the light of morning. We begin with a gloomy twilight and end with optimism and the potential for life.

From a Western perspective, this nexus of associations evokes the *Logos Spermatikos* of John's Gospel: "In the beginning was the Word, and the Word was with God, and the Word was God," God, of course, being characterized by light. The Western mythos also suggests the morning sun rises, drawn by Apollo's celestial horses. But the connection between the horse and light go back to pre-Vedic times in Asia, to the symbology of the heavenly solar horse fertilizing the Earth. In ancient India and China, the symbolic intercourse of the white horse and the terrestrial queen were major state rituals. In Korea, Pak (*Palg*) Hyŏkkŏse, mythic founder of Silla, was hatched from an egg laid by a heavenly white horse.

Back in 1981, Lee was a writer fully conscious of the connection between words and light; he demonstrates it in "The Dreaming Beast," in the medium of text. More than twenty years later, he literally projects light onto a blank screen in the medium of film, making manifest the same trope he explores in the story. Given Lee's ongoing fascination with the meaning and medium of light, I was not surprised to learn that his entry at Cannes this year is *Miryang—Secret Sunshine*.

Five Poems by Chonggi Mah

Translated by Brother Anthony of Taizé

The Fall of Paterson

"The great city split into three parts and the cities of the
nations collapsed." (Rev. 16:19)

1

The streets of Paterson, New Jersey
are so dangerous you cannot walk alone even by day.
Flowers and squirrels, pigeons and clouds,
parks and benches and lawns are all rotting
and what poets called "beautiful things" have left.

The city's little waterfall used to sing a high-pitched chorus,
the sky above the waterfall where a doctor strolled in the 1940s,
within that sky the water daily becoming a rainbow, but
now even the fresh foam is a dumping ground of dry ruins.
City of poverty, crime, drugs, and AIDS,
only hatred, insomnia, and gunshots of fear remain.

People's glares make the smoky city shake.

Bloodstains die a second time under the wheels of automobiles.
I cannot stand upright in your city
and with a horrified heart I hastily tear to shreds poems about heaven.
In the collapsing city sterile children are dying,
and meanwhile all the nation's cities are collapsing.

2

Los Angeles by night, late April 1992,
the City of Angels engulfed in the dark flames of hell,
in Korea Town, raised by the efforts of immigrant Koreans,
sweat and tears, hope and promises were all trampled underfoot.
Days, years of arson, plundering, murder,
and the city collapsed into an ash-heap of despair and shame.

Once driven out in an endless struggle against poverty,
their homeland too far away, bullets daily grazed their ears.
Shouting in a mixture of English and Korean,
tears of frustration welling in their bloodshot eyes,
even with the shield of machine guns mounted on the roofs,
it was still hard to hold back the high waves of lawlessness.

I long for your new songs
as you cover and rebuild the fallen city.
The rainbow swiftly rising heavenward,
"beautiful things" as people of every race join hands and dance.
Sweet sighs of admiration for this new Paterson.
And look: all the water drops composing the rainbow
come pouring down, enveloping us in unity.

Translator's Note: Paterson *is the title of one of the most famous works by William Carlos Williams, poet and doctor, pioneer of modern American poetry.*

358

Calling Names

Are we still calling out to one another?
One blackbird sitting on a branch
kept calling out with a desolate song
then after a time a similar bird came flying along
and, feigning indifference, settled on a nearby branch.
So close that its wings stirred up a breeze.

Are they still calling out to one another?
That second bird stopped coming, I don't know when.
No matter how often its name was called, it failed to show—
talking in its sleep on still, dry nights
from the same branch, that bird still seeking its mate.

Indoors, full and heavy, prejudice sinks down deep
as the sound of a faraway train whistle, moss-covered, strangely
pierces the interstice between night and night then vanishes.
Streetlights are going out one by one.
And broken hearts roam the sidewalks.
With even their names concealed, they all find themselves alone.
Are we still calling out to one another?

1

Until you came
there was nothing but a sound of waters,
nothing but a pea-green sound of waters
flowing from melting high icy slopes.
It was only when you came onto the scene
that fireweed blossomed in bright and dark shades of pink,
covering mountains and valleys.
Then, belatedly, the wind arrived.

The pink flowers went dancing with the wind,
while spruce trees stood on the shady side
rocking as they kept time to the beat.
The boisterous flowers at last grew still
as evening fell. That is the truth.
Until you came here
there was nothing but a sound of waters.
Nothing in the world was moving
except for the sound of waters.

2

You say you simply raised your head for a moment
and took a look around?
It was only when you came that the blue sky appeared.
That is the truth. And the cotton balls of days gone by,
clouds appeared in the sky.
The flowering weeds seemed to bob their heads just once,
and a pink-hued path opened through them.

A path stretching from that lofty above all the way down here,
and along that path no one had walked
you approached, offering reconciliation.
That is the truth. When I held your hand,
it felt warm and comforting.
I could see the path remaining for me to follow,
full of tenderness, and sure as in days of old.

If you examine the summits of ice-decked mountains,
each is like a plate.
On it sit great winds
that have as yet been unable to fly away.
Do not awaken them, those pallid seasons on the plate,
those small black bugs, dashed expectations
that only live in the eternal ice of frozen mountains
as if nonexistent, each one prostrate in the moss.
Do not awaken that wide-eyed, cold obsession.

Those bugs can never fly away, even when summer comes,
they cannot set off, though they grow old as we do.
If their six frozen legs and frozen necks ever stir
that lonely ice will break without hesitation.
The wind, hastily preparing to set off, is donning its clothes.
A sound of melting ice goes rushing down toward the villages.

The salmon that have returned, struggling far upstream,
their bodies changing color, all dark red,
gather in water too shallow to cover them fully
and mate to the sound of flapping
then even before they have finished mating
their bodies flail as they are devoured by bears.
This is not Purgatory; what an expression!
Shaking off the stains of blood, summer is departing in haste.

After the stench of blood has been borne downstream,
wild plants beside the stream stand gray-haired, suddenly aged.
Where is the widespread fragrance they had at their peak?
Feigning boredom, they turn their backs, comb their hair, and die.
It was the artist who used to make invisible things visible, wasn't it?
Not realizing they have died, they keep calling out to other wild plants.
The breeze, familiar to our ears, now blooms into autumn flowers.

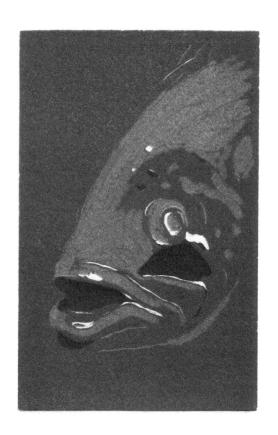

Five Poems by Song Ch'an-ho

Translated by Wayne de Fremery

AN OLD TALE TAKEN FROM A TRUNK

Our house has some awfully old smudges.
Scrub and scrub and still
the smell of pale yellow—
pale yellow stains,

the unremembered
are oldest in our house.
The forgotten, rustling,
smell of mint.
Want some candy, little one? No thank you,
Grandma,
you've been dead ten years!

365

CAMELLIA

Why would those folks
drag their boats
into the hills?
The skate is ripe, too ripe,
the hootch already gone from the jars.

With their little mudskippers in the buck
in tow and briny salt sacks stowed,
why would they weave paths through
rough reeds and trees
for the hills,
the hills?

In the name of that flower,
some other shore?
Along a path to see it,
along a path through mountain passages,

singing and crying,
they row into the hills.
The skate is ripe, too ripe,
inland spring gone too.

Why would they
want to walk these mountain trails?
I picked a rock from the path
and placed it on a pile of other prayers—
a camellia with its neck broken.

Finally, the lion rises straight to its feet,
a flower in full bloom—
four feet into emptiness,
a red mane from—

I have to finish this sentence.
Before the wind snaps
that camellia in its teeth and springs for the ground.

Autumn came in a yellow taxi. It was the first time I'd seen fall looking so fresh. He wore the latest fashion in wedding tuxes. His new yellow shoes, new yellow watch, his smart bowtie seemed to hold him fast to the listless life he was fleeing, but just barely.

Trying to shed the clods clinging to his new shoes, slightly slow-witted, he paced for a time at the entrance to the orchard, not knowing what to do. I saw them then, the apples' foreheads reddening beyond the hedge.

Finally, he reached through. Shall I jab him? Shall I jab him? The thorns of the bitter orange trees were clearly conflicted. It's the way it was. They had raised the apples, washed and cradled them in the wind with their own hands.

It's so. And now they're grown. So, if not the thorns of the bitter orange trees, then who could know the contours of their ripened figures? Who could tell the secret stories, faded like dark sunspots, in their cores?

Whatever they know, the thorns of the bitter orange trees are busy stitching final touches in gowns fitted for the apples at their ends. They must be finished before they are picked.

Ah, what sin is there in youth? Autumn has already tasted their sweetness; life's promises are already fleeing the season on big, backward steps.

Finally, at last, the camellias fall.
Returning again to the yard
with my brush-clover broom,
there, already, more
weight in red light,
let go and recumbent,
than a hundred bags can hold.

Friend, where are you reading this fine day?
You push away red lips, bright like that,
decline even the healing wines.
Beginning with
mornings such as these,
try the sacred text
of this broom
sweeping blossoms
into sack after sack.

Peter H. Lee

A portrait of the scholar as a young man—the year Peter H. Lee completed his M.A. at Yale University. (Summer 1953 in New Haven, CT)

Peter H. Lee:

Fifty Years with Korean Literature in America

Interview by Mickey Hong

This interview was conducted on March 6, 2007, and took several hours from late morning to mid-afternoon at the Faculty Center at the University of California, Los Angeles. Prof. Peter H. Lee has been a faculty member at the university since 1987. Academics in Korean studies outside Korea know Peter H. Lee as the resilient, meticulous scholar who is mostly responsible for establishing the field of Korean literature in the English-speaking world. However, in this interview he reveals a glimpse of his personal life, rich with encounters and experiences.

Mickey Hong: What were your memories of childhood? What colors, smells, and sounds do you remember? What did people wear? What did you wear? What kinds of food and drink were popular?

Peter H. Lee: I don't really remember colors, except those of girls' dresses. Smells and sounds, I think, are quite important because smells can be good or bad, and some are exotic. When I was about five, my grandfather took me to Mitsukoshi department store to buy me a school uniform. Back then you had two uniforms: one for winter and spring, and another for summer and maybe early autumn. So that was the first time I set foot in Mitsukoshi, which was across the street from the Bank of Korea, *Chōsen Ginkō*. When I entered the building, I smelled a strange but pleasant odor, unlike any I was used to. It was a combination of perfume, naphthalene, and other scents. From then on I always associated that odor with Japanese stores. It struck me as strange because I had never smelled anything like it. But when I went to Hwasin later on, there was a similar smell, though not as strong.

When my father took me to a Japanese restaurant, again I encountered an odor different from what I was used to at home—maybe a combination of Kikkoman *shōyu* and other Japanese condiments. We never used *shōyu*. We used homemade Korean-style soy sauce. Also you could tell the difference because if you add Japanese *shōyu*, the soup becomes dark. I didn't like that. In the restaurant I encountered a second unusual odor, very different from the Korean odors at home. Although I wasn't allowed into the kitchen, the aromas wafted out and I could tell what they were cooking—beef soup, roast fish. But the smells from Mitsukoshi and the Japanese restaurant were different.

Our family occasionally went to a restaurant on the third or fourth floor of Hwashin department store where I experienced other smells—of curry rice, omelet rice, and some Western dishes. I think I first ate a Western-style sandwich in August 1945 in a Chongno restaurant. Other sounds and smells struck me as a child at the Chongno night market (*yasi* before 1945) with its many brightly lit stalls and ocean of people. Some fruit stalls sold exotic items like bananas and pineapples!

In Honmachi (Ponjŏng, what is now Myŏngdong), the Japanese area, there was a small store owned by a White Russian that sold butter, cheese, and bread. I was ten or eleven when I was sent there by my father or aunt to buy some bread and butter. When I walked into that store I encountered an entirely different odor. A very different odor. And I met the White Russian, who had a lot of hair.

Out in the street, different smells mingled, of food, people passing by, tram cars, buses. Tram cars had a distinctive smell, as did buses. When I rode in a taxi (an old Volvo, as I recall), there was yet another smell.

On the top floor, the fourth or fifth, of Hwasin department store, there was a small cinema that showed films primary and secondary school students could watch. I went there occasionally to see Japanese films, which always began with newsreels. Some of these films were quite good. Inside the movie house there was another odor, one that I cannot begin to describe.

Back then, educated persons, the intelligentsia, all wore Western suits. Old people still wore *kat* and Korean costume. Even up to the mid-1930s, I rarely saw mature women wearing Western-style skirts and shoes. That was rare, but in the late 30s you did see some women with short hair or permanents wearing Western dresses and carrying handbags. The men, the intelligentsia, however young—if they were at least thirty and if they could afford it—normally carried a cane for style. My father, who always carried a cane, had many of them for different occasions, like accessories. My grandfather also had a cane, but he wore Korean-style clothes.

A sound I remember at home was when my grandfather would ring a bell in the evening to signal that we had a "guest," which meant that Japanese police were raiding homes to make sure we weren't eating white rice. We had to eat mixed-grain rice instead. Many things were rationed once the war started. Sugar, I remember, was scarce.

MH: What were your impressions of your first time in Europe? What things were fashionable in Europe at the time? What were you carried away by?

PHL: Fribourg, Switzerland, was the first place I went to in Europe from the States. I arrived there in 1954, mainly to improve my French, so I took some courses in French literature. I also took a series of courses in Indian philosophy. The town was small, and there was no concert hall or anything like that except for the university auditorium. Occasionally, someone would come and give a concert.

After that I went to Milan in the fall of 1955. And to La Scala. At the time, they sold student tickets. I would go there early in the morning, 7:30 or 8:00, and stand on line so I could buy tickets for the opera. It couldn't have been expensive if I could afford it. So I went there regularly while I was in Milan studying, and I heard Maria Callas performing the role of Violetta in *La Traviata*, and she did very well. On that day every box, the ceiling, and the walls of La Scala were decorated with real roses. It was just absolutely breathtaking. The fragrance and the color—red! I thought, "Oh my goodness!" Only Italians could think of doing that. Callas was slightly taller and bigger than ideal for portraying Violetta, who is petite and has TB. Anyway, she sang well and I vigorously applauded her. I forgot what other operas I saw there, but I went to La Scala quite often, like twice a month. I saw several operas, but that's what stays most in my mind because of the magnificent setting. Particularly on that evening, women came in their best gowns—so beautifully dressed. It was quite an experience.

Of course Milan has a famous cathedral but it also has a modern shopping arcade that's completely enclosed by glass—with a high ceiling. I used to go there with my friends and take a walk and have coffee, known in Italian as *quattro passi in galleria*, which means you are making four steps, or going there and taking a walk.

And then I went to Florence, which was my ideal city, and still is today. I was completely captivated by the cultural heritage they have. I would take a walk every day through a certain section. Maybe two blocks every day. I would look at the buildings, and sometimes touch the walls because almost every building in Florence has some historical significance. I ate well in Florence. I found a small restaurant, a trattoria, run by an Italian couple. As I began to have every lunch and dinner there, they somehow took a liking to me, and the owner's wife would take me into the kitchen and show me everything, asking, "You like this? You like that?" I paid weekly or fortnightly. They kept track of what I ate. They would tell me, "You ate this much," and I would pay. It was a nice arrangement.

But in Florence there are many good restaurants. It's out of this world the way they eat—the setting, the way they serve the food, the food itself. René Wellek came to stay in Florence for a month or two while he was writing his book. He took me once to a nice restaurant for lunch, so I took him out to dinner. One of the well-known dishes in Florence is called *Fiorentina ai ferri*, which is actually a cut of Florentine beef barbecued on top of the grill. There is one place that is well known for this dish, so if you go there, you have to have it. It's the only thing they serve. We went there and they served us a flattened beef steak on a huge plate. It was very tender and thin. And that's it. So we had a good meal, maybe with some salad.

It wasn't expensive as I recall, about three dollars because the exchange rate was so favorable in 1956, six hundred Italian lire to the U.S. dollar. I think I paid two thousand lire for the meal. So it cost a little over three dollars. We had that magnificent meal for three dollars! So I enjoyed Florence every day. I would meet with my friends who were mostly painters from Israel, Spain, Sweden, and Germany. Finally, toward the end of my stay in Florence, one Japanese painter showed up, and he didn't speak a single word of Italian. Somehow he came to the table next to where our gang was sitting. I was the only Asian there, until that other guy. So I went over and talked to him and learned that he was from Japan, and I helped him find an atelier in Florence. We looked around, and he finally chose one, a nice place.

After Florence I went to Perugia. There's a university for foreign students where they gave you intensive training in Italian grammar, composition, conversation, and culture. Five to six hours every day. You met at nine, and there was a class on grammar, then on reading. Every weekend they organized a tour. You paid little and they took you to all the cultural places near Perugia. Of course, Perugia is in

AZALEA

An
Interview
with
Peter H.
Lee

A poem
written in
Lee's youth
(opposite)
and recently
hand-copied on
his customary
5"x9" index
card. See "Bust"
on page 378 for
a translation.

Umbria, so there were many small, well-known places. My time there passed quickly. After that I went to Munich, Germany. I was studying German poetry, particularly Rilke, but I also did East Asian studies, Sinology, and Japanology. Again, I had a group of close friends with whom I would meet once a week. We would take walks, go out to eat, and discuss books.

During my sojourn in Munich I also went to concerts, operas, and plays on a regular basis. One thing I recall is attending a performance of Wagner's *Parsifal*, a long piece lasting four to five hours. When I entered the hall, I noticed formally dressed nurses lined up with stretchers on both sides. I was told that they were ready if someone fainted during the performance—and sure enough, one lady behind me fainted, and had to be removed by the nurses. And the audience was not supposed to clap at the end of the performance—it was supposed to be akin to a religious experience (at least for the Germans).

It was pleasant in Munich because at that time it was the most international city in Germany—open-minded and liberal. For example, in the English Garden—a main feature of the city, a huge park of I don't know how many acres, with streams, lakes, pavilions, and lots of trees and greenery—from April to September you saw completely naked sunbathers, and they didn't care! They were all lying down and completely naked! They didn't care about passersby.

And then I went to Oxford to speak with Sir (Cecil) Maurice Bowra, who was the Warden of Wadham College. I went to see him, and it was like an advanced conversation on the books I read. We met once a week and he entertained me with a huge afternoon tea with a lot of biscuits and sandwiches. We'd eat and talk; sometimes he asked me questions and I answered, and then I asked him questions and so forth. It was a civilized way of spending time.

MH: How did you feel as one of the very few Asians studying abroad? Did you encounter any difficulties?

石膏

달빛 쪼으며 눈물지으는 외로운 女人

떨으리이 흐르고 부허이 흐르면

안 개같이 나리는 追憶에 목이 메어

긴 한밤 외진 고으을 홀로 헤맨다

삐들어진 墓石처럼 싸느런 가슴

파리한 두보로 흐르는 구슬

오오 버려진 女人… 깨여진 花甁!

너를 살리기이 하여 바닿으 사람이

그 다지 스러음은 지니는게요?

너는 무슨 種族으로 태여나썼기에

네 가슴에 피를 흘렸구나

無情한 女人아!

무어운 쇠사슬은 끊지 옷하냐?

장미빛 黃氏도 푸른 달님도

너의 動脈은 너이 가슴에 꽃어주마

네 肺臟을 부르게 울드릴수 있다면

기다리도 슬고 時計도 점드는 밤 빠으로 부빈다

슬프도 古月를 껴안고

PHL: No, actually by the time I was in Munich in 1956, there were about five or six Koreans, most of them studying music—piano, violin, or cello. They were girl students from Seoul National University. Also there was one student studying law. We seldom got together because we didn't have time. I was there to learn German culture, so I would speak to my German friends.

In 1955, I spent one summer in Paris on my own, trying to listen to the Parisian accent and the way they talk. The language spoken in Fribourg is French, so I was in a French-speaking part of Switzerland. However, there's a difference between Swiss and Parisian French. So going to Paris was quite useful.

Another summer I went to Spain on my own and looked around. That's how I spent my European sojourn of seven years. Then toward the end of my seventh year, I was communicating with Donald Keene, whom I had known earlier. He knew that I had gotten my Ph.D. in the meantime and was looking for a job, and he told me there was a possibility that Columbia University would hire someone in my field. I waited and finally a letter came from him

BUST

The lonely woman who weeps while picking up moonlight
When the stars flow and the owl hoots

Choking from memory that decends like fog
She wanders the long deep night in a secluded alley

The heart that is as cool as the crooked gravestone
The beads that flow down on two pale cheeks

Oh, foresaken woman . . .
A shattered vase!

As what race were you born
That you must possess such sorrow?

To revive you, many have
Spilled their blood upon your chest

Can't even rose-color twilight or blue moon
Break the heavy iron chain?

Heartless woman!

If I could dye your heart in red
I will stick into your chest a vein from my heart

In the night when even crickets have gone in hiding and clocks are
    asleep
She embraces the sad bust and rubs her cheek against it.

Translated by Mickey Hong

asking me to send him my CV. I did and then maybe after about a month I received an official letter that I had been appointed an assistant professor of Korean literature with an annual salary of $6,500. That wasn't much. I was single, but my monthly check was about $300 after they deducted taxes and everything. But it was okay because I had to study and prepare my lectures and write my books. $300 was enough. At that time no matter how many years they had been teaching, every assistant professor in the humanities received the same salary of $6,500—that was it. Because they seemed to say, "You should be thankful that you are at Columbia. Don't even think about money!"

MH: Which films did you enjoy? Who were your favorite film stars?

PHL: Europeans have this terrible habit of dubbing. Humphrey Bogart would speak in French or Italian, which is horrible. I saw several Japanese films while I was in Italy, including *Seven Samurai*, and all seven samurai spoke Italian. So it was kind of funny. I don't really recall the actors and actresses. The Italian neorealist films directed by Vittorio De Sica—*The Bicycle Thief* and *Open City*—some actors in those movies. At the time, Silvana Mangano acted in a movie called *Bitter Rice, Riso Amaro*. Also Gina Lollobrigida. In French movies at the time, the well-known male actors included Jean Gabin and Charles Boyer. A woman actress who was still beautiful and popular was Danielle Darrieux. I don't know exactly when but Catherine Deneuve began acting at the time.

MH: What was your relationship like with your parents and grandparents?

PHL: When I did my homework well, such as memorizing a chapter from a Confucian canonical text, my grandfather would take me out and buy me candies, nicely wrapped hard candies. The interesting thing is that neither my grandfather nor my parents ever asked me to study. They completely left me alone. I was absolutely free to do whatever I wanted with my time. But because I was a studious type, I studied hard even in grammar school, middle school, and senior year. I did so well in all my courses, including math, which was my worst subject, that I didn't have to pay tuition, even if it wasn't much, because I was an exceptional student.

I was always studying in my room. They might say, "Why don't you go out and take a walk or something?" but they never told me to study. I suppose they knew I *was* studying. Grammar school sent your grades home anyway, so they would look at them. My parents and grandfather never interfered with how I used my free time. If I had any, I would go out and take a walk and so on, but there was homework in middle and high school, even back then. There were two exams—midterms and finals—that I had to prepare for. In middle and high school, there were even biology and agriculture, all kinds of strange subjects. And Chinese—we had to learn to speak with the correct tones. I was not good at memorizing tones at the time, but I had to memorize everything. Somehow I passed. I was so glad that I no longer had to take exams. However, when I came to this country, I did have to take exams again. At university, I had to write papers, but exams I disliked intensely.

HM: What were some of your favorite concerts, lectures, travels, and notable encounters and meetings?

PHL: One memorable event took place in the winter of 1956 when Martin Heidegger came to the University of Munich and gave a lecture one evening in a big hall. I sat in the front row because I didn't want to miss anything he said. We were all eagerly waiting. Townspeople came, too, so there were people standing everywhere, and some sitting in the aisles. We kept waiting and waiting, and finally somebody appeared and I thought, "Who is *that*?" He was a ruddy-faced and stout man, not exactly what you would think of as a typical German philosopher. Heidegger looked like a stout peasant, with his rugged face and broad shoulders. But the moment he opened his mouth, we were completely intoxicated because he knew how to manipulate the language just as he did in writing. Heidegger wrote famous essays on Hölderlin, the German poet. His lecture was about language and he said that to speak about language as language by means of language is beyond language. He repeated the same key words in their different functions. *Sprach* is a noun, and *sprechen* is a verb, and he used those words five or six times in different syntactical locations. That's why you really had to pay attention, because if you missed something, you would be completely confused. Heidegger gave a good talk and that was a memorable event during my stay in Munich.

MH: Passing on wisdom for future Koreanists, how should one study, manage interpersonal relations, and keep motivated, etc.?

PHL: When beginning in literary studies at age seventeen, I communicated with my seniors whose books I had read and whom I respected by writing letters to them. I'm so-and-so and I would like to meet you, so may I visit you at your home. Then invariably, they answered. By that time we already had phones, so if I could find out their phone numbers, I could call them. But most writers active at the time didn't have phones at home, because they were living far away in small houses. So I had to go out to meet these people. When they answered my letters, I would ask them to send me a map of how to get to their place. They usually wanted me to come to their homes early in the morning, because around nine or nine thirty, they would leave. If some didn't want me to come to their home, they would say come to such-and-such a tearoom or bookstore. I would go there and see them. And that's how I began to meet most writers.

I met Chŏng Chiyong, Im Haksu, Kim Tongsŏk, Kim Tongni, Cho Yŏnhyŏn, and Sŏ Chŏngju. I met a number of active poets and fiction writers, as well as critics. In addition to meeting creative writers, I was also contacting those who studied English literature and were teaching the subject. By 1945, I had read most basic English textbooks on my own so I was able to read a novel in English, but I didn't have any books because my father's field was law. So I contacted these people and asked if I could borrow their books. They told me to go ahead and look around their studies and take whatever I wanted. Some had beautifully bound leather books with cases that they had never opened, and which were there only as decoration. So they would let me borrow them. I was a junior scholar of English literature and a junior writer, but they said it's OK. They had complete trust in me. That's how I met important scholars of English literature. Some of them even showed me their dissertations they had submitted at Keijo Imperial University (which existed in Seoul, Korea, from 1924 to the end of World War II), or Tokyo [Imperial University], or wherever. If I went to their house early in the morning, inevitably they would ask me to eat breakfast with them but I never did because I always ate before I went.

Sometimes, we would leave their home together and go to a well-known coffee shop. We would sit down and other writers would join us and that's how I met A, B, C, D, and so on, and new writers, and they were all very kind to me. I felt good that they were not condescending. They listened and responded to me. We discussed books that were popular at the time. Actually I bought all the books published from 1945 to 1948, so I had a first-rate library of first editions illustrated by well-known painters, but during the [Korean] War, part of our house was burned down and they were all destroyed. Gone. Books were not expensive at the time, so whenever a new book appeared, I bought it.

From 1945 to 1948, the political Left and Right co-existed. So one evening you attended a lecture by a right-wing author and the following evening, you went to a lecture or poetry reading by a left-wing author. It was a exciting period. I could go to all these meetings. There were also concerts and recitals. I met leftist composers and singers who were educated in Japan. There was one composer named Kim Sunnam who set to music mainly poems by Korean poets like Kim Sowŏl and others. When he had composed enough pieces, his practice was to choose a singer, a tenor or a baritone, and have him try them out for the first time. I went to a public performance of Kim Sunnam's work, and I met the composer as well as the singer. I don't know what happened to the singer. He was a nice man. His name was Pak Ŭnyong. I also borrowed a lot of books from him. He had a good collection of Japanese authors as well as Korean authors in Japan writing in Japanese, such as Kim Saryang. I borrowed those works and read them.

It was an exciting period, very dynamic. Of course there were many demonstrations and assassinations, but we had nothing to do with those kinds of things. For a while, from 1945 to 1946, North Korea stopped supplying electricity to the South as a kind of retaliation. So we had to use candles. The city of Seoul allocated electricity in such a way that it came on only during supper time, from five to seven, and it was off. So you had to eat your supper quickly. But we still went out in the darkness. Tea rooms were still open. On every table there was a candle and we talked with our friends, friends of both sexes. Women were also students of literature and writing their own poems. It was interesting to talk to them and discuss what they had read. We sometimes exchanged books. The zeal for reading was really strong at the time, particularly among the young intelligentsia. If you were on a tram or bus, you would seldom see a young man of my age group or students who were not reading. They all carried a pocket edition. These days I don't see that in Seoul. They read the newspapers and popular genres, but not Goethe, Andre Gide, or Thomas Mann, which we used to read on trams or buses. It was really amazing. The moment you got onto the tram, you saw that everyone was reading, except for commoners. It was a good phenomenon at the time.

I followed the same practice of contacting scholars in Europe when I went there, in Switzerland, France, Italy, or Germany, and meeting them. I met a number of German poets, very good ones, that way. I went to see Arthur Waley in London. That's how I spent my free time: contacting these people and meeting them, sizing them up, seeing what they were up to. In 1951 I sent a group of poems in English to Wallace Stevens. I used to go see him in Hartford, and I met W.H. Auden in New York. I met well-known critics who came to Yale to give talks. In this way I came in contact with well-known writers and critics. I enjoyed that. I wanted to know what kind of person writes a certain kind of poem. And usually the person is completely different than you imagined.

For example, you would think Wallace Stevens was very fine and frail. He *was* well-dressed, but he was a big man. A *big* man. After reading Sŏ Chŏngju's poems, you would envision somebody entirely different from the real Sŏ Chŏngju. When you met him, you . . . [sigh]. Chŏng Chiyong, the same thing. You would think . . . but he was a short man, very short. He came up to around here [points to chin]. Bespectacled, but sharp-tongued. That's how I met a number of active writers on both the right and left, especially from 1945 to 1948. I saw Yi T'aejun, Im Hwa, Yi Yong'ak, Kim Namchŏn, and Sŏl Chŏngsik. At the time they were much above me, because I was only in my late teens and they were in their early forties, established. But they were generous with their time. I'm grateful that they gave me that kind of time.

The important lesson is this. In order for Koreans to make Korean literature known, first of all we have to make connections. That means we have to be able to point to some Western works or Chinese and Japanese works as parallels or contrasts, so the reader will say, "Ah hah!" this work belongs to the genre of Montaigne's *Essays*. For example, *P'aegwan chapki* (Ŏ Sukkwŏn's *The Storyteller's Miscellany*)—to which genre of prose do you compare it? Because that kind of literary miscellany is a unique form, containing biographical, autobiographical, and critical writing—narratives. So you have to think how we can tell readers about the corresponding Western prose form. In order to do so, you have to read a certain number of books.

384

I read quite widely from Greek and Latin literature to modern literature, so I was able to find comparable writers from ancient times through the sixteenth century (when Ŏ Sukkwŏn was active) and the seventeenth. So that's how it should be done. Particularly when one is writing on twentieth-century Korean writers, you have to bring in other twentieth-century writers—Western, Chinese, and Japanese. That way the reader is better able to situate a given work: "Ah hah, this work belongs to this, it's like this," which makes the reader better prepared. I would strongly recommend this because our approach, when we wish to introduce and propagate Korean literary works, has to be comparative. If a Korean work just stands by itself, it's hard to attract the attention of Western readers because they won't have time to pick up that book unless it's distinguished in some way, by unique features or those it shares with well-known Western works. That's the reason why we have to do it.

I suppose twentieth-century works are easier to treat in this comparative way because modernism is an international movement. To do it with pre-modern texts, traditional Korean literary works, takes time, but still we must do so. To me, that really is the first step, and the reason why few classical Korean works are being translated and introduced, and few secondary studies on classical Korean literary texts are readable is because those who teach classical Korean literature in Korea do not read even one Western language. So they don't have a comparative perspective. They're only introducing these works to a Korean audience, and a limited one at that. So that's why when I pick up a secondary source on classical Korean literary work, I learn little. So we have to somehow try to change the way Korean scholars approach classical Korean literary works. They have to open up, they have to read what's out there, but very few of them make that conscious effort. Many of them might think they are too old to pick up one new Western language. To make Korean literature better known, the work has to begin with Korean scholars in Korea. Isn't that so?

MH: Yes, they have to expose themselves to what's out there so they have a context for comparison.

PHL: Yeah, that kind of work is rare in Korea. It will take considerable reading of Western literary works, but if scholars are not trained in literary theory and criticism, then it's difficult for them to understand such works. I think that's the main reason why Korean literary studies are not as advanced as Chinese or Japanese literary studies. At the graduate workshop on Korean humanities at UCLA, for example, Carter (J. Eckert) said that the younger generation will surely be larger than our generation, and they should be able to share their reading and contacts among themselves, but we have to see if they can do that. The simple fact that there are more students studying Korean literature now doesn't necessarily mean they will produce a better result. I think that's important to acknowledge.

Always seek out those from whom you would like to learn. With colleagues, too, take the initiative. Until the late 1980s, because there was really no one with whom I could talk about Korean literature, my main interactions were with scholars of English, comparative, Chinese, and Japanese literature. This is the way you learn, and in turn you impart something to others to make them aware of the existence of Korean literature. So you have to talk to everybody, not just those in your field. You always have to go out of your way, you have to reach out. That's important. Reach out. Reach out. Always. I think that's very important. Reaching out.

MH: How do you keep notes, organize your files? What are your personal habits and rituals?

PHL: Whenever I read a book, I take notes, even today. I keep these notes, which have all the page numbers, so that means I don't have to go back to the book again. I can simply refer to my notes. I have card files like these [pointing to 5 x 9 index cards] in five boxes. But because those cards are too small, I began to type my notes on 8 x 11 paper. I have maybe eight or nine folders of those. I file them alphabetically, by subject or by author's name, so then I can go back and take a look. That saves a little time. Of course taking notes takes time, but you don't have to look for the books in the library and check them out again. Many times the books are not there anyway. That's my practice. My personal habit.

MH: You have been so prolific, are there things you'd still like to do? Personally, academically? What's next?

PHL: There are many books I haven't been able to read because I didn't have the time. When I was teaching, the books I had to read were mostly critical studies and theoretical works. I would like to spend more time reading actual literary works that I didn't find time to read in the past. Not only in Korean but also in Japanese and Western languages. That will take time. Then I will think of some project and go back to certain classical works that strike me, works I haven't had time to look at carefully. *Ch'unhyang ka* (*The Song of Ch'unhyang*) is one good example. I will continue to do something—reading, thinking, and writing.

MH: How would you describe your lifelong relationship with literature?

PHL: I think this is a good question because my attitude has always been grave and solemn. Because when you pick up a volume of verse or work of fiction, you immediately grasp that a tremendous amount of suffering, hard work, and imagination went into making that book. You are even more aware of this when you yourself are a creative writer and you know how much time you spend writing a single poem. You have to go though ten or twenty revisions. You mumble a poem to yourself, even when you're walking or on the bus, because you're thinking of how to improve a particular line. That's how I feel

Peter H. Lee
(opposite)
before giving
his Faculty
Research
Lecture, the
highest honor
UCLA bestows
on faculty
(Royce Hall,
UCLA, April
2000)

whenever I pick up a book—I have respect for that author, I identify with him or her. My attitude *is* grave and solemn. I don't treat books lightly, but solemnly. It's something precious. That single book is imbued with an author's soul and blood. We cannot treat such a thing shabbily. That's the key attitude when dealing with a literary work; we respect the author who spent time, who suffered, who imagined, who wrote, and who wants us to take part in that experience.

There are some books for which one reading is not enough, so you have to go back. That's the attitude with which you have to treat books. Then some day, as a reader, you will begin to see a new world and acquire a new sensibility. Our literary sensibility has to be refined and polished continuously. We cannot just ignore it, or let it stagnate, because then it begins to rust. We must keep on refining and polishing that sensibility. If you keep on training yourself this way—I use the word *hullyŏn*—it's a kind of education, and even without knowing it, you begin to acquire certain criteria which are almost faultless. Then whenever you pick up a book and read, you can say, "Ah hah!" You begin to see the whole dimension. Not just layer by layer, but you begin to see the whole thing. It's a concrete object right there. It consists of a sound system, a meaning system, and a metaphysical system. It's all there. You are able to perceive that multi-dimensional work at first glance. And that should be the goal for all students of literature. One day, you will reach that level from which you can deal with a literary text meaningfully and fruitfully without missing much. A full engagement with the text. At all levels. If you want to do that, then you need *hullyŏn*. Those who have never produced any creative writing do not understand it very well. Those who have had the experience understand it better. Even if it's not much, it's good to do some creative writing. Not because you want to be a Shakespeare, Goethe, Valéry, or Rilke, but to experience the creative process.

Peter H. Lee retired as an active professor at the end of the spring semester in 2007 and the conference "Celebration of Continuity," a

commemoration of his career, was held on June 1, 2007, at UCLA. He is now professor emeritus and continues to do what he does best: read, write, and think, and make others do the same.

Of all the lessons from Prof. Lee, the harshest is also the most valuable and proves to be truer with passing time—that being a lover of literature is entirely demanding. Prof. Lee warned that literature is a jealous lover, and I must give it all of my attention. My attitude toward literature changed, not because he admonished me, but because of his infectious passion for literature—how he gives himself wholly to his work.

Orhan Pamuk in Insadong with Nana Lee.

Korea From the Outside

Orhan Pamuk

"What is your first impression of Korea?"
"What does Korean sound like to you?"

This was my first visit to Korea. When people began asking me such questions within ten minutes of my arrival at Incheon International Airport, I realized that Koreans are similar to Turks. Like Turks, they are very curious about what other people think of them. Like Turks, they are grappling with issues of national identity and nationalism, but these concerns are not as intense, dangerous, or destructive in Korea as they are in Turkey. Korea's economic miracle over the past twenty years has reduced anxieties about identity, and Koreans generally seem happier and have a more positive and open outlook on life. Speaking to world-renowned writers at the Seoul International Forum for Literature, Korean intellectuals and literary scholars expressed disappointment about how little-known their work is outside of Korea and asked what can be done about this. During these discussions Koreans openly displayed their pride by stating such facts as "our country's gross national product ranks twelfth in the world." The feeling of

[*] This is a translation of Orhan Pamuk's short essay about his impressions of Korea that was published in Turkey's leading newspaper *Sabah Gazetesi* on June 5, 2005, after Pamuk attended the second Seoul International Forum for Literature. Nana Lee, who has translated many of Pamuk's work into Korean, translated the original Turkish into Korean, which was then translated into English by Jessica Ji-Eun Lee.

joy shared by Koreans when the world validates their country's achievements was also apparent when Korean medical researcher Hwang Woo Suk successfully reproduced stem cells that may one day help patients suffering from incurable diseases. When President Bush expressed reservations about Hwang's research on human cloning, Koreans were united in support of science and pride for their country. In response to President Bush's negative remarks, the Korean government and its citizens supported and encouraged Dr. Hwang.[†]

Another topic mentioned during the forum was the issue of Japan apologizing to Korea. Japan's brutality toward Koreans and Chinese during World War II is understandably difficult to forget. Atrocities such as forcing Korean women to serve as sex slaves for Japanese soldiers are still remembered by Koreans, and the international community knows that in recent years tension has been building between the two nations. Japanese writer Ōe Kenzaburō, one of the participants in the forum, believes that Japan, as a democratic country, has a duty to apologize for its past crimes. However, his benign, cordial tone changed when he talked about Japan's ultranationalists and conservative politicians. It was clear that he disagreed with the nationalists' contention that Japan had not committed a crime, and even if it had, should not apologize. It seemed to me that Korea and Japan discuss their past in a more flexible and humanistic way than Turkey and the Middle East address theirs. The reason Korea has become more tolerant and confident in looking at its history may be linked to the extraordinary wealth it has enjoyed in recent years. In Seoul I saw magnificent buildings unlike any I have seen elsewhere in the

---

[†]   Editor's Note: After Orhan Pamuk's visit to South Korea, Dr. Hwang's research on stem cells became the target of investigation and Seoul National University announced in January 2006 that his papers on human cloning were fraudulent. Dr. Hwang was indicted on embezzlement and bioethics law violations linked to faked stem cell research and afterward he was stripped of his professorship, and the government rescinded its financial and legal support for him. However, many nationalistic Korean supporters of Dr. Hwang have not changed their position even after his indictment.

world (they were built with a great sense of style), wondrous hotel lobbies (some of the world's most beautiful elevators are in Seoul), and bookstores. I met many people who spoke about the affluence and economic growth of Korea—some spoke happily about working twelve hours a day; women complained about being lonely because they don't see their husbands enough; and some talked about enjoying Saturday afternoons walking through crowded bookstores. Although I saw homeless people lining up to be fed at soup kitchens on the same blocks where name-brand department stores line the wide, luxurious streets of Seoul, the gap between rich and poor in Korea is definitely not as great as in Turkey.

As I have witnessed at many of these kinds of seminars, writers who were invited to the Seoul International Forum for Literature— world-famous writers whose books are sold in huge bookstores—ate breakfast in the hotel cafeteria by themselves, looking depressed and lonely. I am well known around the world for writing postmodern and experimental novels. I recently chatted over coffee with Robert Coover, one of the writers I respect and admire. But the topic of our conversation wasn't postmodernism. Instead we talked about the time when Coover was serving in the U.S. Navy and brought the Sixth Squadron into Izmir (a city in Turkey) and went out with friends to hunt for wild boar in 1954.

The gravest problem facing Korea today is North Korea. Struggling with starvation, isolated from the rest of the world, that bizarre authoritarian regime, like a troubled sibling, threatens us all. It recently announced to the whole world that it has nuclear weapons, behaving like someone brandishing a gun and claiming that they are going to shoot everyone, including themselves. Other writers at the forum visited Panmunjom but I chose not to. Instead, I went to Donghae with my friend and Korean translator of my novels, Nana Lee (my novel *Snow* was recently published in Korean), and his friends. We ate seaweed soup, sashimi, and shellfish and drank *soju* [Korean vodka]. My uncle fought in the Korean War, so I spent my childhood listening to his stories about

Korea. Because of that, Korea has always been a country that I've felt close to. In both Korea and Turkey, children with cute rabbit-like teeth shout "hello! hello!" to tall foreigners who pass by, then look at each other and giggle.

Orhan Pamuk in Kangnŭng.

Peace, Poetry, and Negation‡

Korea
From
the
Outside

Robert Pinsky

A Buddhist foundation in Korea invited poets from around
the world to gather for a conference on peace in the
summer of 2005. The undertaking seemed less quixotic and more
practical after I learned a little about the figure from whom the
Manhae Foundation takes its name.

In Manhae (born Han Yong-un), Koreans can celebrate a
great modernist poet who is also a central figure in Korean
religion, culture, and politics. An American poet reads with some
astonishment that Manhae, a monk and religious reformer who
profoundly influenced Buddhist thought and practice, was also a co-
author of the Korean Declaration of Independence. Accomplishments
comparable to those of Thomas Jefferson, Walt Whitman, and Ralph
Waldo Emerson, achieved by someone born in 1879 (the same year
as the American businessman-poet Wallace Stevens).

This unusual, comprehensive centrality of Manhae may tempt
even Western poets to feel some tiny glint of reflected glory. It
also intimidates us: what can one offer in the context of such an
imposing model? At that gathering in Seoul, where poets from
around the world were invited to think about the somewhat vague
ideal of peace, the challenge was perhaps the more poignant for

‡ The original form of this essay was presented at the Paektamsa Temple, South
Korea, in 2005, and published in RARITAN (Summer 2006).

Azalea

*Peace,
Poetry, and
Negation:
Robert
Pinsky*

those of us representing languages that have had no Manhae, no single figure who so thoroughly included the worlds of art and practical politics. That occasion, and the writing of Manhae, inspired the questions I will try to consider here.

On a grand scale, what is the place of poetry in the needy world, where a deficiency of peace for much of the population means hunger, violence, and disease? On an immediate, personal scale, what might be the social or religious or political place of the next poem one writes, in relation to the formidable accomplishment of Manhae in a language and culture we can only begin to understand?

In the context of such questions, and the diffidence they inspire, it is a great relief to turn toward Manhae's poems. These poems present not the political rhetoric of triumph, but intricacies of doubt; and not the religious rhetoric of peace achieved, but peace as the goal of struggle; not salvation, but longing. Far from separating individual psychology from politics or religion, the poems seem determined to blur, or even wipe away, any such distinctions. And it appears to be a poetry that attacks its own means, that sometimes creates an image or a metaphor only to tear at the creation. Here is Francisca Cho's translation of the poem "Cuckoo":

The cuckoo cries its heart out.
It cries and when it can cry no more,
It cries blood.
The bitterness of parting is not yours alone.
I cannot cry even though I want to.
I'm not a cuckoo, and that bitterness can't be helped either.
The heartless cuckoo:
I have nowhere to return, and yet it cries,
"Better turn back, better turn back."

Regret, exile, discomfort: these feelings, whether they are understood as personal, erotic, historical, or all of the above, here dramatize themselves by how the poem expels its own notions:

"I'm not a cuckoo," "I have nowhere to return," "I cannot cry." These negatives are like the legend of the bird that grieves till it emits not a voice, but blood.

"I haven't seen your heart," says the refrain of a poem called "Your Heart." "Don't," says the refrain of "First Kiss." "It's not for nothing that I love you," says "Love's Reasons." Even a poem of devotion has the refrain "Don't Doubt": "If you doubt me, then your error of doubt / and my fault of sorrow will cancel each other." There are negatives, too, in a poem called "Don't Go": "That's not the light of compassion from Buddha's brow; it's the flash from a demon's eyes / That's not the goddess of love who binds body and mind, and tosses herself into love's ocean, caring nothing for crowns, glory or death; / It's the smile of the knife." The refrain of "Don't Go" is "Turn around—don't go to that place. I hate it."

Ah yes, the negative! It cheers me up, and in a certain way it is near the heart of poetry itself. Through negation poetry implicitly says to politics, no, you are not all there is, there is also the human body; and to the human body, no, you are not all there is, there is also spiritual yearning; and to spiritual yearning, no, you are not all there is, there is also sexual pleasure; and to sexual pleasure, no, you are not all there is, there is also politics.

The art says no to all, and includes all. Unruly, it welcomes conflict, paradox, and negation. This may be what the Yiddish poet Zische Landau had in mind who said, long ago, that whatever Yiddish poetry might be it would not be merely "the Rhyme Department of the Jewish Labor Movement." That is, poetry does not merely put particular feelings and ideas into language, but creates an experience that reminds us of something beyond any particular feelings and ideas: always beyond, always in process, always headed somewhere new.

In the old Soviet days of Eastern Europe, a Polish poet has said, the most ambitious poet was the State: it wanted to control all the metaphors. Poetry, to the contrary, wants every metaphor to remain open.

I am angry at my country's government much of the time, often in relation to this very notion of peace. When I try to think of how that anger is related to poetry in general, or to my poetry in particular, it is helpful for me to think of my task as reopening and questioning metaphors. Not to be an expert in foreign policy, but rather in the contradictions and reversals of language.

In this light, one wonders if Manhae's reputation for writing poems that can be read as erotic or nationalistic, psychological or political, personal or communal, represents not a taste for allegory or some delight in poetry's hidden or multiple meanings, but rather the embodiment of poetry's quality of inclusion: not that a love affair is a secret code for patriotism, but that poetry is peculiarly able to understand how the human soul enacts both.

Great rhetoric may talk as though there is only politics. Great erotic passion may talk as though there is only eros. Poetry, in contrast with these, somehow acknowledges or implies the All—or, if that sounds too misty, it checks the box "All of the Above." Less confident of settled knowledge than any language purely of love or purely of politics or purely of psychology, poetry is more confident in its inclusive, sweeping ambition. It excludes nothing. Irritably, it looks beyond everything.

The poet in English who is often presented as having successfully included political reality in his work is William Butler Yeats, Manhae's senior by only nine years and, like Manhae, associated with the Indian poet Rabindranath Tagore. The refrain of Yeats's poem "Easter 1916" combines the all-including terms "utterly" and "all" with the negative paradox of beauty that is terrible: "All is changed, changed utterly: / A terrible beauty is born." The poem touches on the disparate realms of social class (the poet on the way to his club, unlike the conspirators coming from "counter or desk"), poetic ambition ("rode our winged horse" and "might have won fame in the end"), personal affections ("some who are near my heart"), and includes even a natural scene along a stream where "hens to moorcocks call" and "birds . . . range / from cloud to tumbling cloud."

Peace is certainly one of the subjects raised by this Irish poem about a violent, doomed uprising. Yet also somewhat strange, precisely in its quality of peace, is Yeats's comparison for his own poem about that violent, unsettling Post Office takeover:

To murmur name upon name,
As a mother names her child
When sleep at last has come
On limbs that had run wild.

He likens his arrangement of names into poetry—"I write it out in a verse, / MacDonagh and MacBride / And Connolly and Pearse"—to the way a mother murmurs the name of her child after the child has fallen asleep.

The anger and sexual jealousy that makes him call one of these "a drunken, vainglorious lout"; the confessed social snobbery that contrasts "counter or desk" with "Around the fire at the club"; the violent deaths and executions of the event itself; the pragmatic political calculation of whether "England may keep faith"—none of this is transcended by the incantation of peace, the calm and maternal sound of a name: not transcended, but included. The beauty—a poem, or a child, or a historic act of rebellion—is born, and it is also terrible.

This peculiar embrace of the beautiful with the terrible, peace not avoiding violence and struggle and terror, not rising above them but somehow including them, seems to me one of the central, if mysterious, gestures of art. If it were not so unsettling and contradictory, I would call it familiar. It associates opposites: in Yeats's lines, Peace and Wildness, but maybe more accurately Peace and Struggle, perhaps even Peace and Conflict. Gerard Manley Hopkins says of peace, having in mind Christ as a dove, and exploiting "brood" as a word that indicates both hatching the young and a kind of strained, dark meditation: "And when Peace here does house / He comes with work to do, he does not come to coo, /

He comes to brood and sit." Emily Dickinson seems to say that the harbor of Peace is an illusion, but then reasserts its promise:

AZALEA

Peace,
Poetry, and
Negation:
Robert
Pinsky

> I many times thought Peace had come
> When Peace was far away—
> As Wrecked Men—deem they sight the Land—
> At Centre of the Sea—
>
> And struggle slacker—but to prove
> As hopelessly as I—
> How many the fictitious Shores—
> Before the Harbor be—

"How many the fictitious Shores": the infinite, manifold possibilities of imagination. This vision of multiplied wreckage and struggle articulates the opposite or absence of peace, just as Yeats's evocation of a mother who names her sleeping child is the opposite or negation of the objective violence and subjective passion that are the subject of his poem.

I perceive a similar process of opposition and stress in Manhae's poem "Come." This remarkable poem begins with images of peace:

> Come in to my garden, the flowers are blooming there.
> Should anyone chase you, hide in the blossoms.
> I'll turn into a butterfly and light upon the ones you hide among.
> Then your pursuer won't find you.
> Come, please come. It's time.
> Come in to my arms, my breast is soft there.
> Though I'm soft as water, I'm a golden sword and an iron shield
>   to protect you.

The sweet peacefulness of these early stanzas includes the refrain: "Come, please come. It's time." But the concluding stanza transforms the meaning of that refrain:

Come in to my death, my death is always ready for you.
Should anyone chase you, stand behind my death.
In death, emptiness and omnipotence are one.
Love's death is at once infinite, everlasting.
In death, battleship and fortress become dust.
In death, the strong and the weak are companions.
Then your pursuer won't catch you.
Come, please come. It's time.

This resolution in the absolute of death is in a way conventional (the poem was apparently inspired by Tagore's "The Gardener, 12" as Francisca Cho suggests in her note) and in another way unexpected and radical. In his poem "Reading Tagore's Poem 'Gardenisto,' " Manhae writes, "You're a song of hope within despair, sung while picking fallen flowers for a garland." But in another, similar transformation he rejects or criticizes that sweet image of hope in a faded garland: "You say the scent of death is sweet, but you can't kiss the lips of dry bones. / Don't spread a web of golden song over that grave, but plant a bloodstained banner."

Restlessness, not stasis. Conflict, not repose. Or rather, conflict when repose is expected and repose when conflict is expected. The artist, above all, wants to bring something new into the world: art, if saying so is not too circular, aspires to creation.

There is the slogan that the artist "speaks truth to power." Yes, and we can hope not only the artist does that; we would truly despair if we thought only poets were capable of speaking truth to power. Eminently, governors and magistrates should speak truth to power. Art has its own way of speaking.

In the week of the poets' conference in Korea on the subject of peace, the Irish Republican Army officially renounced violence. The coincidence brings to mind another poem by Yeats:

"On Being Asked for a War Poem"

Peace,
Poetry, and
Negation:
Robert
Pinsky

I think it better that in times like these
A poet's mouth be silent, for in truth
We have no gift to set a statesman right;
He has had enough of meddling who can please
A young girl in the indolence of her youth,
Or an old man upon a winter's night.

The author of "Easter 1916" and "Meditation in Time of Civil War" says "We have no gift to set a statesman right." I remember trying to say this poem by memory once, on a hike up a mountain, and I could not recall one of the words: "He has had enough of *something* who can please / A young girl in the indolence of her youth, / Or an old man upon a winter's night." He has had enough of *glory* who can please? He has had enough of *striving* who can please?

On that mountain trail in California's Trinity Alps, I could not wait to get down to a bookstore and check. What I learned is that Yeats's actual word, "meddling," was tougher, meaner, more irritable than my "glory" and "striving." That pugnacious note, and the reservations an Irish poet might have about the English war cause, together qualify the line "We have no gift to set a statesman right." To some extent, the line means that art does more than set a statesman right about this policy or that. By pleasing, by waking up, art may question the very terms of peace and war. A "terrible beauty" is beyond or above "meddling."

All politicians after all say they are for peace. And so they may be on their terms, as Adolf Hitler was. The poet may choose to demonstrate that peace is as unexpected, as many-sided, and as rooted in conflict, as those poems of Manhae's that say in death, the strong and the weak are companions.

The savagery in the word I could not call up—"meddling"—for

me embodies how passionate and angry Yeats's refusal to write a war poem is, though cloaked in the manners of modest calm: the young girl in the indolence of youth, the old man, the winter night, the "pleasing." As in the poems of Manhae, erotic energy, the time of year, and the domestic or individual scale of indolence and old age have an intricate figurative and literal relationship with the other idea of "meddling" and "setting a statesman right."

But as the context of an international conference on peace reminded me in new ways, I am an American, and, poet or not, that fact puts me in a special relation to the concept of peace. In this time of immense American power, military and economic, in the wake of an American invasion of Iraq, removing a government there, bombing and occupying in the name of peace, do I not have particular, urgent responsibilities? Nor is war the only opposite to peace: starvation, corruption, disease . . . all these global contraries of peace are national matters for my country, because of our massive power.

Possibly because that political, economic, and military power is so immense, it is sometimes said that contemporary American poets are slow to speak about causes like peace. This criticism is amazing to me. In 2003, shortly before the invasion of Iraq, Laura Bush planned a reception for poets at the White House. The event was finally canceled—not because of the many refusals to attend, but because of plans to present a petition against the planned invasion, with thousands of signatures of poets. The Web site "Poets Against the War" calls itself (this is a little embarrassing, I concede) "the largest poetry anthology ever published." It now contains twenty thousand poems.

At the moment of that planned White House reception, American poets in large numbers demonstrated that they could have "set a statesman right": mistrust of the grounds for mounting a precipitate, catastrophic invasion turns out to have been a justified mistrust.

But quantity is not quality. Are there American poems that serve the ideal of peace in a way worthy of comparison to Manhae's

AZALEA

Peace,

Poetry, and

Negation:

Robert

Pinsky

incorporation of the negative, his inclusion of the erotic? I think at once of Allen Ginsberg ending his Cold War poem "America" with a—precisely—disarming declaration of his sexuality and his patriotism, in the cause of peace. After his hilarious parody of xenophobia and paranoid Red-baiting, he concludes his poem with a mockery of himself, mockery of conventional categories and terms, of the standards for military service—laughing at everything but his quite sincere, wholehearted, and unironic willingness to serve his country:

> It's true I don't want to join the Army or turn lathes in
> precision parts factories,
> I'm nearsighted and psychopathic anyway.
> America I'm putting my queer shoulder to the wheel.

This poem is exhilarating and penetrating because it does not omit parts of life in order to serve a political rhetoric: the conflicts in Ginsberg's heart are not apart from the world but a manifestation and epitome of the world. He is patriotic, and contrary.

And here is Robert Lowell, in the last stanza of "Waking Early Sunday Morning," using the word "peace" with the saddest irony imaginable:

> Pity the planet, all joy gone
> from this sweet, volcanic cone;
> peace to our children when they fall
> in small war on the heels of small
> war—until the end of time
> to police the earth, a ghost
> orbiting forever lost
> in our monotonous sublime.

This anger of 1967 expresses itself not in rant or posturing but in an even, mournful meditation on the ghostly, joyless—and

404

contradictory—sublime: negative, as well as monotonous.

Lowell's lines and Ginsberg's—meditative or manic—are efforts to attain peace by almost physical means: a modern, poetic equivalent of the chanted magical charms that might be at the anthropological roots of our art. The animal, fearful or needy, vocalizes to create an audible artifact that might bring the peace it craves: an incantation, that does not so much describe the world as it is at any moment as it tries to bring about by words the world as it potentially, maybe essentially, can be. One could hardly find a more apt expression of this aim than the poem "Incantation," by the late Polish poet Czeslaw Milosz. Here is my own translation:

> Human reason is beautiful and invincible.
> No bars, no barbed wire, no pulping of books,
> No sentence of banishment can prevail against it.
> It establishes the universal ideas in language,
> And guides our hand so we write Truth and Justice
> With capital letters, lie and oppression with small.
> It puts what should be above things as they are,
> It is an enemy of despair and a friend of hope.
> It does not know Jew from Greek or slave from master,
> Giving us the estate of the world to manage.
> It saves austere and transparent phrases
> From the filthy discord of tortured words.
> It says that everything is new under the sun,
> Opens the congealed fist of the past.
> Beautiful and very young are Philo Sophia
> And poetry, her ally in the service of the good.
> As late as yesterday Nature celebrated their birth,
> The news was brought to the mountains by a unicorn and an echo,
> Their friendship will be glorious, their time has no limit,
> Their enemies have delivered themselves to destruction.

AZALEA

* All original images are digital photos & prints

K.E. Duffin

Visitor. 2006,Watercolor, 7″ x 10″ 60
Memory. 2006, Linocut, 4″ x 6″ 58
Divide. 2007, Watercolor, 4″ x 6″ 166
Watcher. 2007,Watercolor, 6″ x 6″ 214
Twin. 2006, Watercolor, 6″ x 6″ 26
Silver Fish. 2006, Linocut, 6″ x 4″ 364

Joe Savitzky

A Beer-can House. October 1953. 249
War Orphan. January 1954 in Seoul. 250
Having Fun. June 1953 in Seoul. 251
Farm Scene. November 1953 somewhere north of Seoul. 252
Farm Scene II. November 1953 somewhere north of Seoul. 253
A Village. 254
Three workers. July 1953 at railroad track near Seoul. 255
Tomorrow's Leaders. June 1953 in Seoul. 294
Sport Day Gathering. October 1953 near Singongdŏk, Seoul. 304
Selling Fruit on Sport Day. October 1953 at Singongdŏk, Seoul. 309
Left Alone. June 1953 at the T'oegyewŏn Temple near Seoul. 310

Chung Zuyoung

Puram Mountain no. 4. 2006, Oil on linen, 79″ x 118″ 78
Puk'ak Mountain no. 1. 2006, Oil on linen, 75″ x 83″ 282
Puk'ak Mountain no. 2. 2006, Oil on linen, 75″ x 83″ 282

* *AZALEA* generally adheres to the McCune-Reischauer system in transcribing Korean into English. However, many Korean contributors have not followed this convention, and we respect their way of writing their names in English.

Brother Anthony of Taizé was born in England in 1942 and completed studies in medieval and modern languages at Oxford. He is a member of the Community of Taizé and has been living in Korea since 1980, where he taught medieval and renaissance English literature at Sogang University (Seoul) for many years. More than twenty volumes of his English translations of modern Korean literature have been published. A Korean national, his Korean name is An Sonjae.

Chung Zuyoung works and lives in Seoul. She studied at Seoul National University and Kunstakademie Düsseldorf, Germany, where she earned a Meisterschüler degree. Her work has been internationally exhibited at numerous museums through solo and group exhibitions and collected by Shinsegye Gallery and Artsonje Center in Seoul. She teaches at the School of Visual Art of the Korean National University of Arts.

Don Mee Choi, born in South Korea, has studied modern Korean literature and literary translation in Seattle under the guidance of Bruce Fulton. She has translated *Anxiety of Words: Contemporary Poetry by Korean Women* (Zephyr, 2006) and *When the Plug Gets Unplugged: Poems by Kim Hyesoon* (Tinfish, 2005). More of her translations of Kim Hyesoon's poetry are forthcoming from Action Books, 2008. Her original poems have appeared in *Cipher, Tinfish, Action Yes,* and *La Petite Zine.*

Ellie Choi has a dual B.M./B.A. in classical piano and English literature from Northwestern University and an M.A. from UCLA in Korean literature. She has taught at WPI in Worcester, Mass., and at Yonsei University in Seoul, and is currently finishing a dissertation at Harvard University in modern Korean intellectual history entitled, "Travel and the historical imagination: Yi Kwangsu's vision of Chosŏn during the Japanese empire."

K.E. Duffin is an artist and writer living in Somerville, Massachusetts. She studied at the School of the Museum of Fine Arts, where she learned printmaking. Her work has been exhibited internationally and is in the collections of the Boston Athenaeum, the Boston Public Library, and the DeCordova Museum. In 2005 she received a Massachusetts Cultural Council Artist Grant, and her first book of poems, *King Vulture*, was published by The University of Arkansas Press.

Heinz Insu Fenkl, born in 1960 in Pup'yŏng, is a novelist, translator, and editor. His autobiographical novel, *Memories of My Ghost Brother*, was named a Barnes and Noble "Discover Great New Writers" selection in 1996 and a PEN/Hemingway Award finalist in 1997. He has also published short fiction in a variety of journals and magazines, as well as numerous articles on folklore and myth. His most recent work is *Cathay: translations and transformations*, which includes his own fiction as well as T'ang poetry and the opening of Kim Man-jung's seventeenth-century Buddhist classic, *Nine Cloud Dream*. He currently teaches at the State University of New York in New Paltz.

Wayne de Fremery, a native of northern California, is a Ph.D. candidate in the Department of East Asian Languages and Civilizations at Harvard University. He currently lives in Koyang, a northern suburb of Seoul, with his family.

Ha Seong-nan (Ha Sŏng-nan), born in 1967 in Seoul, studied creative writing at Seoul Institute of the Arts. She debuted in 1996 with her short story "Grass," and won the prestigious Dong-in Literary Award, the Yisu Literary Award, and the Hankook Ilbo Literary Award. She has published several volumes of fiction.

Janet Hong is a writer and translator living in Vancouver, Canada. In 2001, she won the grand prize for her translation of Ha Seong-nan's "The Woman Next Door" in the Modern Korean Translation Contest. Since then, her translations have appeared in *Kyoto Journal*, *Koreana*, and Jipmoondang's *Portable Library of Korean Literature*. She lives in Vancouver, British Columbia.

Mickey Hong is a Ph.D. candidate in Korean literature at UCLA. Her dissertation topic is 1930s Korean modernist poetry.

Huh Su-gyung (Hŏ Su-gyŏng), poet, novelist, essayist, and translator, was born in Chinju in 1964, and first published her poems in *Silchŏn munhak* in 1984. In 1992, she moved to Germany to study archaeology at the University of Münster. She has published four collections of poetry, a novel, a collection of essays, and a translation. She was awarded the Tongsŏ Literary Award in 2001.

Hwang In-sook has published five books of poetry and six books of prose. She has won two major poetry awards in Korea. Ever since the appearance of her first collection of poems, *The Birds Let the Sky Free* (1988), she has been widely acclaimed as a poet of strikingly innovative and vivacious imagination. Although she is one of the leading poets of Korea today, her works have not yet been translated into other languages, perhaps because of her reclusiveness and the difficulty of her poetic language. She lives in central Seoul, in an area overlooking the downtown area, where she takes care of her ever-proliferating kittens.

Hwang Jiwoo began his poetic career in 1980, the year of the Kwangju massacre, and immediately became a leading poet in an "age of poetry" that spanned the 1970s and 80s in Korea. He published several collections of poetry, including *Even Birds Leave the World*, *Lotus Blossom in the Crab's Eye*, *Sea Gleaming As Night Falls*, and *Someday I'll Be Sitting in a Dingy Bar*. He was awarded several literary awards, including the Kim Suyŏng Literary Award, the Sowol Literary Award, and the Daesan Literary Award. He is president of Korea's National University of Arts.

Hwang Sunwŏn, born in 1915 in Daedong, Pyŏng'annam-do, made his literary debut as a poet during middle school in 1931. He studied English literature at Waseda University in Japan. After 1937, however, Hwang Sunwon devoted himself exclusively to writing fiction, producing many collections of stories and several novels. A member of the Academy of Arts since 1957, Hwang was the recipient of such honors as the Asia Freedom Literature Prize and the Academy of Arts Award and the March First Culture Prize. He died in 2000.

Kang Hong-Goo was born 1956 in Sinan, Chŏllanam-do, and lives in Seoul. He studied at Hong'ik University, where he earned a B.F.A. and a M.F.A. His work has been exhibited internationally and collected by numerous museums, including Musée des Beaux-Arts de Tours (France), National Modern Art Museum (Korea), and Samsung Leeum Museum (Korea). He also published five books, including three essay collections.

Kim Jean Young has a Ph.D. in Russian literature (Yale University) and is a professor at Yonsei University, Korea. A specialist in Pushkin and nineteenth-century Russian literature, she has a deep interest in the comparative study of Korean and Russian literatures, and has published a Russian translation of Chŏng Hyŏn Jong's poetry (*Tak malo vremeni dlia liubvi*, St. Petersburg, 2000). The English translation project devoted to Hwang In-sook's poems emerged during her sabbatical year at Harvard

University in the course of a friendly discussion with Prof. David McCann on modern Korean poets.

Kim Aeran was born in Incheon in 1980 and studied theater and drama writing at the National University of Arts. She began writing fiction in 2003 and was awarded a number of literary prizes, including the Hanguk Daily News Literary Award. She published her first collection of stories, *Run, Dad!* in 2005.

Kim Chiha, longtime symbol of the political dissident poet in South Korea, was born Kim Yeongil in 1941 in Mokp'o, Chŏllanam-do. In 1970, he published the poem *Five Bandits* (Ojŏk), which satirized contemporary Korean society. This led to his arrest and indictment for violating the Anti-Communism Law. He served seven years in solitary confinement. He has published many books of poetry and essays, most of which have enjoyed great popularity. He has been honored with many prizes, including the Asia-Africa Authors' Association Lotus Prize, the "Grand Poet Prize" at the International Poets' Conference, and the Yisan Literary Award.

Kim Jung-Hyuk was born in 1971 in Kimcheon, North Kyongsang Province. He began his literary career with the publication of his short story "Penguin News" in the literary quarterly *Munhak kwa sahoe*. "Penguin News" later became the eponymous work of his 2006 short story collection and Web site: http://www.penguinnews.net.

Kim Hyesoon has received numerous prestigious literary awards, and currently teaches creative writing at Seoul Institute of the Arts. Translations of her poetry are available in *When the Plug Gets Unplugged* (Tinfish Press, 2005) and *Anxiety of Words: Contemporary Poetry by Korean Women* (Zephyr Press, 2006). A collection of her selected poems in translation is forthcoming from Action Books, 2008.

Kim Seung-Hui (Kim Sŭng-hŭi) has published nine volumes of poetry, including her most recent, *Naembineun dungdung* (Beating pots), which appeared in 2006. *I Want to Hijack an Airplane*, a volume of English translations of her poems, was published in 2004 by Homa & Sekey. She has won several major awards and is currently professor of Korean language and literature at Sogang University, Seoul.

Kim Wonsook is a painter and sculptor whose work is widely known in Korea and other parts of the world. She has to her credit more than forty solo exhibitions mounted in New York, Chicago, Los Angeles, Tokyo, Hamburg, Bologna, and many other cities. She holds an M.F.A. from Illinois State University.

Kim Young-ha, born in Seoul in 1968, published his debut novel *Nanen nareul pagiohal gweolliga itda* (*I have the right to destroy myself*) in 1996. The novel was translated into French as *La Mort à Demi-mots* (Editions Philippe Picquier, 1998) and published in English in 2007 by Harcourt/Harvest. A prolific writer, he has written more than seven books as well as a significant number of essays and film reviews. His works are being translated into many languages and he was awarded many literary prizes, including the Contemporary Literature Prize, the Hwang Sunwon Literary Award, the Tong'in Literary Award, and the Yisan Literary Award. He was the host of a daily radio show on books and authors, and has taught at Korea's National University of Arts.

Ko Un, born in 1933, is a world-famous figure, and has published more than 130 volumes of poetry and other writings, including twenty-three of the monumental *Maninbo* (Ten thousand lives) series. An edition of English translations of poems selected from the first ten *Maninbo* volumes, *Ten Thousand Lives*, was published by Green Integer in 2005 and *Flowers of a Moment* was published by BOA in 2006. A full selection of his poems, *Songs for Tomorrow*, will be published by Green Integer in 2007. A new edition of his Zen poems *What?* will be published by Parallax Press in early 2008.

Kyong-Mi Kwon is a Ph.D. candidate in modern Korean literature at Harvard University. Kwon received translation fellowships from the International Communication Foundation (ICF) in 2002 and the Korea Literature Translation Institute in 2005-2006. She has also published a translation of Yi Mun-yŏl's short story entitled "Tugyŏp ŭi norae" (aka "Twofold Song") in 2004. She is currently conducting her dissertation research in Tokyo, Japan, as a Fulbright Research Fellow.

Lee Chang-dong, born in Daegu in 1954, is an award-winning film director and writer. He served as Korea's minister of culture and tourism from 2003 to 2004. He began writing fiction in 1980, went on to publish several books, and then, to many people's surprise, debuted in 1997 as a film director with *Green Fish*. He gained international attention with his second film, *Peppermint Candy*. His third film, *Oasis,* won the Best Director's Award at the Venice Film Festival and the Chief Dan George Humanitarian Award at the Vancouver Film Festival in 2002. His recently released fourth film is *Secret Sunshine*.

Lee Hye-kyung, born in Poryŏng, Ch'ungchŏngnam-do, studied Korean literature at Kyunghee University. She has published many works of fiction, including the novel *Kil wi ŭi jap* (A house on the road), and a collection of stories, *Kŭ jip ap* (Front of the house). She has been awarded many literary prizes, including the Tong'in Literary Award, the Hyundae Literary Award, the Hankook Ilbo Literary Award, and the Today's Writer Award.

Lee Hyung-Jin received his M.A. in comparative literature from SUNY, Binghamton, and his Ph.D. in comparative literature from Pennsylvania State University. He has taught Korean and Asian literature at Rice University. He is now assistant professor of translation studies in the English department at Sookmyung Women's University.

Jessica Ji-Eun Lee received her B.A. in political science at Wellesley College. She is a candidate for an M.A. degree in the Regional Studies East Asia program at Harvard University.

Ji-Eun Lee is currently a postdoctoral fellow at the University of Minnesota, Twin Cities campus. She received a Ph.D. degree in Korean literature from Harvard University and has taught and worked at the University of Toronto, Dartmouth College, and the University of British Columbia.

Nana Lee has translated Orhan Pamuk's novels into Korean. Currently she teaches Turkish Literature at the Turkish Department, Hankuk University of Foreign Studies.

Lee Moon-jae, born in 1959 at Kimp'o, Kyŏnggi-do, studied Korean literature at Kyunghee University. His poems first appeared in *Siundong* in 1984, and he has published four collections of poetry and an essay collection. He was awarded the Kim Talchin Literary Award, the Si wa sihak Young Poet Award, and the Sowŏl Literary Award.

Lee Sang-Wha is a professor of English Literature at Choong-Ang University. Her specialty is utopias in literature and she has published a study of British utopian novels in the twentieth century. She has also translated six literary works from English into Korean.

Lee Si-Young (Yi Si-Yŏng), born in Kurye, South Chŏlla Province in 1949, began publishing poetry in 1969, and his first volume *Manwol* (Full moon) appeared in 1976. Since his second book, *Param sokŭro* (Into the wind, 1986), he has published many volumes of poetry. He received the Sorabol Literature Prize, the Jŏng Ji-Yong Literature Award, and the Paek Sŏk Award.

Young-Jun Lee received a B.A. from Yonsei University, as well as an M.A. and Ph.D. from Harvard University in modern Korean literature. He has taught at the University of California, Berkeley, and Harvard University.

David R. McCann is Korea Foundation Professor of Korean Literature at Harvard University. He has translated the work of many Korean poets—including Kim Chiha, Sŏ Chŏngju, Ko Un, and Kim Namjo—and is the author or editor of many books, including *The Columbia Anthology of Modern Korean Poetry* and *The Way I Wait for You*, a collection of his own poems.

Chonggi Mah (Ma Chong-gi), born in 1939, grew up in war-torn Korea and studied medical science at Yonsei University, Seoul. In 1966, he left Korea to work as a doctor in the United States and continued to compose poetry in Korean throughout his medical career. A volume of English translations of his work, *Eyes of Dew*, was published in 2006 by White Pine Press.

Jenny Wang Medina is a doctoral student in modern Korean literature and culture at Columbia University. Her translation of Oh Jung-hee's *The Bird* was published by Telegram Books in 2007, and her most recent work, a translation of Ch'oe Yun's *Mannikin*, received the grand prize in the 2006 Modern Korean Literature Translation Awards.

Kevin O'Rourke, an Irish priest (Columban Fathers) and one of the foremost translators of Korean literature into English, has lived in Korea since 1964. He obtained a Ph.D. from Yonsei University in Seoul and has since taught at Kyunghee University in Seoul. He has published numerous translations of Korean literature, both premodern and modern, most recently *The Book of Korean Shijo* (Harvard University Asia Centre, 2002).

Orhan Pamuk, Turkish novelist, the recipient of international literary awards, was awarded the Nobel Prize in Literature in 2006. His work has been translated into more than forty languages. Currently he teaches at Columbia University.

Park Min-gyu was born in 1968 in Ulsan, a metropolitan city in southeast South Korea, and graduated from Jungang University. His first novels, *Chigu yongung chonsol* (Legend of the world's superheroes) and *Sammi syuposuta oe majimak paenkullob* (The Sammi Superstars' last fan club), were both published in 2003 and earned him both the Munhak Dongne New Author Award and the Hankyorye Literary Prize in the same year. The short story "Komawo, kwayon neoguri-ya" (Raccoon world) was included in the 2005 Yi Sang Literary Award Collection. His most recent novel, *Ping Pong*, was published in 2006.

Robert Pinsky, poet, essayist, literary critic, and translator, has published nineteen books, most of them collections of his own poetry, including critically acclaimed translations. He served as Poet Laureate Consultant in Poetry to the Library of Congress from 1997 to 2000, and teaches at Boston University, where he is director of the M.A. program in creative writing.

Joe Savitzky was born and raised in New York City, and attended the University of Illinois, graduating in 1951 as an architectural engineer. He served in Korea in 1953/54 as an engineering officer in the U.S. Army, based just north of Seoul. He went on to obtain a master's degree in city planning at M.I.T in 1958, and then began working in Israel in 1960, where he has stayed until retiring in 2004. He is now living in Tel Aviv.

Song Ch'an-ho, a native of northern Ch'ungch'ŏng Province, is the author of three books of poetry: *Hŭk ŭn sagakhyŏng ŭi kiŏk ŭl katgo itta* (Soil with memories of a square, 1989)*, 10-yŏn tongan ŭi pin ŭija* (A seat left empty for ten years, 1994), and *Pulgŭn nun, tongbaek* (Crimson eyed, camellias, 2000). His most recent collection was awarded the Kim Su-yŏng Literary Award, as well as the Tongsŏ Literary Prize.

Ronald Suleski obtained an M.A. in Chinese studies and a Ph.D. in modern Chinese history from the University of Michigan. He has published about Manchuria in the 1920s and 1930s. Korea has been a special interest since his first visit while serving with the U.S. Army in the 1960s. He has returned there many times. He is the assistant director of the Fairbank Center for East Asian Research at Harvard University.

Sung Suk-je (Sŏng Sŏk-che), born in 1960 in Sangju, Kyŏngbuk Province, made his literary debut as a poet in 1987 and published two collections of poetry. In 1994, he shifted gears and began writing fiction with the publication of *Kŭ kot enŭn ŏchŏguni dŭri sanda* (Ridiculous things live there). Sung has since published several collections of stories and novels, including *Hollim* (Possession), *Hwang Mankŭn ŭn irŏke malhaetta* (Thus spoke Hwan Mankŭn), and *Ingan ŭi him* (Power of human). He was awarded several literary prizes, including the Hankook Ilbo Literary Award, the Tong'in Literary Award, the Yi Hyosŏk Literary Award, and the Hyŏndae Literary Award.

Scott Swaner graduated from the University of Utah, received his M.A. from Cornell University and his Ph.D. from Harvard University, and was in the third year of his appointment as assistant professor of Korean Literature at the University of Washington in Seattle when he was diagnosed with pancreatic cancer in early 2006. He died on December 20th of that year.

Yoo Hui-sok is professor of English education at Chonnam University, South Korea. In addition to Korean literature, his major field of research is nineteenth-century American and English literature. He has published a wide variety of articles on twentieth-century Korean literature and American writers.

Yoon Sung-Hee, born in Suwŏn in 1973, graduated from the creative writing program of Seoul Art College. After publishing her first story, "A House Made of Lego Blocks," in 1999 in *Donga Ilbo*, she published three collections of stories, *A House Made of Lego Blocks, Are You There?*, and *A Cold*. She has been awarded many literary awards, including the Yisu Literary Prize and the Hyŏndae Literary Award.

Yun Dae Nyeong (Yun Tae-nyŏng), born in 1962 in Yesan, Ch'ungch'ŏngnam-do, graduated from Tan'guk University with a major in French literature. A series of stories, "Silver Trout Fishing Network," "Miari, 9 January 1993 Network," and "Once in a While, a Cow Visits a Motel," established his reputation as a writer who captures the ethos and sensibilities of Korean people in the 1990s.

Dafna Zur is a Ph.D. candidate at the University of British Columbia majoring in Korean language and literature. Her translations have been published in *The Columbia Anthology of Modern Korean Literature*, *Manoa*, and *Words Without Borders*. Her research interests include Korean children's literature, North Korean science fiction, and contemporary Korean women's fiction.